ARBEITEN ZUR KIRCHENGESCHICHTE

MARTIN SCHNEIDER

**Europäisches Waldensertum
im 13. und 14. Jahrhundert**

Gemeinschaftsform — Frömmigkeit — Sozialer Hintergrund
Groß-Oktav. XII, 157 Seiten. 1981. Ganzleinen DM 64,—
ISBN 3 11 007898 8 (Band 51)

DIETRICH WÜNSCH

Evangelienharmonien im Reformationszeitalter

Ein Beitrag zur Geschichte der Leben-Jesu-Darstellungen
Groß-Oktav. XII, 282 Seiten, 11 Grafiken und 1 Faltatabelle. 1983.
Ganzleinen DM 142,— ISBN 3 11 008600 X (Band 52)

DIETMAR WYRWA

**Die christliche Platonaneignung in den
Stromateis des Clemens von Alexandrien**

Groß-Oktav. X, 364 Seiten. 1983. Ganzleinen DM 84,—
ISBN 3 11 008903 3 (Band 53)

KARL CHRISTIAN FELMY

**Die Deutung der göttlichen Liturgie
in der russischen Theologie**

Wege und Wandlungen russischer Liturgie-Auslegung
Groß-Oktav. XIII, 509 Seiten, 19 Abbildungen. 1984. Ganzleinen DM 136,—
ISBN 3 11 008960 2 (Band 54)

E. I. KOURI

**Der deutsche Protestantismus und die
soziale Frage 1870—1919**

Zur Sozialpolitik im Bildungsbürgertum
Groß-Oktav. X, 256 Seiten. 1984. Ganzleinen DM 108,—
ISBN 3 11 009577 7 (Band 55)

Preisänderungen vorbehalten

Walter de Gruyter · Berlin · New York

ARBEITEN ZUR KIRCHENGESCHICHTE

REINHARD SCHLIEBEN

Christliche Theologie und Philologie in der Spätantike
Die schulwissenschaftlichen Methoden der Psalmenexegese Cassiodors

Groß-Oktav. X, 132 Seiten. 1974. Ganzleinen DM 50,—
ISBN 3 11 004634 2 (Band 46)

HANS SCHNEIDER

Der Konziliarismus als Problem der Neueren Katholischen Theologie
Die Geschichte der Auslegung der Konstanzer Dekrete von Frebonius bis zur Gegenwart

Groß-Oktav. VIII, 378 Seiten. 1976. Ganzleinen DM 133,—
ISBN 3 11 005744 1 (Band 47)

GERHARD MAY

Schöpfung aus dem Nichts
Die Entstehung der Lehre von der creatio ex nihilo

Groß-Oktav. XII, 196 Seiten. 1978. Ganzleinen DM 90,—
ISBN 3 11 007204 1 (Band 48)

GERHARD SIMON

Humanismus und Konfession
Theobald Billican, Leben und Werk

Groß-Oktav. XII, 260 Seiten, 1 Abbildung. 1980. Ganzleinen DM 98,—
ISBN 3 11 007862 7 (Band 49)

Text — Wort — Glaube
Studien zur Überlieferung, Interpretation und Autorisierung biblischer Texte — Kurt Aland gewidmet
Herausgegeben von Martin Brecht

Groß-Oktav. VIII, 397 Seiten, Frontispiz. 1980. Ganzleinen DM 128,—
ISBN 3 11 007318 8 (Band 50)

Preisänderungen vorbehalten

Walter de Gruyter · Berlin · New York

THE DIET CHEF'S GOURMET COOKBOOK

THE DIET CHEF'S GOURMET COOKBOOK

Myles Omel

Frederick Fell Publishers, Inc.
New York, New York

Copyright © 1981 by Myles Omel

All rights reserved. No part of this work covered by the copyright may be reproduced or used in any form or by any means—graphic, electronic, or mechanical, including photocopying, recording, taping, or information storage and retrieval systems—without permission of the publisher.

For information address:
Frederick Fell Publishers, Inc.
386 Park Avenue South
New York, New York 10016

Library of Congress Catalog Card Number: 80-70958
International Standard Book Number: 0-8119-0328-1

MANUFACTURED IN THE UNITED STATES OF AMERICA
1 2 3 4 5 6 7 8 9 0

Published simultaneously in Canada
by Fitzhenry & Whiteside, Limited, Toronto

CONTENTS

Introduction **ix**
The Basic Techniques for Low-Calorie Cooking **1**
Seasonings **6**
Appetizers and Snacks **16**
Soups and Stocks **26**
Eggs and Cheese **44**
Combination Main Dishes **51**
Meat **55**
Poultry **101**
Seafood **131**
Vegetables **166**
Salads and Dressings **211**
Sauces and Marinades **230**
Breads and Cereals **244**
Garnishes **250**
Desserts **255**
Beverages **270**
Menus **274**
Weights, Measures, and Equivalents **278**
Glossary of Cooking Terms and Foreign Phrases **285**
Index to Recipes **303**
Index **309**

DEDICATION

To my family, for their patience.

INTRODUCTION

Whether you're a disillusioned diet dropout or a first-time novice, by opening the pages of this book you have made a resolution to do something about your weight. As diet chef for the world's most famous spa, I have helped thousands of dieters lose unwanted pounds and inches. And with the recipes, cooking, and diet information in this book, I can do the same thing for you.

What makes my book different from other cookbooks is that it is not merely a collection of diet recipes. There are no exotic, time-consuming extravagances to contend with or easy-on-the-waistline substitutes made with artificial sweeteners. Rather, this is a general cookbook designed specifically for dieters. The guidelines and suggestions on selecting, buying, storing and preparing foods, along with the majority of the recipes and cooking tips, relate directly to kitchen-tested low-calorie cooking procedures.

This is a cookbook for dieters who appreciate good food and who find pleasure and relaxation in the kitchen. It is a book about calories, but more importantly, it is a book that will show you how to lose weight and maintain your ideal weight without giving up your favorite foods or restricting you to monotonous diet menus.

Using this book as a guide, you will learn how to eliminate the unwanted extra calories from any dish or recipe. You will achieve the slim, attractive figure you want, and best of all, you will establish sensible cooking and eating habits that can keep those lost pounds from returning once your true goal is obtained.

The hundreds of books and articles that have been written about reducing are testimony to the fact that no one regimen for losing weight works for everybody. Some dieters, for numerous reasons, are able to lose weight faster than others. The fact is that the rate at which you lose weight is really unimportant—it only seems important at the time. In the end, what is important is not how much weight you're able to lose or how fast you're able to lose it, but rather how successful you are at maintaining your new lower weight once you've reached it.

No matter how hard you try, you just can't ignore the word calorie. So exactly what is it? A calorie, simply defined, is a unit of heat that measures the energy-producing value of food. All foods except plain water have calories, but they differ in the number of calories each provides for a given weight. Proteins and carbohydrates, for instance, have about 4 calories per gram. Fats, on the other hand, have about 9 calories per gram. Obviously, the foods with the highest concentration of fats are going to be highest in calories for any given amount of weight.

If you consume more calories in your daily diet than your body needs to function, the excess will be stored as body fat, and you will gain weight. If you consume fewer calories than your body needs, then your body starts to burn up its own fat reserves, and you will lose weight. A clearer description of the relationship between calories and the body's metabolic functioning is best left to the dietetic experts. But understanding what a calorie is makes it easier to grasp the principles of weight loss and weight gain. It's up to you (with some good advice from your doctor) to use this knowledge for safe and successful dieting. There are several alternatives.

Your first choice is to go it on your own and make up a low-calorie diet with the help of a calorie-counter, faithfully listing everything you eat each day and adding up the totals. This isn't as hard or as monotonous as it sounds because, in all likelihood, you already know the caloric value of most of the more common foods.

The advantage of calorie-counting is its flexibility. You can eat what you want, when you want it, as long as you continue to lose weight. And if you overindulge one day, you can make up for it the next day by eating less or exercising more. But the disadvantages in such a flexible method of dieting, where success is contingent on your willpower and constraint, are numerous.

First of all, it doesn't take into account some of the psychological factors that cause failure. For most dieters, self-control is a difficult thing at best. It's easy to become discouraged by temporary setbacks. A slight gain in weight—or simple standing still on the scale—can trigger a whole set of emotional rationalizations that can force a dieter to stray from his diet.

Another disadvantage to the self-designed diet is that in all probability it wouldn't be nutritionally balanced. While cutting down calories to lose weight is your immediate goal, the elimination of essential nutrients brought about by a poorly planned diet could have disastrous effects on your health in the long run.

A second alternative to weight control that has merit is to rely on the skills of a professional and follow one of a multitude of carefully planned low-calorie diets. These diets work and are guaranteed to be nutritionally sound. Better yet is to conform to a plan designed by a doctor or dietician specifically for you. The calories will be counted by the nutritionist rather than by you, and there's the satisfaction of knowing that the diet is the best one for your health and well-being. Chances are you would stick to a diet designed by others longer than one you designed yourself.

But a major disadvantage of a fixed diet of this kind is its lack of flexibility. You soon grow tired of the same foods on the menu, and sometimes it's just impossible to obtain the exact items needed.

Another disadvantage is that most fixed diets demand some cooking skills and the breaking of old culinary habits. You would have to know where to purchase specific items and the best methods of storing them.

Finally, there's the major problem of preparation and the possibility of having to purchase new pieces of cooking equipment needed for specific techniques (a microwave oven, for instance). After all, for the dieter, just one failure in the kitchen is sometimes justification for abandoning a diet altogether.

A third method for losing weight is to put yourself in the hands of experts and register for a week or two at an expensive health and beauty spa. Everything from diet to exercise will be carefully and individually laid out for you in exact detail. After a few weeks of this kind of regimentation and pampering, you're bound to feel slimmer, trimmer, and more attractive. This is definitely a program you can stick to, while it lasts, that is. The cost alone is probably the greatest motivation in the world.

No matter what choice you make, you should consult with your physician first and get his approval. After a thorough examination about the state of your health, he'll be in the best position to advise you on any special precautions you should take. The doctor can also help you choose a diet that's right for you. So, to lose weight and stay healthy, my advice is to arm yourself with a diet prescribed to you by your doctor, then learn to prepare low-calorie foods properly by reading this book from cover to cover.

Your doctor can tell you to lose weight for your health and happiness. A dietician can lay out a diet that is interesting, imaginative, and most important, nutritionally sound. But it takes the expertise of a skilled cook to make low-calorie foods look and taste attractive. Take the trouble to create new and exciting meals, and you'll be reinforcing your incentive to lose weight. Eliminate the unwanted calories in the foods you love, and you'll be less likely to continue the faulty eating habits that put on the weight.

But it's difficult to change a lifetime of habits, especially eating habits. Most overweight people got that way simply from overeating the wrong kinds of foods. They constantly consume more food than their bodies burn up. For years, they have been able to utilize this extra fuel through heavy work, constant activity, and exercise. But in later years the metabolism changes and the body doesn't burn up fuel the way it used to when they were younger. Also, physical activity had been reduced to the point that what they believe to be the normal amount of food to maintain their weight has now become excessive, and the overabundance turns to fat.

It's my personal feeling that it's the quantity of food a dieter is so used to consuming each and every day that is the hardest thing to give up, and attempting to live with a crash diet, that restricts caloric intake by cutting down the total volume of food, won't last long. It's like trying to lose weight and stop smoking at the same time. Trying to do too much at once is almost impossible to live with.

My suggestion for permanent weight loss is to keep eating the same volume of food you're used to. Eat that satisfying bulk that gives you that "full" feeling and you won't leave the table feeling emotionally and physically deprived. The trick is to learn how to appease your hunger and cut your appetite with filling, low-calorie foods. As you reduce your total caloric intake slowly but surely, those extra pounds will disappear. Remember that a diet is not something you go on to lose weight and then forget. The chances of keeping lost weight from returning are improved when you stay with a diet program long enough to make low-calorie, sensible eating a habit. I'm not afraid of the word "diet." For some (and that includes myself) it is a life-long proposition.

Bear in mind that my remarks and observations about dieting and nutrition are strictly that of a layman and, for the most part, reflect my personal and professional experiences with weight control. As a diet chef, I've had to expand my knowledge of nutrition past my own immediate needs. And since diet and nutrition bear a correlative relationship with the preparation of low-calorie foods, I feel my personal comments are both necessary and proper. They should in no way, however, conflict with specific instructions on diet, nutrition, or food preparation given you by your own physician or dietician.

In my opinion, too many low-calorie cookbooks present recipes that are designed for hospital patients or food faddists rather than for dieters. These books are quickly read and then forgotten. In contrast, the recipes you will find here are simply low-calorie versions of traditional dishes—foods you know and like. You don't have to deprive yourself of your favorite foods or starve yourself to control your weight. Once you've learned a few basics of calorie-conscious food preparation, you can eat what you wish and still be able to keep your weight under control. Use these techniques long enough to make low-calorie cooking and eating a habit, and your weight problem will be solved for a lifetime.

Here are my four criteria for weight control:

1. *You must be motivated:* You must have a genuine, sincere desire to

control your weight and be willing to suffer the ordeals of dieting for the pleasure of being healthier and more attractive. You must be willing to change your attitudes toward eating in order to control your overindulgences and obsessions with food and be willing to adjust to new cooking and eating habits. And finally, you must give up your freedom to eat as much as you want, whenever you like, and be convinced that nothing, but nothing, can prevent you from attaining the slimmer, trimmer figure you want. In the final analysis, you alone make the choice to be fat or thin.

Dieting requires willpower and resolve. Don't expect to succeed overnight. And don't panic when you slip now and then. Properly motivated, you will quickly compensate for these overindulgences because you have made enough changes in your life so that overeating becomes the exception rather than the rule. As long as your motivation is strong and stays that way, you will never be overwhelmed by rich, high-calorie foods again.

2. *You must count calories*: Why? Because calorie-counts give you a frame of reference from which to operate, so you know approximately how much food you should eat to lose weight or to maintain your weight loss. The alternative is to follow a prescribed diet that counts the calories for you, something most of us find difficult to stick to without adequate supervision. Calories do indeed count, but the key to successful weight control is understanding the long-term relationship between calorie intake and calorie expenditure.

One pound of body fat contains approximately 3,500 calories. To lose two pounds a week—the recommended maximum amount for most dieters—you must consume 7,000 fewer calories than your body uses, which means eliminating about 1,000 calories a day from your total calorie intake. By taking in fewer calories than your body needs, you're forcing it to draw its energy requirements from stored-up fat.

While basic calorie requirements vary according to an individual's size, age, sex, and activity level, your body's caloric need is roughly 15 times your weight in pounds. If you weigh 150 pounds, for example, and are moderately active, you'll maintain your present weight on 150 multiplied by 15, or about 2,250 calories per day. To lose those two pounds, you would need to reduce your calorie intake to 1,250.

When you're making every effort to lose weight, don't be discouraged if your weight loss is inconsistent. Your body is simply adjusting to your new eating habits and sometimes it takes its time about catching up. As long as you don't cheat and faithfully stick to your diet plan, you are burning fat and losing real fat weight no matter what your scale indicates. Also, as you approach your ideal weight, your maintenance level will change, and in order to continue losing at the same rate, you will need to lower your calorie intake still further or increase your calorie requirements by increasing your physical activity. Most nutritionists seem to agree that your ideal weight at age twenty-two should be the guideline for your weight throughout life.

3. *You must eliminate unwanted calories whenever you can:* Once you realize that the whole subject of weight gain, loss, and maintenance depends upon the relationship between daily calorie intake and your body's energy requirements, and you know what your optimum daily calorie intake should be, take the next step; learn how to modify the amount and the kinds of food you eat in order to stay within the bounds of your caloric allowance. Remember, it's the total number of calories you consume, not when, how, or why you consume them, that shows up on the scale.

Start by monitoring the amount of food you eat. Eat normal portions, but don't take seconds. If at the end of the first week your weight remains unchanged, then reduce the size of your "normal" portions until the scale shows that you are losing weight.

Next, choose foods that tend to have a lower calorie content. Fish, chicken, veal, and lamb, for instance, all generally contain fewer calories than the equivalent amount of beef. Diet margarine and skim milk have half the calories of butter or whole milk. Avoid most convenience and obviously fattening foods such as potato chips, cookies, gravies, and candy.

And finally, learn to use the low-calorie preparation techniques I've outlined in this book to keep your weight at the desired figure. By eating the right types of foods in the proper amounts and adding as few calories as possible in their preparation, you can enjoy eating and still lose weight without any starvation or extraordinary sacrifices.

4. *You must be totally conscious of everything you eat:* You must face the fact that your unwanted overweight is primarily the result of eating too much of the wrong kinds of foods and consuming more calories than your body needs. To attain your desired weight, you must learn to control your daily caloric intake and establish sensible eating habits that allow you to stay within your caloric needs. Sound impossible? It is, if you approach dieting as a penance and think of it as something you *should* do rather than as something you *want* to do. You must be absolutely convinced that a trimmer, healthier, more attractive body is what you really want. It is only when nothing, not even the emotional pleasure and satisfaction of eating, is more important to you than your will to become thin that you will be able to reach your goal. But if you're sufficiently motivated, no amount of boredom, idleness, anxiety, craving, or temptation can make you deviate from your diet plan. The sooner you realize that there are many things more important in life than the pleasure of food, the quicker you'll reduce and stay reduced.

You'll find this book easy to use. It is divided into the usual food groups based on menu sequences—appetizers, soups, desserts, beverages, and so on. The important chapters for meat, poultry, fish and vegetables, however, are further categorized by the various low-calorie cooking methods of preparation.

Bonne chance and *bon appétit*!

THE DIET CHEF'S GOURMET COOKBOOK

THE BASIC TECHNIQUES FOR LOW-CALORIE COOKING

The principles and procedures of low-calorie cooking are not a radical departure from the accepted classic methods of preparation. Actually, the reverse is true. I have relied heavily on the standard methods and have modified them only when, by doing so, it was possible to reduce or eliminate unwanted calories.

It is said that "variety is the spice of life." It is also the nucleus of low-calorie cooking. Cooks who prepare foods by the same one or two methods day after day will soon become bored with cooking in general, and especially with the foods they're preparing. By giving you principles and techniques which you can apply to all kinds of foods, I hope to make low-calorie cooking exciting, challenging, and worth perfecting.

Cooking is the process by which we subject raw foods to the action of heat in order to make them tender and more digestible. Cooking also seals in or extracts the natural juices and flavors in foods, and when enough heat is applied, acts to sterilize and make safe the foods we eat.

The various procedures used in preparing foods are each related to a specific type of heat and are divided into dry-heat and moist-heat methods. Cooking by dry heat is used in roasting, baking, broiling, panbroiling, and sautéing and is effected by trapped heat in an oven (convected heat), by radiant heat from a broiler or charbroiler (radiant heat), or by direct heat from a hot, dry surface (conducted heat). Low-calorie moist-heat cookery methods include boiling, simmering, poaching, steaming, braising, and stewing. These methods entail the cooking of foods submerged in liquid or surrounded by steam. Moist-heat cookery is generally done on top of the stove and is employed for foods that require low temperatures and an extended period of cooking to make them tender.

Just as there are no "magical" foods that will painlessly "melt away" our unwanted pounds, there is nothing magical or secretive about the procedures used in low-calorie cooking. I am convinced that what every weight-conscious cook needs is not another collection of diet recipes, but rather a thorough understanding of the basic dry- and moist-heat methods of cooking and how these methods—together with the new techniques I have described at the end of this chapter—can be used to lower the calorie content of our favorite foods.

Why not make your adventure in low-calorie cooking as easy as possible? Use the recipes you have and enjoy the kinds of foods you're used to eating. Simply learn to substitute low-caloried ingredients for the high-caloried ones, and everything you cook will be nothing more than a variation on the basic preparations.

Become familiar enough with these principles and techniques to be able to modify and perfect any recipe to your personal caloric requirements. But learn to be creative, and use your own ingenuity to substitute the ingredients and seasonings in a recipe to your own tastes and preferences.

LOW-CALORIE DRY-HEAT COOKING METHODS

ROASTING is the cooking of food, uncovered, in an oven. Although the terms *roasting* and *baking* are almost synonymous, "to roast" originally meant to cook food on a spit before an open fire. Today, roasting is generally done in an oven, but large roasts and big birds are referred to as being "roasted," while vegetables and breads are said to be baked.

As a general rule of cooking, large roasts and big birds, which take a relatively long time to cook, are prepared at low temperatures (325°F.) to prevent them from overbrowning before they are cooked through. Small roasts and birds, which require a shorter cooking period, are prepared at higher temperatures (400°F.) to facilitate browning and prevent them from drying out.

BAKING is the cooking of food with dry, indirect heat, covered or uncovered, in an oven. Poultry to be baked is cut up, rather than trussed and cooked whole as in roasting. Few vegetables can withstand exposure to dry oven heat. Tough-skinned vegetables, such as potatoes, eggplant, and winter squash are notable exceptions.

BROILING is the cooking of food under or over direct heat. As a cooking process, broiling is similar to roasting (foods that are tender enough to be roasted are also excellent when broiled), but in broiling, the food is being cooked one side at a time.

Broiling is a quick method of cooking and is used primarily for steaks, chops, and shish kabobs. The exact cooking times for broiled foods vary considerably, and depend on the source of heat, the kind of food, the tenderness, texture and thickness of the food, and finally, on the desired degree of doneness.

PANBROILING, a variation of broiling, is a method used to cook lean cuts of red meat in a hot, dry, heavy skillet over direct heat without added fat. The pan is never covered and excess fat extracted from the meat as it cooks is poured off as it accumulates.

SAUTÉING is a method of cooking small, tender pieces of meat, poultry, fish, or vegetables that requires a combination of intense heat and quick cooking to keep them tender. It is considered a dry-heat method of cooking, because a large open pan or grill is used to dissipate any moisture surrounding the food, and also because no liquid is added until after the surface of the food has been seared or until it has been removed from the pan.

Sautéing should not be confused with *frying*, which is a method of cooking food partially submerged in fat. Although the procedures appear the same, in frying, or panfrying, a great deal more fat is used (at least one-half inch in depth) and the food usually requires further cooking at a reduced heat after being browned.

The technique that really distinguishes a true sauté, however, is a constant tossing or stirring of the food while it is being cooked. (Thus the name sauté, from the French word *sauter*, which means "to jump.")

A familiar form of sauté is the method of Oriental cooking known as stir-frying. A special round-bottomed pan called a *wok* is generally used, but the cooking process is basically the same as the classic French method.

Sautéing is one of the most common methods used in all of cookery, yet because of the high calorie count associated with anything "fried," most diet cookbooks choose to ignore it completely. I find this restriction absolutely unnecessary. The techniques and procedures of a basic sauté can easily be adapted to low-calorie cooking by using food-release agents and nonstick cooking surfaces whenever possible. Granted, there are times when a small amount of oil, butter, or margarine (seldom more than one tablespoon for four servings) is needed for proper searing and browning, but they are rare exceptions rather than the rule.

LOW-CALORIE MOIST-HEAT COOKING METHODS

BOILING is the process of cooking food in a large amount of liquid at a temperature of 212° F. Boiling is a quick, efficient method of transferring heat to food, but in practice, very few foods are actually cooked at a sustained boiling temperature. Eggs, pasta, rice, and foods prepared in a pressure cooker (as high as 250° F.) are notable exceptions to the rule. Whole fruits, fresh vegetables, and legumes are cooked at a gentle boil. Essentially, all methods of cooking in liquid use the same principle and are simply various stages of the overall *boiling* process.

SIMMERING is the cooking of large or whole pieces of meat, chicken, turkey, fish, or shellfish in a large amount of liquid just below the boiling point, between 180° F. and 210° F. In simmering, the cooking is initiated in boiling liquid to expel unwanted elements from the food and to seal in the valuable juices and flavor; the heat is then reduced to a simmer until the food is done. Salt, herbs, spices, and aromatic vegetables are usually added during the cooking process to prevent unnecessary leaching of the flavor compounds and nutrients from the food by osmotic pressure.

The cooking time required for foods prepared in this manner will depend on the kind of protein (meat, poultry, or fish), its quality, tenderness, and the size and quantity of the pieces being cooked.

The various moist-heat methods by which protein foods are cooked in liquid (simmering, poaching, braising, and stewing) essentially differ in the size of the meat pieces and the quantity of liquid used rather than in the cooking temperatures employed. You'll find that most foods, except for starches, are cooked at "simmering" temperatures.

POACHING is a term used to describe the simmering of eggs, fruit, or portion-cut pieces of fish in a small amount of liquid. This method of cooking is identical to *simmering*, except that the poaching liquid is almost always reduced and thickened and used as a sauce.

BRAISING is the cooking of foods with a small amount of flavored liquid in a covered pot, either at a simmering temperature on top of the stove or in a slow to moderate oven. The flavored liquid, enhanced by the addition of aromatic vegetables, spices, and the juices extracted from the cooked food, becomes the sauce.

Braising differs from the other low-calorie moist-heat methods of cooking in that the food is generally seared and browned in a hot skillet, under the broiler, or in a hot oven before any liquid is added. White meats and fish are not browned (white meats may be quickly seared in a hot oven to tighten the outside surface) and can be braised in much less time than required for tougher protein foods.

This method contributes to the tenderness of foods, but it's only the tough foods that have to be braised to become tender. Tender foods, such as poultry, sweetbreads, pork, veal, lamb, and fish are sometimes braised for a variety in taste and flavor. Vegetables prepared by this moist-heat process are also said to be braised.

STEWING is the braising of food in small, uniform pieces. It is a moist, braising process used mostly in the preparation of less tender foods. Tender foods should be sautéed rather than stewed. As in braising, the reduced or thickened cooking liquid becomes the sauce. A stew may or may not be browned, depending upon the type of food being cooked.

The same principles and procedures used for braising are used for stewing, except that for stewing, the food is cut considerably smaller and the cooking time is short compared to the braising of steaks or roasts.

SEASONINGS

The recipes in this book are not new or even exotic in nature. They are based on ingredients that are familiar and readily available to all of us and, for the most part, are simply decalorized versions of our more traditional favorites. My intention is not to give you another collection of recipes, but rather to show you how almost any recipe can be made lower in calories by substituting low-calorie ingredients for high-calorie ones and by changing the method of preparation.

For most cooks, however, learning to prepare foods without benefit of the usual highly flavored but fattening ingredients is an awakening experience. In all probability, dishes will seem bland and almost unrecognizable in taste. But if the creative instincts are sufficiently challenged and the desire to lose weight strong enough, the disillusioned cook will persist in his efforts until the desired results are obtained. This requires patience and discipline. It also requires a knowledge of the various types of seasonings—herbs, spices, vegetable flavorings, and extracts—and the important role they play in diet cooking.

The world of seasonings and the preparation of low-calorie meals are almost inseparable, for one seems so totally deficient without the other. Seasonings, after all, are simply flavor enhancers. They are not essential ingredients, nor do they change the chemistry in a recipe. They can be added or subtracted at will. But judiciously and artfully used, seasonings are capable of transforming otherwise plain and monotonous diet dishes into ingenious gourmet delights. They give a subtle but distinctive flavor to almost any dish and succeed in making low-calorie cooking a challenging, creative experience.

The proper use of seasonings is an art that can be acquired only through constant practice and a loving devotion to cooking. It is a creative means of expression that one cultivates over a period of years in the kitchen and cannot be thought of in terms of measurement or formula. In the end, one's own experience and perception rather than a strict adherence to recipes must determine how a dish is flavored. Moreover, you must be extremely careful when seasoning food not to overdo it. What tastes right to one person may be quite objectionable to another. Our sense of taste varies, which is why it is difficult to follow any particular recipe exactly. Unless a recipe calls for a certain predominant flavor—curry and chile dishes for instance—seasonings should be used with discrimination and restraint. The best advice I can give is to use as delicate and subtle a touch as possible, especially if it is a new flavor. You can always add more if desired, but it's almost impossible to correct an overseasoned dish.

Improper buying and storage can rob seasonings of their flavor. Buy them in the smallest amounts possible, especially those you don't use very often. Whole herbs and spices keep their aroma and flavor longer than those that are ground or powdered. For convenience, keep your seasonings as close to the stove as possible, but not so close that the heat is able to dry them out. And finally, keep them tightly covered and away from light.

CITRUS JUICES AND RINDS

Most of us are familiar enough with the flavoring characteristics of citrus fruits to appreciate the marvelous contribution they make to cooking. The addition of a small amount of citric juice, or more specifically citric acid, to a dish almost invariably enlivens and accentuates its flavor. At the same time, citric juice brings a refreshing and rewarding taste to the palate; tames sweetness; adds freshness to the taste of unsalted foods; cuts oil and fat; helps tenderize meat and poultry; keeps seafood white and firm; acts as an emulsifier in salad dressings; substitutes for wine or vinegar in a recipe; makes dairy products more digestible; and enhances the flavor of vegetables. The list is long indeed!

What is not generally understood, however, is that while citric juices like lemon juice, orange juice, and lime juice are excellent seasoners or flavoring agents, they have very little aromatic flavor, and the fruit taste actually comes from the heavy concentration of aromatic oil in the rind. This is usually taken with a hand grater or a special tool called a zester. I personally like to remove large portions of the rind with an old-fashioned potato peeler and cut them into fine slivers with a sharp French knife.

Be sure to use only the colorful outer coating of the fruits, as the white pith beneath it is bitter. A twist of citrus peel over a hot or cold beverage is yet another way to capture these essential oils for flavor. Easy and effective

HERBS

Herbs come from the leaves and sometimes the stems or flowers of small, succulent annual, perennial, or biennial plants grown in temperate climates. Among the most common are basil, bay leaf, marjoram, mint, oregano, parsley, rosemary, tarragon, and thyme.

Although most of us, including myself, are satisfied with the assortment and availability of dried herbs, there is, without doubt, a charm and fascination about using them fresh. A few fresh herbs, like parsley, are always available, but most are so difficult to find in stores that about the only way to always have a selection of fresh herbs on hand when you want them is to grow them yourself. Fortunately, herbs can be grown almost anywhere; they even grow well indoors in pots or window boxes if they are provided sufficient sunlight. Some herbs that grow well indoors are oregano, mint, and chives. Freezing and drying are the common methods for preserving fresh herbs for later use. (There are few things as alluring as an herb-scented kitchen). Incidentally, if you own a microwave oven, it is especially good for this purpose.

Fresh herbs are not as concentrated in flavor as dried ones, so when substituting fresh herbs for the dried varieties in a recipe, use three to four times the amount recommended for the dried volume.

Dried herbs that are left whole will retain their characteristic flavor and aroma longer than if purchased already ground or powdered. However, if they are adequately protected from exposure to moisture, heat, and light, the deterioration of preground herbs can be delayed.

MUSHROOMS

Mushrooms are a gastronomic delight, both as a food and as a seasoning. They are delicious by themselves—either raw, cooked, or pickled—or they can enhance the flavor of other foods; they provide excitement and savor to almost every facet of diet cookery; they add a touch of elegance to any dish; and they are good for dieters because they are low in calories (one pound of raw fresh mushrooms has about 66 calories), without fat or carbohydrates, yet high in proteins, vitamins, and minerals.

If you really adore the taste and bouquet of mushrooms, try mixing dried and fresh mushrooms together in the same recipe. Dried mushrooms, used extensively in European and Asian cooking, are wild, not cultivated varieties, and are often better for flavoring than fresh ones. Prepare dried mushrooms by soaking them in warm water, or in wine, until soft. And be sure to save the liquid in which they soak and use it as part of the stock. Unlike fresh mushrooms, which should not be added to a cooked dish until the last ten minutes of cooking, dried mushrooms can withstand longer cooking without detriment and can be added to a dish at the beginning of the cooking period. They have a different texture, however, and should not be indiscriminately used as a substitute for fresh ones.

Canned mushrooms, on the other hand, may be substituted when fresh are not available, but they have very little flavor and are usless as a seasoning.

ONIONS

Of the various vegetable flavorings used in cooking, none is more important or versatile than the ubiquitous onion. It has been cultivated for thousands of years and is still the basic seasoning ingredient in all the great cuisines of the world. In low-calorie cooking, onions add a maximum amount of flavor and aroma and a minimum amount of calories—only four calories a tablespoon. So feel free to use onions as a seasoning, but don't get carried away; they can easily add an additional 50 to 75 calories to the total caloric value of a dish.

Onions come in a wide variety of sizes, shapes, and colors, from the more common dried yellow, white, and red varieties to the less frequently used shallots, garlic, chives, green onions, and leeks. Most are marketed dry—but dry only in the sense that they are cured in sunlight and air for several days before being harvested and stored. Inside they should be sweet-tasting and juicy. Chives, green onions, and the thick-stemmed leeks, like other green vegetables, are marketed fresh.

DRY ONIONS

Because of their tremendous keeping qualities, most types of dry onions are available from storage year around, but many of the milder varieties, like the large red and white Spanish and Bermuda types, are grown in limited amounts and appear only seasonally.

The pungent, full-flavored Globe or Creole type onions are far and away our most popular dried onions. These are the onions that can be used in so many ways in the kitchen, from sliced to diced—either raw or cooked. Although usually yellow in color, you will find white, red, and brown varieties offered. They're always available and will give you the most flavor at the lowest cost.

Other types of onions that are marketed dry include the mild-flavored pearl and white onions. These are the flaky white to silver-skinned onions that measure from one-half to two inches in diameter and are so delectable in stews, braised dishes, and casseroles. They're not a separate variety, however, but simply white onions harvested very young.

Shallot

The shallot is a member of the onion family which produces small clustered bulbs instead of a single one. It is pungent yet delicate in flavor and combines some of the characteristics of both onion and garlic. Like garlic, the bulbs separate into papery brown-skinned cloves.

Shallots are still difficult to find in this country, except in the professional kitchen, but they have been used extensively in Europe for centuries, and you will find them to be an important flavoring for most of the classical preparations of *haute cuisine*.

Used primarily as a flavoring and blending agent in low-calorie cooking, shallots emulsify better than onions and help bind pan sauces together, thus reducing the need for calorie-laden starch thickeners.

If you can't find shallots in your supermarkets, minced Globe onions or the white portion of scallions can be substituted in equal proportions to the shallots called for in the recipe.

Garlic

A head of garlic is a bulb, like the onion, encasing individually wrapped cloves in a tissue-thin white skin. It is the strongest, most pungent member of the onion family and is without question an extraordinary and certainly a most controversial seasoning.

Though aggressive in flavor and aroma when eaten raw, cooking subdues its pungency, and long-cooked garlic becomes delicate and mild in taste and can be enjoyed with impugnity. However, like shallots, garlic should never be browned or burned as, unlike onion, it develops a disagreeable, bitter flavor.

GREEN ONIONS

Chives

Chives have the most refined flavor of all the onions and are used where a mild onion flavor is desired. They combine well in egg and cheese dishes and are especially invaluable, both as a garnish and seasoning, in hors d'oeuvre and dip mixtures and sprinkled into soups, salads, and vegetable dishes. Unlike the other members of the onion genus, only the hollow, cylindrical leaves are eaten.

Chives are perennial, easy to grow, and at their absolute best when used fresh. But freeze-dried and frozen chives are also available, and, admittedly, are convenient to have on hand when needed.

Chives have a lovely flavor by themselves and also mix well with other herbs. They are included as one of the classic *fines herbes* used in French cookery—namely, parsley, tarragon, chervil, and chives. Other herbs, however, are commonly used as a substitute in particular recipes.

Scallions

Scallions (sometimes called green onions) are not a separate variety of onion, simply young onions which are pulled when their bulbs are less than one-half inch in diameter. They are second to chives in delicacy of flavor and may be eaten raw in vegetable hors d'oeuvres or dips, in salads, or cooked.

As a seasoning, green onions lend their flavor and color to many low-calorie dishes and are an excellent substitute for shallots.

Leeks

Leeks are onionlike plants that resemble large green onions in shape, with long, thick cylindrical stems averaging one inch in diameter, and very little bulb formation at the root end. They have a milder, more subtle flavor than the standard Globe onions and are used primarily to flavor soups and stews. The long, flat dark-green leaves, which are usually discarded in the family kitchen, are used by the professional chef as an added seasoning in stocks and court bouillons.

Used extensively in Europe, leeks, unfortunately, have never been very popular in this country, and because of the lack of demand, are always inordinately expensive.

SALT

Salt as a seasoning is familiar to all of us. It is one of the most fundamental of all the tastes in food, and along with sweet, sour, and bitter, is perceived as a true taste by the tasting organs in the mouth. Salt is neither an herb nor a spice, but a mineral used to intensify the natural flavor of foods to which it is added. It is a primary and necessary seasoning, one that is contained naturally in most foods—and in virtually all processed foods, I might add. Food without salt is often dull, but it will absolutely ruin a dish if overdone.

A word of caution, however. The unrestricted use of salt can be catastrophic to your diet and your morale. This is because the body tends to store sodium (salt is technically a compound known as sodium chloride), which in turn produces a proportionate amount of fluid retention in the tissues. And since every pint of fluid retained in the body is equal to one pound of weight, it is indeed possible for you to be losing fat and gaining weight at the same time!

Use salt only in cooking. Break yourself of the unconscious habit of salting everything before you even taste it (it's an insult to the cook anyway). Also, avoid prepared foods that have an obviously high salt content, such as pretzels, potato chips, and pickles. Stay away from prepackaged and fast-food items and prepare everything from scratch. After all, isn't that what this book is all about?

The best salt for cooking is sea salt, since iodized or ordinary table salt is diluted with cornstarch for easy pouring. It generally comes in coarse crystals and is ground fresh as needed. Both salt mills and sea salt can be found at health-food stores and gourmet cooking stores.

You will find that for most recipes I have simply stated "salt and pepper to taste." That's because the amount that is "to taste" varies so widely with each individual cook. Also, it allows cooks who are not on a salt-restricted diet to season as they choose.

Remember, the role of salt as a seasoning is not to give a special taste of its own to food, but to give emphasis to and intensify other flavors.

SOY SAUCE

Authentic soy sauce is made from a fermented mixture of water, soy beans, wheat, and sea salt. A staple in Oriental cuisines, soy sauce is used primarily to heighten the flavor and color of cooked food. But it is also a predominate ingredient in many cold dishes, marinades, and dipping sauces. In cooked dishes, it should be added shortly before the end of the cooking period, as too much heat affects the flavor.

There are two principal types of soy sauce—light and dark. For dieters I recommend using light soy sauce, specifically the Kikkoman brand—a Japanese-style soy sauce that, ironically, is made in the northern United States. Light soy sauce tends to be less salty and less bitter than other imported or domestic types marketed; it is also the most delicate in flavor. This is good for dieters because less sweetener is necessary than would be used with stronger and heavier sauces.

Remember that soy sauce is essentially the Oriental substitute for the American salt shaker, so whenever you use it, be sure to cut down on the salt.

SPICES

True spices are the dried, aromatic parts of perennial plants and trees grown in tropical climates. Allspice, cinnamon, cloves, ginger, mace, nutmeg, pepper, and turmeric are among the most commonly used spices in American cookery. Spices, like herbs, lose their fragrance and strength when exposed to heat, light, or air for any length of time, so it is best to buy them whole and in small quantities and preferably in metal containers.

You will recall that I said that seasonings are not essential ingredients and for this reason can be altered in a recipe without affecting the basic mixture. Spices vary considerably in flavor and pungency. Our individual sense of taste, likes, and dislikes also vary. Thus when you're cooking with spices, don't feel as though you have to follow a recipe exactly. (This doesn't hold true for baking recipes, however.) Rely on your own personal taste to determine the kind and the exact amount of seasoning to use. And remember to use spices with restraint, for they generally increase in strength during cooking. This is especially true in diet cooking where we often allow liquids to evaporate and subsequently thicken a dish by reduction.

For diet dishes that require a long cooking time, add whole spices at the start. If they are ground, add them during the last half hour of cooking. If the cooking time is short, add the spices from the start.

VANILLA

I doubt whether there is any flavoring as important to diet cooking as vanilla. It makes sugar sweeter and heightens the natural flavor of most fruits. Vanilla sugar—made by placing a dried vanilla bean in a canister of sugar—or vanilla extract, when used in combination with unflavored sugar, can reduce the amount of this high calorie ingredient in a recipe by at least one half, sometimes more. You will discover that vanilla can be used in the same way with artificial sweeteners and helps to eliminate the aftertaste that is usually associated with these synthetic products.

Vanilla flavoring is available in three forms: dried pods or beans, pure vanilla extract, and imitation vanilla flavoring or *vanillin*. For the most and the best vanilla flavor, use the dried bean or the extract. Imitation vanilla flavoring has the bouquet of vanilla, but like most chemical substitutes and seasonings, it lacks the depth and quality of the real thing.

Vanilla extract has about ten calories per teaspoon, which comes from the alcohol used in the fermenting process. To save calories without destroying its flavor in foods that are heated, add the extract just before a dish is removed from the stove. The alcohol will evaporate, thus eliminating the calories, while the vanilla flavor will infuse the liquid and enhance the ingredients.

VINEGAR

We don't often think of it as such, but ordinary household-variety vinegar is an excellent low-calorie seasoning. It is a convenient, inexpensive, easy-to-use ingredient that adds an unusually delicate flavor and aroma to foods when it is carefully and unobtrusively used. Originally the product of good wine gone sour (thus its French name, *vin aigre*, meaning sour wine), today there are many types of vinegars to choose from. These include, in addition to wine vinegar, cider vinegar, made from fermented apples; malt vinegar, made from sour beer and ale; and distilled white vinegar made from grains. There are many others, but one of my personal favorites is rice vinegar from Japan. It is very mild, with a very pleasant taste, and is especially suited to salad-making.

For cooking and for salads, the wine vinegars, both red and white, are the most agreeable and the most versatile. Red is robust, white more delicate, and both are excellent seasoners. A fine cider vinegar, either plain or herb-flavored, can also be exceedingly good, but don't be afraid to cut it with water if you find it to be overly acidic.

Distilled white vinegar is more common for pickling and preserving. It is very strong and should be diluted when a milder vinegar taste is desired.

Malt vinegar (so very good with fish) has a distinctive taste and is usually used in recipes of English origin.

In cooking with vinegar, remember to go easy at first. How much you eventually use is strictly a matter of taste, but too much can overflavor and give a harsh quality to the dish.

WINE

Wine used in cooking does wondrous things to food and can frequently transform a mundane diet dish into a gourmet delicacy. The alcohol contained in the wine (it's the alcohol that yields the calories) is volatilized by the heat in cooking, and what remains to flavor the dish is the residual taste and aroma.

The key to cooking successfully with wine is to use it at every opportunity in your favorite recipes (I hope the recipes in this book will soon become your favorites), for only experience with wine cookery will make you skillful in its use. You will be surprised how just a small amount of wine cooked slowly in a dish can change its flavor completely. Seasoning with wine can perform culinary magic and give added flavor to practically every course on your menu; it can also become one of your most important allies in the kitchen.

Cooking with wine is more an art than a science and, as a creative low-calorie cook, you should be adventurous and enjoy experimenting. But don't overdo it. Too much of a raw wine taste will give a harsh and unpleasant quality to a dish. You should follow a wine recipe exactly for the first time, especially if an unfamiliar type of wine is called for, until you become knowledgeable enough with the characteristics of the combined ingredients in a dish to be able to adjust them to your own taste. When properly used, wine will enliven the flavor of a dish, while at the same time imparting a subtle but distinct flavor of its own, without adding calories.

Essentially, cooking with wine—and other spirits used as a seasoning—amounts to cooking away the alcohol rather than cooking with it. If your finished diet dish tastes strongly of alcohol, chances are you have used too much or you haven't allowed enough cooking time for the alcohol to evaporate. Usually ten minutes is a sufficient amount of time to accomplish this. When both wine and herbs are called for in a dish, I frequently combine them in a small saucepan and reduce the mixture by half before straining it into the food. This way, you can add wine and herb seasonings to a dish without worrying about the evaporation of the alcohol. As with other seasoning agents, wine adds greatly to the overall flavor of a dish, but is most effective when used with restraint.

The moderately priced table wines commonly served as a beverage are excellent choices for low-calorie cooking. These wines, however, must be fully cooked to be edible. Fortified and aperitif wines are exceptions to the rule. They are stronger and have a more concentrated flavor than table wines and are primarily used for their characteristic body and bouquet. They're always added toward the end of the cooking period and are never really cooked for any length of time. Also, the quantities used with fortified wines and aperitifs are considerably less than required for the more commonly used table wine recipes. Remember that, except for a few important exceptions, most table wines, both red and white, are interchangeable and any wine you enjoy drinking or serving with a particular dish should also be fine for cooking.

All alcoholic ingredients used as a seasoning—wine, liquor, beer, liqueurs, and flavoring extracts—will lose their alcoholic calories when subjected to sufficient heat to cause their alcohol to evaporate. But beer, liqueurs, and dessert wines leave behind a carbohydrate residue that contains calories, and these calories should be counted as part of the total caloric value of a dish.

As a final reminder, wine must be sufficiently cooked to be edible, for it is the highly concentrated residual extract that seasons a dish and not the alcohol.

APPETIZERS AND SNACKS

In diet cooking, appetizers—the name I have chosen to embrace the entire range of hot and cold appetizers, hors d'oeuvres, relishes, savories, spreads, dips, and tidbits served before a meal or as the first course of a meal—serve two important functions: Preceding a meal as a cocktail, luncheon, or dinner appetizer, they are meant to stimulate the appetite and set the stage for the courses to follow. Eaten between meals in the form of snacks, their purpose is to supplement the diet or curb the appetite until the next meal. They can be as simple or as elaborate as you choose. The varieties are endless. But whether the appetizers are before-the-meal starters or between-meal "pacifiers," they should enchant the eye, please the palate, and above all, be in character with the occasion.

The recipes that follow are decalorized versions of the more popular appetizers. They are all made from nutritious, low-calorie ingredients and can be enjoyed in moderation without undermining your diet.

CLAM DIP

2 cartons (8-ounce) low-fat cottage cheese
1 cup buttermilk
1 can (8-ounce) minced clams, drained
1 teaspoon Worcestershire sauce
1 teaspoon lemon juice
1 teaspoon onion salt
½ teaspoon Tabasco sauce
⅛ teaspoon white pepper

Makes 3 cups at 14 calories per tablespoon.

CRANBERRY DIP

1 cup plain yogurt
1 can (8-ounce) low-calorie cranberry sauce
2 tablespoons cream-style horseradish

1 teaspoon sugar
½ teaspoon cinnamon

Combine all ingredients in a blender. Blend well and refrigerate.

Makes 2 cups at 10 calories per tablespoon.

CURRIED AVOCADO DIP

2 large avocados
1 cup plain yogurt
4 tablespoons lemon juice
1 teaspoon curry powder

⅛ teaspoon garlic powder
⅛ teaspoon salt
dash of Tabasco sauce

Mash avocado pulp. Add remaining ingredients and beat until smooth.

Makes 3 cups at 18 calories per tablespoon.

CURRIED HORSERADISH DIP

2 cups plain yogurt
1 tablespoon prepared horseradish

2 teaspoons curry powder
2 teaspoons lemon juice
dash Tabasco sauce

In a small mixing bowl, blend all ingredients with a wire whip. Chill thoroughly to allow flavors to blend before serving.

Makes 2 cups at 20 calories per tablespoon.

DIETER'S PLAIN SOUR CREAM DIP

2 cups low-fat cottage cheese
1 cup buttermilk
1 teaspoon lemon juice
dash of salt

Combine the buttermilk, lemon juice, and salt in a blender. Blend for 5 minutes. Put blender on low speed and add cottage cheese a little at a time. Put the blender on high speed and blend 2 to 3 minutes, forcing the sour cream down into the blades with a rubber spatula. Keep covered in the refrigerator.

Makes 2 cups at 11 calories per tablespoon.

FLAVORED SOUR CREAM DIP

2 cups low-fat cottage cheese
1 cup buttermilk
1 teaspoon lemon juice
1 packet dry onion soup or dip mix
dash of salt

Make the sour cream by combining the buttermilk, lemon juice, and salt in a blender. Blend on high speed for 5 minutes. Reduce to low speed and add cottage cheese a little at a time. Return to high speed and blend 2 to 3 minutes, forcing the sour cream down into the blades with a rubber spatula. Put sour cream in a small mixing bowl and stir in dry mix. Cover and refrigerate before serving.

Makes 2 cups at 11 calories per tablespoon.

Chef's Cooking Tip:
If the sour cream thickens too much, thin with either skim milk or additional buttermilk. If you like it thicker, blend in more cottage cheese.

FRUIT DIP

1 carton (8-ounce) plain yogurt
1 pint fresh strawberries
2 teaspoons honey
½ teaspoon cinnamon

Combine all ingredients in a blender and purée until smooth and creamy.

Makes 1½ cups at 12 calories per tablespoon.

ONION DIP

1 carton (8-ounce) plain yogurt
1 tablespoon onion soup or
   dip mix
2 tablespoons chopped chives

Combine ingredients in a small mixing bowl. Mix well and chill thoroughly before serving.

Makes 1 cup at 10 calories per serving.

SEAFOOD COCKTAIL DIP

1 bottle (11-ounce) dietetic catsup
2 teaspoons lemon juice
1 tablespoon creamy horseradish
1 teaspoon Worcestershire sauce
¼ cup minced celery
¼ cup minced chives

Combine all ingredients in a small mixing bowl and chill before serving.

Makes 1½ cups at 6 calories per tablespoon.

TANGY LEMON DIP

1 carton (8-ounce) plain yogurt
1 tablespoon sugar
½ teaspoon grated lemon peel

Combine all ingredients. Blend with a small whip and chill before serving.

Makes 1 cup at 11 calories per tablespoon.

DEVILED EGGS

4 hard-cooked eggs, shelled
2 tablespoons imitation
   mayonnaise
1½ teaspoons prepared mustard
¼ teaspoon Worcestershire
   sauce
⅛ teaspoon celery seed
⅛ teaspoon onion salt
pepper to taste
paprika

Cut the eggs in half lengthwise, then combine scooped-out yolks with remaining ingredients. Refill whites. Sprinkle with paprika and chill.

Makes 8 servings at 50 calories per serving.

STUFFED CELERY

1 carton (8-ounce) low-fat cottage cheese
¼ cup buttermilk
1 teaspoon lemon juice
¼ teaspoon onion salt
¼ teaspoon garlic salt
¼ teaspoon Worcestershire sauce
4 celery ribs, washed, peeled, and chilled
12 green pepper strips
dash paprika

Combine cottage cheese, buttermilk, lemon juice, onion salt, garlic salt, and Worcestershire sauce in a blender. Blend until smooth and creamy. Refrigerate for at least one hour. Cut celery ribs into 3-inch pieces. Fill each piece with one tablespoon of filling mixture. Garnish with pepper strips and paprika.

Makes 12 servings at 11 calories per serving.

BACON-WRAPPED WATER CHESTNUTS

20 water chestnuts
¼ cup soy sauce
1½ tablespoons honey
10 slices lean bacon

Drain water chestnuts thoroughly. Combine soy sauce and honey in a small bowl and marinate chestnuts for 30 minutes. Cut the bacon slices in half, crosswise, then wrap bacon around each water chestnut and fasten with a toothpick. Place the appetizers on a rack in a shallow pan. Bake in a preheated 375° F. oven for 20 minutes or until bacon is crisp. Drain on paper toweling.

Makes 20 servings at 35 calories per serving.

BAKED STUFFED MUSHROOMS

24 large fresh mushrooms

DUXELLES MUSHROOM STUFFING MIXTURE
1 pound chopped mushrooms with stems (include stems from mushroom caps)
4 shallots, peeled
1 tablespoon butter or margarine
1 tablespoon vegetable oil
1 tablespoon minced parsley
salt and pepper to taste

Clean large mushrooms with a damp cloth. Remove and reserve the stems for stuffing mixture. Clean and trim the additional one pound of mushrooms. Add stems from reserved mushroom caps and chop coarsely. Chop peeled shallots. Place chopped mushrooms and shallots in a food processor (or mince with a French knife) and whirl for about 5 seconds or until finely chopped. Heat the fat and oil in a large skillet and sauté the vegetables until the moisture has evaporated. Season with salt, pepper, and minced parsley. Fill the mushroom caps with the duxelles mixture and bake in a preheated 350° F. oven for 15 to 20 minutes.

Makes 24 servings at 30 calories per serving.

RAW MUSHROOMS AND ROQUEFORT

½ pound large firm mushrooms
1 package (0.70 ounces) Italian salad dressing mix
⅔ cup water
⅓ cup cider vinegar

4 teaspoons Roquefort cheese, crumbled
2 teaspoons diced pimiento
1 head bibb or butter lettuce

Wipe mushrooms with a damp cloth. Slice mushrooms. Combine with dressing mix, water and vinegar, cheese and pimiento. Cover and chill for at least 4 hours. To serve, drain mushrooms and serve on lettuce cups. Strain marinade and spoon cheese and pimiento over mushrooms. (Reserve strained marinade to use with other salads.)

Makes 4 servings at 30 calories per serving.

Chef's Cooking Tip:
Fresh mushrooms can be successfully frozen if you wash and dry them quickly in a little acidulated water (water with a small amount of lemon juice added) and store them in plastic bags until needed. They can be used right from the freezer without defrosting.

RUMAKI

¾ pound chicken livers, halved
10 water chestnuts, halved
½ pound lean bacon
½ cup soy sauce

1 tablespoon honey
1 tablespoon shredded fresh ginger root

Wash and drain livers. Pat dry with paper toweling. Cut the bacon strips in half, crosswise. Fold liver halves around halved water chestnuts, wrap with a half slice of bacon and secure with a toothpick. In a shallow baking pan, combine the soy sauce, honey, and shredded ginger. Place the appetizers in the sauce and marinate for several hours, turning frequently to coat all sides. Place on a rack in a shallow pan and broil under moderate heat until the bacon is crisp, about 7 minutes. Turn at least once while cooking. Serve immediately.

Makes 20 servings at 50 calories per serving.

Chef's Cooking Tip:
Rumaki can be prepared ahead and refrigerated or frozen until serving time. Simply undercook. When ready to serve, finish the cooking in a 375° F. oven until the bacon is crisp.

HAM-WRAPPED PICKLES

8 slices luncheon-type cooked and smoked ham, thinly sliced

24 whole sweet gherkins

Cut ham slices into approximately 1¼-inch by 4-inch strips. Wrap each strip around gherkins. Spear with a cocktail pick and chill.

Makes 24 servings at 30 calories per serving.

LOW-CALORIE CREAM CHEESE SPREAD

2 cups low-fat cottage cheese
1 cup buttermilk
2 teaspoons sugar
1 teaspoon lemon juice

½ teaspoon onion salt
¼ teaspoon Worcestershire sauce
1 teaspoon alginate powder

Allow the cottage cheese to reach room temperature. Combine the ingredients in a blender and whirl 3 to 5 minutes or until smooth and creamy. Use a rubber spatula if needed to push the cheese into the blades. Refrigerate at least one hour before serving.

Makes 2 cups at 11 calories per tablespoon.

NOTE: Alginate powder is a non-caloric, vegetable-based thickener and emulsifier used by many vegetarians as a substitute for gelatin. It is available in most health food stores and some drugstores.

LIVER PÂTÉ

1 pound chicken livers
2¼ cups water
1 chopped apple
1 teaspoon minced onion

½ teaspoon salt
½ teaspoon pepper
⅛ teaspoon garlic powder

Clean the chicken livers thoroughly. Simmer in 2 cups of boiling water until firm, about 7 to 10 minutes. Do not stir. Drain and rinse. Peel and core apple. Combine livers, onion, apple, and seasoning in a blender. Add ¼ cup of cooking liquid. Blend until smooth, adding more liquid if too thick. Refrigerate.

Chilling should thicken pâté to the proper consistency to use as a spread or as a paste to be piped through a baker's bag.

Makes 2 cups at 25 calories per tablespoon.

SARDINE SPREAD

1 cup low-fat cottage cheese
1 can (4-ounce) boneless sardines
2 tablespoons chopped parsley
2 tablespoons minced onion
4 tablespoons diet catsup

1 teaspoon lemon juice
1 teaspoon Worcestershire sauce
1 teaspoon garlic salt
dash of Tabasco sauce

Combine all ingredients in a blender. Blend well and refrigerate.

Makes 1¾ cups at 20 calories per tablespoon.

FRUIT COCKTAIL

1 cup watermelon balls
1 cup cantaloupe balls
1 cup honeydew melon balls

1 cup cranshaw melon balls
4 fresh mint sprigs

Arrange melon balls in sherbet glasses. Garnish with sprigs of mint. Chill thoroughly before serving.

Makes 4 servings at 20 calories per serving.

JELLIED CHICKEN BROTH

2 tablespoons unflavored gelatin
½ cup cold water
4 cups hot chicken broth
1 tablespoon chopped parsley
salt and pepper to taste

Soften the gelatin in the half cup of cold water for 5 minutes. Add the hot chicken broth to dissolve the gelatin. Season with salt, pepper, and parsley. Pour liquid into a nonstick baking dish. Chill. When set, cut into squares and serve in cold bouillon cups.

Makes 4 servings at 16 calories per serving.

Chef's Cooking Tip:
If you're using canned chicken broth, refrigerate the can for a few hours so the fat can be removed from the surface with a spoon or ladle before heating.

JELLIED TOMATO CONSOMMÉ

1 tablespoon unflavored gelatin
¾ cup tomato juice
1 cup consommé
⅛ teaspoon salt
⅛ teaspoon pepper
⅛ teaspoon prepared horseradish
2 tablespoons lemon juice
1 teaspoon sugar

Soften the gelatin in the tomato juice. Place over low heat to dissolve. Remove from heat and stir in the remaining ingredients. Pour into a 2-cup mold or individual dishes. Chill until firm, then unmold in lukewarm water.

Makes 4 servings at 30 calories per serving.

SHRIMP COCKTAIL

1 cup shredded lettuce
½ pound small cocktail shrimps
¼ cup seafood cocktail dip
4 parsley sprigs

Wash shrimp and pat dry. Combine shrimps with cocktail dip in lettuce-lined cocktail glasses. Chill thoroughly before serving. Garnish with parsley sprigs. Serve with Seafood Cocktail Dip (recipe on page 19).

Makes 4 servings at 55 calories per serving.

VEGETABLE JUICE COCKTAIL SUPREME

20 ounces tomato juice
4 ounces carrot juice
1 tablespoon beet juice
½ teaspoon celery salt
⅛ teaspoon onion salt
⅛ teaspoon Worcestershire sauce
dash of Tabasco sauce

Combine all ingredients and chill before serving. Garnish with a lemon or lime slice or a small rib of celery.

Makes 4 servings at 42 calories per serving.

Chef's Cooking Tip:
Beet juice can be readily obtained by draining just the amount of juice you need from a can of sliced beets (to be used later for salads or vegetables) and refilling the can with water so the beets don't dry out.

SOUPS AND STOCKS

At times, nothing's more satisfying than the sight and aroma of a good bowl of soup. Served hot or cold, thick or thin, bland or sharp, soup is a delightful and sensible way to begin a diet meal. It can be prepared with a minimum of calories, yet still be satisfying enough to take the edge off a voracious appetite.

It's interesting how cultural preferences can change the importance and dignity of a dish. In this country, for instance, we think of soup as an appetizer, usually choosing between a modest fruit or seafood cocktail, a cup of delicate, light, clear broth or consommé, or a chilled green salad to appease our appetites and stir up our taste buds before the arrival of the main event. But in many countries, soup constitutes the entire meal and is the mainstay of the diet. The pot au feu and bouillabaisse of France are two classic soups that are meals in themselves and need little in the way of accompaniment—except possibly a small salad and a light dessert.

Soup can be defined as a liquid-based food which derives its nourishment and flavor from the cooking of meat, poultry, seafood, or vegetables. In the case of clear soups—such as broths, consommés and bouillons—the soup is simmered slowly to extract the flavor from the meat and vegetables and transfer it to the broth. Thick soups on the other hand—like cream soups, purées, and chowders—are cooked to tenderize the foods and blend the flavors of the food and its broth. Thick soups are often thickened with the addition of cereals, milk, cream, or eggs, but an electric blender can purée a soup into a creamy smoothness without adding calories.

There are virtually thousands of various soup combinations, and they can be classified in various ways, depending on their basic ingredients, the method of preparation used, their place on the menu (as an appetizer or the major part of the meal), and sometimes simply by the garnish used with the soup.

Basically, there are three major soup classifications: *clear* soups, *thick* soups, and *family* or national soups. Fortunately for the dieter, most soups are light in calories, low in fats, and rich in nutritive value. They are also sufficiently rich in flavor to serve as an appetizer prior to the main course. Your choice of a soup to be served as an appetizer, however, should take into consideration the other dishes on the menu to avoid repeating major flavorings in subsequent courses.

The liquid in which meat, poultry, seafood, or vegetables has cooked in, before it has been clarified, is called *broth*. After this liquid is strained and clarified it is called *stock*. *Bouillon* is primarily thought of as clarified liquid extracted from simmered meat and beef bones. *Consommé* is a clear soup which is derived from the clarification of bouillon, but it can be clarified from other stocks as well.

What you really need to know is that the major difference between broth, stock, bouillon, and consommé is one of clarity. Liquid broths have not been clarified and the *fat* has not been removed. This is usually accomplished by straining the broth and cooling it quickly. The dissolved fat rises to the top of the broth and solidifies. Incidentally, this fat cover helps protect the stock from contamination and should be left intact until the stock is needed. A delightful thing to remember is that for *every ounce of grease that is extracted from the broth, your body has about 240 less calories to contend with.*

For the dieter, then, clear, flavorful, transparent soups are recommended. They will be practically fat-free and will contain important nutrients necessary for a balanced diet.

Canned consommés and bouillons can be used in a pinch, but nothing in a can will impart the rich, appetizing flavor to soup as a carefully prepared homemade stock.

BEEF CONSOMMÉ

To make beef consommé, follow the directions for Basic Beef Stock (recipe on page 40). To clarify (to remove the small particles of food suspended in the stock), reheat the stock and strain it through two layers of wet cheesecloth. Use a saucepan with a small circumference, if possible. The top half of a Pyrex double boiler is ideal for small amounts.

Beat 1 egg white for each 2 cups of stock. Stir egg into stock; bring to a slow boil while stirring constantly. When the stock starts to boil, take if off the heat and let the egg white settle. Return the pan to the heat and bring back to the boil. Carefully skim off the egg "raft" floating on the top, then strain the stock through 3 to 4 layers of wet cheesecloth.

When ready to serve, reheat consommé and serve.

20 calories per 1 cup serving.

BORSCHT

1 small onion
1 carrot
1 turnip
2 celery ribs
3 beets
6 cups beef stock

1 tablespoon lemon juice
1 cup shredded cabbage
1 pound tomatoes, peeled, seeded, and diced
salt and pepper to taste

Clean and finely chop onion, carrot, turnip, celery, and beets. In a large soup kettle, combine vegetables with broth and lemon juice. Bring to a boil, reduce heat and simmer, covered, for 20 minutes. Add shredded cabbage and diced tomatoes. Cover and simmer 20 minutes longer. Season to taste with salt and pepper. Ladle soup into bowls and garnish with a teaspoon of plain yogurt or a sprinkling of fresh dill or chopped chives.

Makes 8 servings at 50 calories per serving.

Chef's Cooking Tip:
This renowned Russian version of vegetable soup is equally good when served cold.

BEEF CABBAGE SOUP

3 cups shredded green cabbage
3 cups beef broth
1 cup diced onion
1 large tomato, peeled, seeded and diced

1 can (4-ounce) sliced mushrooms
salt and pepper to taste

Blanch the cabbage in a large amount of boiling water for 2 minutes; plunge into cold water to stop the cooking process. Drain. Steam the diced onion and tomato in a quarter cup of the broth for 5 minutes. Add the sliced mushrooms, remaining broth. Season to taste. Bring to a boil, then reduce heat and simmer, along with the cabbage, for 10 to 15 minutes to combine the flavors.

Makes 4 servings at 25 calories per serving.

CHICKEN BROTH PARMESAN

1 quart chicken stock
1 tablespoon fresh lemon juice
½ teaspoon grated lemon rind

4 teaspoons freshly grated
    Parmesan cheese

Follow the directions for Basic Chicken Stock (recipe on page 41); remove congealed fat from surface and reheat. To each cup of soup add a dash of lemon juice, a sprinkling of grated lemon rind, and a teaspoon of grated Parmesan cheese.

Makes 4 servings at 35 calories per serving.

Chef's Cooking Tip:
It's easier to grate a lemon before it's cut and squeezed rather than after.

CONSOMMÉ MADRILÈNE

2 cans (10½-ounce) beef
    consommé

1 can (16-ounce) tomato purée
salt and pepper to taste

Dilute consommé with water according to directions; bring to a boil. Add tomato purée, reduce heat, and simmer for 5 minutes. Season to taste and serve piping hot, or refrigerate several hours or overnight and serve chilled.

Makes 8 servings at 35 calories per serving.

FRESH MUSHROOM SOUP

4 cups chicken broth
1 minced shallot
½ pound fresh mushrooms,
    cleaned and diced

½ teaspoon salt
¼ teaspoon white pepper

Reserve two mushrooms for garnish. Combine ingredients in a soup pot. Bring to a boil. Reduce heat and simmer, uncovered, 45 minutes. Strain and discard mushrooms. Serve in cups and garnish with thinly sliced mushrooms.

Makes 4 servings at 30 calories per serving.

Chef's Cooking Tip:
It isn't necessary to peel mushrooms. Simply wipe them with a damp cloth or rinse quickly under cold water before using.

HOMEMADE TURKEY SOUP

2 pounds turkey necks and backs
3 quarts of water
2 chopped onions
2 chopped celery ribs
1 chopped carrot
1 bay leaf
3 parsley stems
1 tablespoon salt

GARNISHING VEGETABLES:
2 sliced carrots
2 sliced celery ribs
1 sliced onion
1 diced rutabaga
1 sliced zucchini

Put turkey necks and backs in a large Dutch oven or soup kettle. Add water, chopped vegetables, and seasonings to the pot and bring the liquid to a boil. Cover tightly and simmer for 2 hours. Remove turkey parts from the broth and set aside; strain broth and discard vegetables. Let broth cool to allow fat to come to the surface. Remove fat. Remove meat from bones; add to broth. Heat until close to boiling. Add all the garnishing vegetables except the zucchini and simmer 15 minutes. Add zucchini and simmer 5 minutes longer. Season to taste.

Makes 8 servings at 100 calories per serving.

JELLIED TOMATO CONSOMMÉ

1 can (18-ounce) tomato juice
1 can (10-ounce) consommé
1 envelope (tablespoon) unflavored gelatin

¼ cup chopped onions
½ teaspoon celery seed
⅛ teaspoon salt
dash Tabasco sauce

Pour ½ cup of tomato juice in a saucepan and sprinkle with gelatin. Reserve. In another saucepan, combine the remaining tomato juice, consommé, onions, celery seed, salt, and Tabasco sauce. Bring to a boil and cook over low heat until reduced by one-third, about 10 minutes. Strain into gelatin mixture, stirring until gelatin is dissolved. Chill until set. Serve with a dollop of yogurt or a lemon garnish.

Makes 4 servings at 35 calories per serving.

LOW-CALORIE VEGETABLE SOUP

½ cup each: diced carrot, turnip, celery, onion, zucchini, mushrooms, or other fresh vegetables

3 cups beef bouillon
1 teaspoon dry sherry
salt and pepper to taste

Put beef bouillon into a 2-quart saucepan and bring to a boil. Add the vegetables and sherry wine. Cook over low heat until the vegetables are tender, about 5 to 7 minutes. Season with salt and pepper to taste.

Makes 4 servings at 25 calories per serving.

Chef's Cooking Tip:
Plan your meals ahead. Knowing there's a low-calorie meal waiting will help you resist between-meal snacks.

ONION SOUP

3 medium onions, sliced
1 tablespoon butter or margarine
1 quart beef bouillon
1 tablespoon freshly grated Parmesan cheese
1 teaspoon Worcestershire sauce

Sauté sliced onions in butter or margarine over low heat until lightly browned and transparent. Add bouillon and Worcestershire sauce and bring to a boil. Reduce the heat to simmer. Cook, tightly covered, for an additional 30 minutes. Top each serving with one-fourth of the freshly grated Parmesan cheese.

Makes 4 servings at 80 calories per serving.

Chef's Cooking Tip:
Cooking onions in a covered pot retards the escape of their flavorful oils and intensifies the flavor of the broth.

OLD-FASHIONED BEEF VEGETABLE SOUP

2½ pounds meaty beef shanks
2 cans (10½-ounce) beef broth
2 cups water
1 cup tomato juice
1 onion, quartered
1 small bay leaf
1 tablespoon salt
6 peppercorns, crushed
⅛ teaspoon thyme
1½ cups diced carrots
1½ cups diced celery
1 cup diced rutabaga
1 can (16-ounce) tomatoes, undrained
1 can (12-ounce) whole-kernel corn, drained

Preheat broiler, Place shanks in an ovenproof skillet; brown under broiler. Place in a large saucepan or Dutch oven with beef broth, water, tomato juice, onion, bay leaf, salt, peppercorns, and thyme. Cover and simmer about 3 hours or until meat is tender. Discard bay leaf. Remove shanks and cut meat into chunks. Skim off all fat from broth. Return meat to pot with remaining ingredients. Cover and simmer about 30 minutes longer, or until vegetables are barely tender.

Makes 8 servings at 90 calories per serving.

VEGETABLE SOUP

4 cups chicken stock
2 carrots
1 leek
1 turnip
⅛ teaspoon each: dill weed, ground oregano, ground rosemary, and ground pepper

1 tablespoon "Maggie" liquid soup seasoning
4 cups canned tomatoes, drained and crushed
¼ cup each: diced carrot, turnip, and rutabaga

Blanch diced carrot, turnip, and rutabaga in boiling water until just tender. Chill under cold water and set aside. Put chicken stock into a 2-quart saucepan. Add coarsely chopped carrots, leek, and turnip. Add seasonings and crushed tomatoes. Simmer, uncovered, until reduced by one-fourth. Remove from heat and purée in blender. Return soup to saucepan and add diced garnishing vegetables. Heat through and serve.

Makes 4 servings at 50 calories per serving.

Chef's Cooking Tip:
Be sure not to fill your blender more than half full at any one time with hot liquid or the lid could blow off. Very messy and very dangerous.

WINE BOUILLON SOUP

1 can (8-ounce) tomato purée
1 can (10½-ounce) consommé
3 cups water
2 whole cloves
½ cup chopped onion
½ cup chopped celery

½ cup dry red wine
½ small bay leaf
½ teaspoon salt
¼ teaspoon pepper
dash Tabasco sauce

Combine ingredients and bring to a boil. Reduce heat and simmer 20 minutes. Strain and serve.

Makes 4 servings at 30 calories per serving.

CARROT SOUP

1 tablespoon butter or margarine
1 medium-size onion, chopped
1 bunch carrots, about 1 pound
3 cups chicken stock
½ teaspoon dill weed
¼ teaspoon nutmeg
salt and pepper to taste
freshly chopped parsley

Melt the butter or margarine in a nonstick saucepan and add the onion. Sauté until almost soft. Add carrots and toss. Sauté with onions for 2 minutes. Add dill weed, nutmeg, salt, and pepper. Stir. Add stock and simmer until carrots are tender. Purée in blender on low speed or force through sieve. Return to cleaned pan and heat thoroughly. Garnish each serving with parsley.

Makes 4 servings at 80 calories per serving.

CREAM OF CAULIFLOWER SOUP

1 large cauliflower
1 chopped leek
1 cup chopped celery
¼ cup chopped onion
2 cups fresh or canned chicken broth
¼ cup skim milk
salt and white pepper to taste
chopped parsley
nutmeg

Cut cauliflower into flowerets. Discard hard stem and green leaves. Place flowerets in a saucepan and add cold water to cover. Do not add salt. Cover and bring to a boil. Reduce heat and simmer for two minutes, no longer. Drain. Add leeks, celery, onion, and broth. Simmer, uncovered, until the vegetables are tender. Strain the soup, reserving the broth. Purée the vegetables in a blender with ½ cup of the reserved broth. This will have to be done in two or three steps, as the blender should not be more than half full with hot liquid at any one time. Return purée to the saucepan. Thin to desired consistency with milk and remaining broth. Reheat. Season to taste with salt and pepper. Garnish with chopped parsley and freshly grated nutmeg.

Makes 4 servings at 50 calories per serving.

FRESH BROCCOLI SOUP

1½ pounds fresh broccoli
½ small onion, chopped
2 celery ribs, chopped
2 cups chicken stock

½ teaspoon Worcestershire sauce
⅛ teaspoon garlic powder
salt and pepper to taste
1 cup skim milk

Wash and trim fresh broccoli. Place in a large saucepan with onion, celery, chicken stock, Worcestershire sauce, and garlic powder; bring to a boil. Reduce heat, cover and simmer 15 to 20 minutes, or until broccoli is tender. Strain soup, reserving broth. Purée vegetables in a blender with ½ cup of the reserved broth. Blend until smooth and creamy. Return the purée to the saucepan. Stir in milk and enough of the broth to thin soup to desired consistency. Heat through and correct seasoning to taste with salt and pepper.

Makes 4 servings at 50 calories per serving.

Chef's Cooking Tip:
Plan to have soup on your menu often. These low-calorie appetizers help to take the edge off your hunger. Thus you won't be as tempted to overindulge on the more high-calorie part of the meal.

FRESH TOMATO SOUP

6 large ripe tomatoes
1 small onion, minced
1 small bay leaf

2 cups beef bouillon
salt and pepper to taste

Peel, seed, and chop tomatoes. In a medium-size saucepan, combine the tomatoes, onion, and bay leaf; cover and stew gently for 15 to 20 minutes. Remove bay leaf. Purée in a blender, one cup at a time. Return mixture to saucepan; add beef bouillon. Heat to a simmer, season to taste and serve.

Makes 4 servings at 35 calories per serving.

Chef's Cooking Tip:
If a soup recipe calls for sautéing vegetables, sear and brown them without fat in a nonstick skillet or in the oven before the liquid is added.

GAZPACHO

2 medium cucumbers, peeled and seeded
2 medium green peppers, seeded
3 cups tomato juice
1 tablespoon vinegar
1 small onion
1 garlic clove
2 ripe tomatoes, peeled and diced
dash Tabasco
salt and pepper to taste

Put the cucumbers, peppers, onion, and garlic in a food processor (or use a large knife) and mince. Combine minced vegetables with remaining ingredients. Cover and chill thoroughly.

Makes 4 servings at 50 calories per serving.

Chef's Cooking Tip:
Gazpacho is twice as good if made one day ahead.

MANHATTAN CLAM CHOWDER

1 can (10-ounce) chopped clams
1½ cups tomato juice
½ cup tomato purée
½ cup diced onion
½ cup diced green pepper
½ cup diced celery
½ cup diced carrot
1 small new potato, peeled and diced
1 firm whole tomato, peeled and diced
½ teaspoon thyme
salt and pepper to taste

Combine all ingredients except clams in a large saucepan. Cover and simmer for 30 minutes, or until vegetables are tender. Add clams and broth from can. Simmer 5 minutes longer.

Makes 4 servings at 80 calories per serving.

PURÉED ASPARAGUS SOUP

This is a marvelous-tasting soup that can be made from the asparagus trimmings that are usually discarded.

2 cups chopped asparagus
½ cup chopped onion
1 cup chicken stock

⅛ teaspoon dill weed
salt and pepper to taste

In a medium-size saucepan, combine asparagus, onion, chicken stock, and dill weed. Cook over low heat until tender, about 15 minutes. Remove from heat and purée in a blender. Return soup to saucepan. Season to taste, heat to simmer and serve.

Makes 4 servings at 50 calories per serving.

Chef's Cooking Tip:
To always stay within your caloric limit, don't eat leftovers just because they're there. Make soup!

SPLIT PEA SOUP

1½ cups split peas
6 cups boiling chicken broth
1 chopped carrot
1 chopped celery rib

1 chopped small onion
1 bay leaf
dill weed
salt and pepper

Combine all the ingredients except the dill weed, salt, and pepper into a large saucepan; bring to the boil. Reduce heat, cover, and simmer gently until the peas are soft and the soup reaches the desired consistency, about 2 hours. Remove from heat and purée in a blender. Return soup to saucepan. If too thick, thin with hot water or chicken broth. Season to taste with dill weed, salt, and pepper, and serve.

Makes 6 (one-cup) servings at 130 calories per serving.

Chef's Cooking Tip:
Although pea soup is relatively high in calories, I decided to include this low-fat recipe because this soup is so popular and nutritious. Remember not to fill your blender more than half full with hot liquid at any one time.

BOUILLABAISSE

3 pounds assorted fish and shellfish (fish: bass, cod, trout, halibut, or snapper. shellfish: clams, crab, mussels, rock lobster, scallops, or shrimp.)
3 cups fish stock or water
1 cup clam juice
1 cup dry white wine
2 minced cloves garlic
2 leeks, julienned (white part only)
1 onion, sliced
2 ripe tomatoes, peeled, seeded, and diced
1 bay leaf
1 teaspoon fennel seeds, crushed
¼ teaspoon saffron
¼ teaspoon thyme
1 tablespoon chopped parsley
salt and pepper to taste
dash of cayenne pepper

Clean, and cut seafood into 2-inch pieces. In a 2-quart saucepan, heat the fish stock or water, clam juice, and wine to boiling. In a 6- to 8-quart soup pot, steam garlic, leeks, and onion in ½ cup of the heated broth for 5 minutes. Add heated broth and remaining ingredients and bring to a boil. Add seafood and simmer, covered, until cooked through, about 15 minutes. Ladle seafood and broth into deep serving dishes.

Makes 6 servings at 210 calories per serving.

CHICKEN IN THE POT

1 (3 pounds) broiler-fryer chicken
1 chopped onion
1 chopped carrot
1 chopped celery rib
water to cover by 2 inches
3 parsley sprigs
½ teaspoon thyme
1 bay leaf
8 crushed peppercorns

GARNISHING VEGETABLES:
2 sliced carrots
2 sliced celery ribs
1 zucchini
1 diced rutabaga
1 diced leek (white part only)
salt to taste

Rinse the chicken inside and out. Truss with butcher's twine. Fill the bottom of an 8-quart soup pot with the chopped vegetables. Place the trussed bird on the vegetables. Wash a 4-inch square of cheesecloth in clear water. Add seasonings and tie cheesecloth into a bag with twine; add bag to pot.

Cover with water; bring to boil. Skim the surface occasionally to remove foam and fat. Allow to simmer 30 to 45 minutes. When juices from the thickest part of the thigh run clear, the chicken is cooked. Remove from the pot; allow to cool slightly. Skin and debone; return the skin and bones to the soup pot. Continue to simmer the stock, uncovered, over moderate heat to reduce and concentrate its flavor. Strain the stock; reheat to boiling in a clean pot. Add the sliced garnishing vegetables to the boiling broth and cook until tender. Use a strainer to facilitate the removal of the garnishing vegetables from the broth.

Divide the chicken and garnishing vegetables into four soup bowls. Ladle the broth into the bowls. Salt to taste and garnish with chopped parsley or chopped celery tops.

Makes 4 servings at 200 calories per serving.

CIOPPINO

4 scallions, diced
1 onion, chopped
1 green pepper, seeded and diced
1 celery rib, diced
1 can (28-ounce) whole tomatoes, chopped coarsely
1 can (8-ounce) tomato sauce
1 cup red or white wine
¼ cup parsley, chopped
¼ teaspoon each: basil, oregano, and garlic powder
¾ pound halibut steaks
¾ pound large shrimp
¾ pound lobster tail
1 can (6½-ounce) chopped clams
salt and pepper

Place scallions, onion, green pepper, and celery in a small saucepan. Add ½ cup boiling water; cover and steam over medium heat for 5 minutes. Drain. Place whole tomatoes, tomato sauce, wine, parsley, basil, oregano, and garlic powder in a 6-quart kettle or Dutch oven. Add the steamed vegetables and mix well; cover and simmer for 20 minutes. Add halibut, lobster, and shrimp; re-cover and simmer an additional 10 minutes. Add the canned clams with liquid; simmer 5 minutes longer to heat through. Season to taste with salt and pepper and serve.

Makes 6 servings at 200 calories per serving.

COCK-A-LEEKIE SOUP

1 chicken (4 pounds)
1 large onion, chopped
2 carrots, peeled and chopped
2 celery ribs, with leaves
2 parsley stems
1 small bay leaf, crushed
1 tablespoon salt
½ teaspoon white pepper
   cold water to cover
4 large leeks, thinly sliced (white part only)
1 large potato, peeled and diced
½ cup barley
2 cups skim milk, scalded

Clean and truss the bird as for roasting. Place it, together with onion, carrots, celery, parsley, bay leaf, salt, and pepper in a 6-quart saucepan. Add enough cold water to cover. Bring to a boil, then reduce heat and simmer, covered, for 1 hour, or until chicken is cooked. Place saucepan in the sink. Fill sink with cold water, but do not exceed the level of the broth. Add more cold water when necessary. Do not remove chicken. When cool, refrigerate without straining for several hours or overnight. One hour before serving, remove chicken from broth. Skim off layer of congealed fat from broth; strain and discard vegetables.

Place 4 cups of the strained broth (the remaining stock can be used when needed) together with leeks, potato, and barley in a 3-quart saucepan. Bring to boiling; reduce heat and simmer, covered, 20 to 30 minutes. Meanwhile, tear apart chicken. Discard skin, gristle, and bones and chop meat. Add meat and scalded milk to soup. Heat through and serve.

Makes 4 servings at 235 calories per serving.

Chef's Cooking Tip:
Remember, with low-calorie dishes the ingredients used are not the whole story. The method of cooking is what makes all the difference. By preparing this soup in two stages you have eliminated hundreds of unwanted fat calories without any effort at all.

SOPA DE ALBONDIGAS
(Mexican-style Meatball Soup)

3 potatoes, diced
2 carrots, diced
1 onion, diced
1 turnip, diced
1 green pepper, diced
1 celery rib, diced
1 clove garlic, minced
1 small bay leaf, crushed
1 can (8-ounce) tomato sauce

2 quarts beef stock
1½ pounds lean ground round
¼ cup raw rice
1 egg, slightly beaten
1 tablespoon chopped fresh mint leaves
1 teaspoon salt
⅛ teaspoon pepper
⅛ teaspoon whole oregano

In a large saucepan or Dutch oven, combine the diced vegetables, garlic, bay leaf, tomato sauce and beef stock; bring to the boiling point; reduce heat and simmer for 5 minutes. Meanwhile, mix the meat, rice, egg, mint, salt, pepper, and oregano together. Form into small meatballs. Drop the meatballs a few at a time gently into the simmering broth. Return soup to boiling; reduce heat and continue to simmer until meatballs are done, about 30 minutes. Skim excess fat from surface before serving.

Makes 6 servings at 275 calories per serving.

BASIC BEEF STOCK

6 pounds meaty beef bones
2 pounds meat scraps
2 veal knuckles, cracked
1 cup red wine
1 onion
1 carrot

1 celery rib
1 garlic clove, crushed
3 parsley stems
water to cover
salt and pepper to taste

Have your butcher crack beef bones and veal knuckles with a cleaver. Place in a roasting pan and brown in a 425°F. oven for 30 minutes. Pour off accumulated fat, then add wine, onion, carrot, and celery; bake 30 minutes longer, stirring occasionally for even browning. Transfer contents of roasting pan to a deep kettle. Add remaining ingredients and bring to a boil. Reduce heat and simmer, covered, up to 12 hours. Skim often to remove accumulated foam and melted fat. Add more water when necessary to keep bones covered. Strain and refrigerate when cool. Leave congealed fat intact until you're ready to use the stock.

Makes 8 servings at 10 calories per serving.

BASIC CHICKEN STOCK

6–8 pounds uncooked chicken bones, gizzards, wings, necks, and backs
1 onion
1 carrot
1 celery rib
3 parsley stems
water to cover
salt and pepper to taste

Place all ingredients in a deep kettle. Bring slowly to a boil. Skim surface of boiling water carefully to remove scum. A small bay leaf, a garlic clove, 2 whole cloves or a pinch of thyme can be added for additional flavor, if desired. Reduce heat and simmer, covered, for 3 to 4 hours, occasionally skimming surface of foam and melted fat. Strain and refrigerate when cool. Leave the congealed fat intact until you're ready to use the stock.

Makes 8 servings at 10 calories per serving.

Chef's Cooking Tip:
For a clearer broth, blanch the chicken parts before you add the vegetables. Place them in a large stockpot and cover with lukewarm water. Bring to a boil, then drain and rinse the chicken parts in cold water. Drain again, rinse out pot, then add vegetables, seasonings, and cold water to cover.

COURT BOUILLON

A court bouillon is a combination of water, aromatic vegetables, seasonings, and one or more food acids (wine, vinegar, or lemon juice) used for cooking fish or shellfish. It should always be presimmered for maximum flavor.

2 cups dry white wine
2 cups water
1 small onion
1 large carrot
1 celery rib
4 parsley stems
4 peppercorns
1 bay leaf
1 teaspoon salt
¼ teaspoon thyme

Combine all ingredients in a saucepan and bring to a boil. Reduce to a simmer and cook, uncovered, 15 to 30 minutes to blend flavors. Use immediately, adding more hot liquid if necessary, or strain, allow to cool, then refrigerate or freeze.

FISH STOCK

3 pounds fish trimmings
1 cup dry white wine
1 onion
1 carrot
1 celery rib

1 bay leaf
3 parsley stems
water to cover
juice of 1 lemon
salt and pepper to taste

Place all ingredients in a large saucepan and bring to a boil. Reduce heat and simmer, covered, for 30 minutes, skimming often. Strain, then refrigerate or freeze.

Makes approximately 4 cups stock.

LAMB STOCK

6–8 pounds meaty lamb bones
1 onion
1 carrot
1 celery rib
1 can (1-pound 12-ounce) tomatoes, undrained

1 clove garlic, crushed
3 parsley stems
water to cover
salt and pepper to taste

Place all ingredients in a deep kettle. Bring slowly to a boil. Skim surface of boiling water carefully to remove scum. Reduce heat and simmer, covered, for 3 to 4 hours, occasionally skimming surface of foam and melted fat. Strain and refrigerate when cool. Leave the congealed fat intact until you're ready to use the stock.

Makes 8 servings at 10 calories per serving.

LOBSTER STOCK

2 pounds leftover lobster shells
1 cup dry white or sherry wine
1 onion, chopped

1 small bay leaf
1 teaspoon butter-flavored salt
water to cover

In a large saucepan, combine all ingredients and simmer over low heat for one hour. Strain through a fine cloth or several layers of cheesecloth.

Makes approximately 4 cups stock.

Chef's Cooking Tip:
Onions, shallots, and garlic cloves can be peeled quickly if they are scalded in boiling water for one minute, then drained and immediately cooled under cold running water. The skins will slip off easily when the root and stem ends are removed.

EGGS AND CHEESE

The egg is said to be the soul of the culinary art, and rightly so, for there is probably no single food that can match its versatility and application in the kitchen. In addition to providing its own good taste, the egg is used to thicken, emulsify, bind, leaven, stabilize, clarify, coat, color, and enrich the flavor of other foods. It lends itself to many aspects of food preparation, from appetizer to dessert, and it can be simply or lavishly prepared.

The egg, of course, is also a nutritionally valuable food. It's low in calories and high in protein, vitamins, and minerals—all elements that are essential to good health. You begin to appreciate the importance of high-quality protein foods like the egg when you realize that, unlike fats and carbohydrates, protein can't be stored in the body for later use and must be replaced regularly on a daily basis.

But it's important to bear in mind that the egg, or more specifically the egg yolk, is naturally high in fat and cholesterol—a substance that some medical authorities believe to be a causative factor in heart disease. This notwithstanding, common sense should tell you that almost any food is permissible in limited amounts on a weight-reducing diet if used wisely.

Egg white, on the other hand, is all protein and, at only 20 calories, can be eaten and used for cooking freely.

When you're on a weight-loss diet, it's especially important that you choose foods that supply the necessary nutrients your body needs for optimum health. The simplest and most pleasant way to obtain these essential elements is by daily selections from a wide variety of foods, with a strong emphasis on body-building proteins. And this doesn't always have to mean meat, poultry, or fish. Dairy products are excellent high-quality alternatives—and this includes cheese.

Like the milk it's from, all cheese—with the exception of cream cheese—is highly nutritious. Unfortunately, the majority of our familiar cheeses are relatively high in butterfat and average a whopping 110 calories an ounce! Soft, fresh, unripened cheeses like cottage, pot, farmer, baker's, and a number of ricottas are exceptions. These are all made from skim milk or whey (the liquid left from milk when the curd solids are removed). They are from 1 to 10 percent fat and range from 20 to 40 calories an ounce. I have found many "imitation" and low-fat cheeses that are quite acceptable, but admittedly it took some time to acquire an affection for their rather bland taste.

It's important to note, when you're talking about cheeses in low-calorie preparations, that because of its concentrated flavor, an average serving of a hard or semi-hard cheese is considered only 1 ounce. In caloric value, this equals approximately 4 ounces of low-fat cottage cheese. The point is, of course, that while you might easily eat three to four times this amount of cottage cheese, you would never eat such a portion of Parmesan, Cheddar or Swiss in one meal.

How do you store the cheese you've selected? Like all dairy products, cheese belongs in the refrigerator as soon as it's purchased. Store it in its original wrapper and keep the cut surfaces tightly covered with foil or plastic wrap after each use. Hard, grating cheese will keep for several months. Soft, unripened cheeses, however, are highly perishable and should be used within three to five days of purchase.

While it is not generally recommended, cheese can be frozen to extend its storage life. The flavor is not affected, but the texture of natural cheeses becomes crumbly and mealy, while soft cheeses tend to separate when thawed. Cheese that has been frozen is best used in salads (where a crumbly texture is acceptable) or used for cooking.

Cheese can add an exciting flavor and texture to your meals, but you must be careful. Like all protein foods, cheese that is heated at too high a temperature or cooked for too long a time will become tough and stringy—when it's melted, it's cooked!

The many pasteurized processed cheeses and cheese foods you find in your supermarket are generally bland in flavor and are poor substitutes for natural cheeses. But there are instances when processed cheese products can be recommended as they blend well with other foods and melt easily and smoothly when heated.

BOILED EGGS

1 medium-size egg
2 cups water

½ teaspoon vinegar

Bring water and vinegar to a boil in a small saucepan. (The vinegar will prevent the egg whites from leaking out if the shell cracks during cooking.) Place the egg in a small strainer basket and gently lower into the water. Cook 3 minutes for soft, 4 minutes for medium, and 10 minutes for hard-boiled. When desired degree of doneness is obtained, drain water and run egg under cold water. For soft-boiled eggs, split the egg with a knife and scoop out the contents with a spoon. For hard-boiled eggs, roll egg around empty saucepan to crack shell into fragments, then peel immediately under cold running water.

Makes 1 serving at 80 calories per serving.

Chef's Cooking Tip:
To prevent the egg white from overcooking and becoming tough, bring the egg to room temperature before cooking. For hard-boiled eggs, the rapid cooling is essential because it prevents discoloration around the yolks.

FRIED EGGS

1 medium egg

salt and pepper

Coat the surface of a 7-inch nonstick skillet with a food release agent. Heat the pan over moderate heat. Break the egg into a cup and slide it gently into the heated skillet. Cook the egg slowly, breaking through the white portion occasionally with the tip of a rubber spatula. Don't disturb the yolk unless you like your egg hard-cooked. This technique allows the steam to cook the egg white before the yolk is overcooked. If you like your eggs firm, cover the skillet for one minute. When the desired degree of firmness is obtained, slide the egg directly from the skillet onto a plate, using the rubber spatula as a guide. Season to taste.

Makes 1 serving at 80 calories per serving.

Chef's Cooking Tip:
Salt tends to toughen eggs, so season egg dishes after they're removed from the stove.

POACHED EGGS

1 medium-size egg
4 cups water

2 teaspoons white vinegar

Combine water and vinegar in saucepan and bring to a boil. Break egg into a cup. Holding the cup as close to the water as possible, gently slide the egg into the boiling water. Immediately reduce the heat to simmer. Cook about 4 minutes. The egg will begin to float to the surface as it cooks. Remove egg with a slotted spoon and rinse under warm water to remove any vinegar taste.

Makes 1 serving at 80 calories per serving.

Chef's Cooking Tip:
Poaching an egg with vinegar added to the water prevents the egg white from shredding, but too much vinegar will give the egg a shriveled-up look and an off taste.

Surprisingly, poached eggs can be made ahead. The night before they're needed, poach the eggs, but undercook them slightly. They'll store nicely floating in cold water in an airtight container in your refrigerator. Then all you have to do is to heat the eggs for just a minute or two in hot liquid before serving.

SCRAMBLED EGGS

1 medium egg

salt and pepper

Coat a nonstick skillet with a food release agent. Heat over low flame. Break the egg into a cup and beat briefly with a fork until the yolk and white are blended. Pour the egg into skillet. Increase the heat to medium and allow the egg to set, about 8 to 10 seconds. Using a rubber spatula, scramble the egg to desired degree of firmness, allowing the uncooked layers to set every few seconds; then continue scrambling. Turn the egg onto a plate. Season to taste.

Makes 1 serving at 80 calories per serving.

Chef's Cooking Tip:
For taste variety and lightness, a teaspoon of skim milk or fruit juice can be blended with the egg before cooking. Be sure to keep the heat low to prevent sticking.

SHIRRED EGGS

1 medium egg
1 tablespoon skim milk

salt and pepper
paprika

Break the egg into a 4-ounce ramekin that has been coated with a food release agent. Add the skim milk, then bake, uncovered, in a 350° F. oven until just set. Season with salt and pepper and garnish with a sprinkle of paprika.

Makes 1 serving at 80 calories per serving.

Chef's Cooking Tip:
A shirred egg is easy to make, but it requires careful watching so it doesn't overcook. To reduce the cooking time, preheat the oven and bring the egg to room temperature before cooking.

CHEESE OMELET AU GRATIN

2 medium eggs
1 teaspoon water or skim milk
salt and pepper to taste

1 ounce shredded low-fat processed cheese

Break eggs into a cup. Add seasoning and blend well with a fork. Coat a 7-inch nonstick skillet with a food release spray. Heat pan over moderate-high heat. Immediately pour eggs into skillet; allow to set 8 to 10 seconds. Using a rubber spatula, lift a portion of the omelet, then tilt the pan and allow the uncooked portion of the egg to run underneath. Spread the shredded cheese over the omelet. Place the skillet under a preheated broiler and cook "au gratin" style until cheese melts. Slide the omelet onto a plate. Fold in half and serve.

Makes 1 serving at 210 calories per serving.

Chef's Cooking Tip:
The au gratin method of cooking eggs cooks the top and the bottom of the omelet at the same time. The added liquid will quickly turn to steam and the omelet will almost double in size.

FRENCH OMELET

2 medium eggs   salt and pepper to taste

Break eggs into a cup. Add seasoning and blend well with a fork. Coat a 7-inch nonstick skillet with a food release spray and place over moderate-high heat. Immediately pour the eggs into the skillet and allow to set for 8 to 10 seconds without disturbing. Using a rubber spatula, lift a portion of the omelet, tilt the pan, and allow the uncooked egg to run underneath. Continue this every 3 seconds until all the egg is cooked. Slide the omelet out onto a plate and fold in half. The center of the omelet will continue to cook after being folded.

Makes 1 serving at 160 calories per serving.

Chef's Cooking Tip:
The secret of making low-calorie omelets that aren't burned or stuck to the pan is in the timing. Give the eggs enough time to set so they won't stick, but not so long that they brown and toughen.

SPANISH OMELET

2 tablespoons chopped onion
2 tablespoons chopped green pepper
1 can (8 ounces) tomato sauce
¼ teaspoon salt
⅛ teaspoon pepper

⅛ teaspoon cumin

OMELET:
4 medium eggs
1 tablespoon water
pepper to taste

In a small saucepan, combine sauce ingredients and simmer about 20 minutes, stirring occasionally. Blend eggs, water, and seasoning in a small bowl with a fork. Coat a 9-inch nonstick skillet with a food release spray. Heat pan over moderate-high heat. Immediately pour eggs into skillet; allow to set 8 to 10 seconds. Using a rubber spatula, lift a portion of the omelet, then tilt the pan and allow the uncooked portion of the egg to run underneath. Place under a preheated broiler and cook "au gratin" style until omelet has doubled in size. Slide omelet onto a serving plate, fill with hot tomato sauce, then fold in half. Garnish with a little more sauce and serve.

Makes 2 servings at 170 calories per serving.

FRENCH TOAST

2 medium eggs, slightly beaten
½ cup skim milk
¼ teaspoon vanilla extract
¼ teaspoon salt

4 slices day-old bread
1 tablespoon powdered sugar
cinnamon

Combine eggs, milk, vanilla, and salt in shallow dish. Dredge bread slices in egg mixture and cook slowly on a nonstick surface. Brown on both sides. Sprinkle with powdered sugar and cinnamon to taste.

Makes 4 servings at 90 calories per serving.

Chef's Cooking Tip:
To remove any pieces of egg shell that may have fallen into the egg mixture, try using a large piece of the egg shell. The smaller piece will cling instantly.

COMBINATION MAIN DISHES

Like hearty soups or stews, main-dish salads, sandwiches, and casseroles make delicious and satisfying low-calorie meals. Often just a light beverage and a well-chosen dessert are all you need to round out a simple but inviting menu. What's more, these are meals that are generally quick and easy to prepare and fun to serve. You'll find that it's easy to stick to your diet when you serve up well-balanced, low-calorie, nutritious meals your whole family will enjoy.

CHEESE ENCHILADAS

2¼ cups water
1 can (16-ounce) tomato purée
2 tablespoons chile powder
2 teaspoons sugar
½ teaspoon salt
¼ teaspoon pepper
⅛ teaspoon cumin

1 pound sharp chedder cheese, grated
1 cup chopped onion
1 can (2¼-ounce) sliced ripe olives, drained
8 tortilla shells
½ cup chopped green onions

To make the sauce, combine water, purée, chile powder, sugar, salt, pepper, and cumin in a saucepan. Bring to a boil; reduce heat and simmer for 30 minutes.

To make the enchiladas, combine all but one cup of cheese with chopped onion and drained olives. Steam the tortilla shells for 2 minutes to soften. Pour ½ cup of the sauce in a shallow casserole dish. Place a large spoonful of the cheese mixture on one side of each tortilla. Roll up tightly and place in the prepared dish, seam side down. Pour the remaining sauce over the enchiladas and sprinkle with remaining cheese. Bake at 325° F. for 25 minutes. Remove from oven, garnish with green onions and serve.

Makes 8 servings at 375 calories per serving.

LASAGNE FLORENTINE

½ pound lasagne noodles
1 box (10-ounce) frozen chopped spinach
½ pound lean ground round
½ cup chopped onion
½ cup chopped green pepper
1 clove garlic, minced
1 can (1-pound 3-ounce) Italian-style plum tomatoes
½ cup water
¼ cup tomato paste
2 tablespoons freshly chopped parsley
1 small bay leaf
1 teaspoon salt
½ teaspoon whole oregano
⅛ teaspoon each: basil and pepper
2 cups pot-style or "baker's" cottage cheese
¼ cup freshly grated Parmesan cheese

Cook the lasagne noodles as directed on the package; rinse and drain well. Cook spinach according to package directions; drain well.

Mix beef with onion, pepper and garlic; brown in a large nonstick saucepan over high heat, stirring occasionally to break up meat chunks. Add tomatoes, water, tomato paste, parsley, bay leaf, salt, oregano, basil, and pepper. Bring to a boil. Reduce heat and simmer 1 hour.

To assemble the dish, pour one quarter of the meat sauce into a 2-quart shallow nonstick baking dish. Add a layer of noodles, half of the chopped spinach, half of the baker's cheese and another quarter of sauce. Repeat layers, ending with a top layer of sauce sprinkled with Parmesan cheese.

Bake in a preheated 350° F. oven for 30 to 45 minutes or until mixture is bubbling. Allow to stand 5 to 10 minutes to set the layers.

Makes 6 servings at 325 calories per serving.

Chef's Cooking Tip:
All or parts of this dish can be made in advance. Put together in the morning or even the day before and keep it covered in the refrigerator until needed. Tomato-based dishes always seem to have more flavor when they are made in advance and reheated.

STUFFED CREPES FLORENTINE

12 diet crepes

SAUCE:
3 cans (8-ounce) tomato sauce
1 tablespoon dried minced onion
¼ teaspoon oregano
⅛ teaspoon pepper

FILLING:
1 package (10-ounce) frozen chopped spinach
¾ pound lean ground round
½ cup minced onion
1 large tomato, peeled and diced
⅓ cup grated Cheddar cheese
½ teaspoon salt
¼ teaspoon pepper
⅛ teaspoon garlic powder
3 tablespoons freshly grated Parmesan cheese

In a small saucepan, combine sauce ingredients; bring slowly to a boil. Allow to simmer, uncovered, for 20 minutes to thicken; set aside. Cook spinach according to package directions; drain well. Coat a large nonstick skillet with a food release agent and place over medium-high heat. Add meat and onion to skillet. Cook, uncovered, about 10 minutes, stirring occasionally, until meat is browned. Remove skillet from stove.

Place about 3 tablespoons of filling in center of each crepe; roll up. Coat the bottom of a 13 x 9 x 2-inch ovenproof baking dish with a food release agent. Place filled crepes, seam side down, in a single layer. Spoon heated sauce over crepes. Sprinkle with Parmesan cheese. Bake, uncovered, in a preheated 350° F. oven, about 30 minutes, or until cheese has browned.

Makes 6 servings at 291 calories per serving.

Chef's Cooking Tip:
Diet crepes can easily be made ahead. If they are to be used within 48 hours, stack and wrap them in foil or plastic and refrigerate. For longer storage, stack crepes with sheets of wax paper between each crepe. Wrap in heavy-duty foil and freeze for up to 3 weeks. Thaw at room temperature or in a 350° F. oven for about 10 minutes.

THE DIETER'S TACO

4 tortilla shells

FILLING:
1 pound lean ground round
¼ cup onion, chopped
1 large tomato, chopped

GARNISH:
1 cup shredded iceberg lettuce
2 large tomatoes, peeled and diced

1 clove garlic, minced
1 small yellow chile, seeded and minced
1 tablespoon chile powder
½ teaspoon salt
¼ teaspoon cumin

2 green onions, chopped (white part only)
4 ounce grated Cheddar cheese
4 ounces salsa sauce

Brown meat in a nonstick skillet over high heat, stirring frequently to break up chunks. Add remaining filling ingredients; bring to a boil. Reduce heat and simmer 10 minutes. When ready to serve, cook tortilla shells on a dry surface over medium-low heat, about 1 minute on each side or until crisp. Fold in half and cook 30 seconds longer. Fill each shell with one quarter of filling mixture. Garnish with vegetables, cheese, and salsa sauce.

Makes 4 servings at 190 calories per serving.

MEAT

Since meat is such an important food, let's take a minute to review the relationship between food selection and calories.

If you're like most overweight people, you're realistic enough to know how you got that way; it was primarily from eating too much of the wrong kinds of foods. Just being able to admit the problem, however, doesn't mean much unless you're really intent and capable of solving it. The task is not easy by any means, but it can be done. The information between these two covers should provide the answers you need to make it happen—for you.

Most dieters start out with the greatest intentions, only to fall back into the same old eating habits that got them into trouble in the first place. Habits, especially eating habits, are hard to break. It takes a great deal of motivation and will power to lose even a few pounds, but most dieters are able to do it, again and again. It takes a great deal more to keep those pounds from coming back, however, and very few people are able to change their eating patterns long enough to accomplish it.

When starting a weight-reduction program, the first thing dieters usually vow is never to eat bread or potatoes again until they have lost the desired amount of weight. They know that meat, for instance, is rich in protein and other essential nutrients, and they are pleased with themselves when they are able to resist "fattening" carbohydrates and opt for a double portion of meat instead. Unfortunately, this strategy will make them gain weight rather than lose it! Here's why.

All meat contains a percentage of fat, and fat has more than twice the calories of either protein or carbohydrate. An ounce of fat contains about 270 calories; an ounce of protein or carbohydrate, on the other hand, contains only 120 calories. By doubling the meat portion, dieters often unwittingly increase their intake of calories more than if they would have balanced their meal nutritionally with carbohydrates. Natural carbohydrates from fruit, vegetables, or grains (as opposed to processed carbohydrates like refined sugar) supply the body with food nutrients and energy and are a necessary part of a balanced diet. When it comes to the calorie count, it's not the slice of bread or the small baked potato that's so bad; it's the high-calorie fats like butter and sour cream that are eaten along with them that adds up so fast.

The way to lose weight is to digest fewer calories than your energy requirements. And if you're seriously anticipating a slimmer you, counting those calories is going to be absolutely essential. Excess body fat has a way of accumulating in mathematical progression; 3500 calories plus 3500 calories equals 7000 calories, etc. (a pound of fat contains 3500 calories). And since most everything you digest contains calories, your metabolic calculator will dutifully compute them, even if you physically do not.

If you gradually increase your intake of the wrong kinds of foods like concentrated fats and sugars without a subsequent increase in the activity you do, your total caloric count is bound to escalate proportionally, and your body will be forced to store the excess calories in the form of fat. Allow this overindulgence to continue over a period of time, and the results will be as unfortunate as they will be inevitable. Without a drastic but sensible change in your food habits or activity level, you'll not only be unable to maintain your present weight, you'll steadily add to it—it's that simple!

To slim down—and stay that way—it isn't necessary for you to periodically starve yourself or even drastically cut down on the *amount* of food you eat. Just learn how to reduce the calories *in* the food so that you end up each day having taken in fewer calories than your body burned up.

Why jump from one fad diet to another or follow rigid menus if you don't have to? Simply apply what you learn about buying, portioning, and preparation techniques in this book to your own recipes and favorite foods, and you'll be on your way to becoming slimmer and staying that way the rest of your life! By substituting low-calorie ingredients for high-calorie ingredients in any recipe and adopting sensible eating habits, you should be healthier, feel better, and live longer.

Cooking is an art as well as a science. The esthetic appreciation of exquisitely prepared food is flattering to the cook, but ruinous to the glutton. Advising those who have a compulsion to eat excessively to cut down on their consumption of high-calorie foods will fall on deaf ears until that person is motivated enough to change careless eating habits into sensible ones.

Meat is the mainstay of the American diet, and we derive the majority of our protein and fat from it. To minimize your fat consumption (and calories) you don't have to stop eating meat. But you do need to become more knowledgeable and selective about the kinds and grades of meat you buy and the best cooking techniques to use with the various cuts. It doesn't make much sense to pay a premium price for Prime or Choice grade steaks and roasts that are loaded with fat calories, when what you're really trying to buy is tenderness. Lean, well-trimmed meat can be every bit as tender as its fattier counterparts if the proper cooking methods and procedures are applied.

MEAT GRADING

When it comes to buying meat, getting the best quality and value for your money isn't always easy. The smartest thing you can do is not rely solely on your own knowledge and abilities, but to get acquainted with the meat dealer behind the counter and let him help you. After all, he cuts and packages meat products every day and has the "know-how" to best judge the products he sells to you.

But you don't have to count on the integrity of the butcher or meat dealer alone. The federal government is also there to help. Most of the meats sold in retail stores are graded for quality by the United States Department of Agriculture. These quality grades are stamped on each carcass and primal cut at the time of slaughter, and then only after the meat has passed a rigid federal inspection for wholesomeness. Few people realize, by the way, that although federal inspection for wholesomeness is a requirement for all fresh and processed meat items sold across state lines or to other countries, the use of grade stamps is strictly voluntary.

Because of the large public demand for leaner meat that at the same time is tender and flavorful, some meat-packing firms have found it necessary to establish their own quality standards apart from the USDA grading system. The only problem I have encountered when buying "brand name" ungraded meats is that it's difficult to know the quality level of the meat without buying and cooking some first. In general, you can count on privately graded meat to fall between USDA Good and USDA Choice grades. Experience and a good communicative relationship with your meat dealer will help to make your meat-buying much more pleasant and rewarding.

To become a calorie-wise meat buyer, you need to know some of the important differences between the various USDA grades.

USDA Prime beef, veal, and lamb (pork is seldom graded because it comes from animals under one year of age, which produces meat of uniform quality and tenderness) is the highest quality grade you can buy. *Prime* graded meat is produced from the best stock. It has abundant "marbling" and a thick outer layer of fat which contribute to the juiciness, tenderness, and flavor of the meat. This grade is seldom found in retail stores. It is sold almost exclusively to high-class restaurants and hotels.

USDA Choice graded meat is of high quality but has less fat than *Prime*. This grade is preferred by most meat buyers because of its tenderness, flavor, and adaptability to most dry and moist cooking methods. Most of the meat available in retail stores is graded *USDA Choice*. Average restaurants and hotels also utilize a large percentage of *Choice* graded meats.

USDA Good graded meat does not have the intramuscular marbling of the higher grades and subsequently has a high lean-to-fat ratio. This is definitely the grade to buy if you're watching your budget, and because it's so lean, it is definitely low in calories. *Good* graded meat is best adapted to moist heat cooking methods because of its low fat content. It lacks the juiciness and flavor of the fattier grades, but is still relatively tender.

BUYING MEAT

Have you ever read that it's the "fat" in meat that determines its tenderness and flavor? More than likely you have, because, unfortunately for those of us who have to worry about the amount of fat and calories in our diets, it's true! The amount of intramuscular fats in meat is one of the accepted standards by which it's graded for quality. When meat is cooked, the thin, delicate strands of fat "marbled" through it dissolve into the muscle fibers and help keep the meat juicy and tender. At the same time, it's the flavor of this interior fat that combines with the protein extractives (flavor components) in the meat fibers during cooking that gives beef, lamb, veal, and pork their own unique flavor characteristics.

To be able to select meat properly, you should learn the important differences between the various kinds of meat and have a basic understanding of how each animal is cut up and marketed. It also helps to know the qualities of the grades and cuts available at the meat counter, whether a particular cut will be tough or tender, and how best to cook it. Surprisingly, there's an easy way to know all this.

For the past few years, butchers across the country have slowly been adopting a standardized identification system for labeling meat sold to the retail customer. I can only add, it's about time! The purpose behind it is to do away with fancy merchandising terms and regional descriptions for meat cuts that are confusing and misleading to the uninitiated buyer. Once you acquire the ability to decipher the package label, it's going to be a lot easier for you to select just the right cut of meat for any meal without spending more than you have to for it.

Walk up to the meat counter in your market and pick out a porterhouse steak. Read the label. What does it say? The first word on the top line should be "Beef." This tells you immediately what *kind* of meat (beef, lamb, veal, or pork) you're buying. The second word on the top line should be "loin," which indicates the name of the primal or wholesale cut the meat comes from. The bottom line is reserved for the trade name for this particular retail cut and tells you what part of the wholesale cut the meat was cut from. In this case, it should say "Porterhouse Steak" (cut from the large end of the short loin).

Easy, isn't it? When you're given the important information about what you're buying and where it came from on the animal, you're in a much better position to judge the quality and tenderness of your purchases before you even get them to the table! If the market you shop at doesn't indicate this kind of information on each meat label, tell the butcher (if you can find one) you've got to have it—and shop elsewhere until he complies. If you and enough of your neighbors complain loud and long enough, he'll do it, believe me.

HOW TO IDENTIFY THE MEAT CUTS YOU BUY

It's reassuring to know that in meat there exists a food we can like and that is good for us at the same time. It is, without doubt, the single most popular food in the world, and the best way to enjoy meat in your diet without going over your calorie budget is to become a knowledgeable meat buyer. You should be able to recognize quality meat cuts by appearance and to know the basic principles of meat cookery that are applicable to each cut.

The first step is to understand an animal's anatomy and the relationship of the nine basic primal (wholesale) cuts to each other in terms of their muscular development and relative juiciness, tenderness, and flavor.

The second step is to learn to distinguish the various retail cuts of meat from one another, and know which primal cut each retail cut is derived from. Once you become familiar with the variety of meat cuts available and are able to determine by description and appearance which cuts are tough and which are tender, you're on your way to becoming a judicious buyer and a successful cook.

Time changes everything. Unlike the old days when the local butcher did most of his own meat slaughtering and cutting, almost all the meat sold in today's markets is butchered in large packing houses, where it is cut and processed into primal cuts and meat byproducts before being shipped to retailers for resale to the consumer.

At the packing house, beef carcasses dressed for market are divided lengthwise into two *sides*. (Consumers who have adequate freezer storage will buy a *side* of beef at a reduced price and have it cut up and wrapped to their personal specifications.) The sides of beef are then generally cut crosswise into two parts called the *forequarter* and the *hindquarter*. It's from these four *quarters* of the animal carcass that the primal cuts originate.

For the purpose of simply understanding the muscular development of the primal cuts, the anatomy of the other meats—lamb, veal, and pork—is basically the same as that of beef. Even the names of the primal cuts are similar to beef, except that "shoulder" in lamb, veal, and pork corresponds to the "chuck" in beef, while the "leg" in lamb and veal (and "ham" in pork) corresponds to beef "round."

Although the bone structure of lamb and veal is the same as that of beef, the method of dividing the carcass for market is a little bit different for these smaller animals. Instead of being *quartered,* lamb and veal carcasses are halved crosswise into a *foresaddle* and *hindsaddle*. Pork, on the other hand, is almost always cut into primal and sometimes retail cuts by the packing houses before being shipped to the retailer.

THE PRIMAL CUTS

A side of beef, as I've mentioned, is divided crosswise into two parts—the forequarter and the hindquarter. From these two quarters come the nine primal cuts.

The forequarter is divided into five sections: (1) the *chuck* from the neck and shoulder muscles is a mobile part of the animal. The meat is juicy and flavorful, but with a large amount of connective tissue and fat. (2) The *rib* is a naturally tender, immobile primal cut located between the chuck and the short loin. (3) The *plate* comes from the lower chest area just below the rib. This primal cut is usually sold as hamburger, stew meat, and short ribs. (4) The *brisket* is located between the foreshank and the plate along the animal's chest. The brisket is a mobile muscle with considerable connective tissue and fat. The lean meat is "stringy" but, at the same time, very flavorful. (5) The *foreshank* is the front leg of the beef. The muscles are tough and gristly. The flavorful lean meat, however, makes excellent soup stocks or hamburger.

The hindquarter is divided into four sections: (1) The *short loin* is located between the rib and sirloin primal cuts or what would be considered the lower back. This is the tenderest part of the animal from which the premium quality steaks and roasts are cut. (2) The *sirloin* lies between the short loin and the rump. Like the short loin, the meat of the sirloin is naturally tender. (3) The *round* is part of the hind leg, a mobile and well-exercised muscle of the animal. The meat of the round is very lean and therefore an ideal cut for the dieter. (4) The *flank* is the muscular wall of the abdomen located between the plate and the end of the sirloin. This is the cut from which the true "London broil" originates.

This short description of an animal's anatomy should help you to select and prepare the best cut of meat at the right price for every meal. The important thing to remember in terms of an animal's muscular development is which muscles are mobile and doing all the work. The lean meat of the frequently used muscles like the legs and neck will be tough and gristly. These cuts will need long, slow, moist heat cooking to make them tender. The primal cuts in the middle of an animal along the backbone (rib, loin, and sirloin) are the least used muscles, and retail cuts from these little-used muscles are naturally tender and need to be cooked only a short time. Ultimately, the price you pay for a cut of meat at the market will be determined more by its tenderness and subsequent cooking convenience than by any other consideration.

TENDERNESS

But even for the dieter who can afford to buy high-quality, tender meats every day, there's something else to be considered. Most of the tender meat cuts are heavily marbled with fat and contain a great deal more calories than the relatively lean tougher cuts. Meat is an important food, but if you want to keep your weight down, you'll have to learn to rely upon some of the other factors that contribute to meat's tenderness besides "fat," and make the most of them.

The age of the animal at the time of slaughter is probably the single most important factor controlling meat's tenderness. Lamb, veal, and pork are marketed under one year of age and are therefore much more tender than beef, which is marketed at ages well over a year. In general, the younger the animal at the time of slaughter, the more tender the meat will be. Keep in mind, however, that these younger animals lack the fat and marbling of beef and therefore require gentler cooking than beef so their meat doesn't dry out and toughen.

Another factor that determines tenderness in meat besides the muscular development, kind, age, grade of the animal and the amount of fat and connective tissue is proper aging and storing after slaughter. The meat you buy in the supermarket is about seven to ten days old. Top quality beef and lamb that restaurants buy, on the other hand, has been *aged* in vacuum-sealed polyethelene bags from one to six weeks at controlled temperatures. This is one of the main reasons why it's so hard for us to duplicate the taste and flavor of a good restaurant steak at home.

HOW MUCH MEAT TO BUY

Knowing which cuts of meat to buy for leanness is important; so is knowing how much meat to buy for the average serving. A dieter's portion of cooked lean meat will weigh between two and four ounces, depending upon the variables within the individual cut, the cooking time and temperature, and the caloric requirements of the particular entrée. It's almost impossible to determine the amount of raw meat to buy with 100 percent accuracy because of the many factors affecting its yield during preparation and cooking. But generally, averaging out the approximate servings per pound is a realistic guide to go by.

One pound of uncooked raw meat with little fat and no bone will serve four. This includes boneless roasts, flank steak, veal cutlets, cube steak, brisket, and ground, processed, canned, and variety meats.

One pound of meat with a medium amount of bone and some fat serves three. This includes bone-in chuck, rib and loin roasts, chops, steaks, and ham slices.

One pound of meat with a large amount of bone and fat will serve two. This includes short ribs, spareribs, back ribs, shanks, and hocks.

Buy the right amount of meat specifically stated in a recipe and you won't be tempted to eat more than you're allowed.

STORING AND HANDLING MEAT

Fresh meat is extremely perishable and must be stored and handled properly to keep it in the best possible condition until it is ready to be cooked. To prolong its wholesomeness and maintain its quality and flavor, meat should be kept under constant refrigeration at a temperature below 40° F. Many home refrigerators have special meat-storage compartments at this temperature. If you do not fully intend to use the meat within two to three days after you bought it, forget the refrigerator and freeze the meat as soon as you get home from the market.

Be sure that your freezer is capable of freezing food at zero degrees or lower. This is the only temperature range that is satisfactory for freezing foods for any length of time. If you have a conventional, one-door refrigerator with an ice-cube compartment, keep in mind that it is not designed to freeze food. The temperature inside the compartment is usually kept between 10 and 20 degrees above zero—cold enough to freeze ice cubes, but not cold enough for long-term storage. Meats and other frozen foods stored at this temperature will slowly begin to thaw. They should be used within a week.

Remember also, that the freezing won't improve the quality of meat that's been allowed to deteriorate in the refrigerator; it can only keep the meat in the condition it was in before it was frozen.

Try to coordinate your meat purchases with a rough menu outline for the week and your storage capabilities. After all, unless you have enough freezer space, buying a large 10-pound roast can only result in pouring a lot of money down the disposal, or putting a lot of monotony on the table!

All meat is at its best when it is cooked the same day it's purchased. For certain kinds of meat—variety or organ meats, fresh sausage, and ground meat—this is absolutely essential, since these are the meats that are potentially the most dangerous in terms of spoilage.

Because of the increased surface areas exposed to the air, cubed or diced meats generally used for stews and casseroles should be cooked within two days of purchase. An even better idea is to buy one large piece of meat (at least you'll know the quality you're getting) and cut it up or grind it yourself.

Small cuts of meat like steaks and chops should be used within two to four days.

Large pieces of meat like roasts will hold in the refrigerator about three to five days. In general, the larger the cut of meat, the better it will store.

Cured and smoked meats like ham, sausage, bacon, and frankfurters will last about two weeks if they are stored, unopened, in their original wrappers.

Storing meat in the refrigerator is only intended to keep it safe from spoilage for a relatively short period of time. Bacteria and yeast mold thrive best in moist or "wet" conditions, and the primary function of your refrigerator is to extend the life of the stored meat by controlling the humidity inside the unit. Mechanically, this is done by maintaining a constant low temperature environment and a continual circulated flow of air. Proper handling and storage techniques, however, are equally important.

Because circulated air tends to dry out food easily, most refrigerated food is covered before being stored. Fresh meat, however, is handled differently. As soon as you get fresh or prepackaged meat home from the market, it's a good idea to loosen the wrapping on the ends to allow the meat to "breath." The cold circulating air will partially dry the surface of the meat and retard the growth of bacteria and mold by minimizing the surface moisture. In general, meat, fish, and poultry benefit and need some air circulation and should be loosely wrapped. Two exceptions are cured, smoked, and ready-to-serve meats, which should be tightly wrapped or stored in sealed containers to prevent them from drying out.

If you usually freeze most of your fresh meat purchases, I would suggest that you locate a wholesale butcher and buy your meat in quantity already frozen. Commercially prepared meat can go right into your freezer without further wrapping, and the fact that it's already frozen helps to keep the other foods in your freezer at a steady low temperature of zero or below.

In contrast to meat wrapped loosely for refrigeration, fresh meat to be frozen must always be tightly wrapped and protected against moisture and vapor loss. If the surface of the meat is exposed to the air for any length of time, the moisture will evaporate and a condition known as "freezer burn" will develop. When this happens, the meat will deteriorate quickly and will eventually be dry, flavorless, and absolutely worthless.

To preserve the quality of frozen meat, it must be carefully wrapped in rigid or flexible plastic, a good freezer-wrap paper, or heavy aluminum foil. "Butcher paper" or the light, clear plastic wraps used in most supermarkets today are not adequate wraps for freezing. For long-term storage, these wraps should be removed and the meat rewrapped properly for freezing.

When preparing meat for the freezer, it's a good idea to wrap small cuts like steaks and chops individually or in single layers. Large cuts or bulk meat like hamburger can be wrapped in meal-size portions. Not only will the meat freeze better this way, but you won't have to thaw more meat than you need for any one meal.

Every package of meat to be frozen should be labeled so that you know what you have stored in your freezer and how long it's been there. Remember that the proper length of storage has a lot to do with the kind and cut of meat that is being frozen, and a "first-in, first-out" method of using up stored meats from your freezer is always the best procedure to follow.

If you have a large amount of freezer space, you can save both time and money by stocking the freezer with your favorite cuts of meat when they're advertised in the supermarkets at "special" reduced prices. This usually happens during the winter months when large amounts of livestock are brought to market by ranchers who find it cheaper to sell at reduced prices rather than bear the cost of feeding the animals through the spring.

Another way to save is to buy a "primal" cut of meat like a short loin or sirloin of beef and have the butcher cut and wrap it for freezing. Unless you live out in the middle of nowhere, buying a side or a quarter of beef just isn't worth it. With today's fuel prices, just the cost of the electricity to operate the freezer would be enough to wipe out any saving you might have realized.

Few homeowners realize that you can't store meat in the freezer indefinitely. Meats that are cured or salted, like ham or bacon, become rancid in a matter of weeks, even though they're frozen solid! The optimum storage time varies with the holding temperature of the freezer and the kind of meat being stored—be it beef, lamb, veal, or pork. Meat should be frozen only as long as it retains its full flavor and quality. This is why a good storage and labeling system is so important.

At 0° F., beef and lamb will retain their quality for six months. But at −10° F., the optimum storage time increases to twelve months.

Veal and pork can be stored for four months at 0° F. and eight months at −10° F. The variety meats are very delicate and should be used within one month. Canned meats should never be frozen. The contents can expand and break the seal, subjecting the meat to contamination and dehydration.

If the proper method of storing frozen meat seems rather complicated and confusing, it's probably because the storage times and handling procedures vary with each kind and cut of meat you put in your freezer, be it fresh, frozen, cured, or cooked. Unfortunately, you will encounter additional problems when it comes time to prepare frozen meat for cooking.

Frozen meat can be put into the oven, under the broiler, or into the skillet, frozen solid as it comes from the freezer, or it can be thawed first in the refrigerator, then allowed to come to room temperature before cooking. The cooking methods are generally the same for frozen and nonfrozen cuts—large or small—but the frozen meat will take anywhere from one-third to three times longer to cook. The actual length of time it takes to cook meat from the frozen state will ultimately depend upon the size and thickness of the cut and the cooking method employed. Because minutes-per-pound cooking tables are based on meats at room temperature, a thermometer inserted into the large cuts during the last stages of cooking will be the only reliable method of determining the degree of doneness.

Unless you're really pressed for time, I would recommend planning your meals far enough ahead to allow frozen meat to thaw completely before cooking. Although there's nothing wrong in cooking meat in its frozen state, preparing fresh or thawed meat is undoubtedly a more familiar procedure, and there's less chance for the meat to be improperly cooked.

To defrost meat in the refrigerator takes about three to eight hours per pound. At room temperature, defrosting will take approximately one to three hours per pound. In either case, the actual defrosting time will depend upon the weight, size, and thickness of the cut.

A very important step in thawing frozen meat is to leave the original wrapping intact to minimize evaporation and drip loss—the loss of water-soluble nutrients and flavorings. Don't try to defrost meat too rapidly. Putting meat in cold water as you would poultry only increases the loss of these valuable juices.

One rather important advantage in taking the time to defrost meat in the refrigerator is that in the event you find your meal plans changed, the meat can be safely refrozen. As long as it has not been completely thawed and still contains ice crystals, the temperature of the meat is low enough to prevent spoilage or excessive drip loss. Completely thawed meat and meat exposed to temperatures over 40° F., on the other hand cannot be refrozen and should be cooked immediately; it can then be refrigerated and used within 2 days or frozen for later use.

Leftover meat and cooked meat dishes should be cooled quickly and stored in tightly covered containers or in airtight wrapping material. If it is warm when refrigerated, leave it uncovered until it cools; then cover. Cooked meats stored in the refrigerator should be used within two days; frozen meat dishes can be stored about four weeks.

COOKING MEAT

Considering today's food prices, being on a diet can be very economical. Meat is an expensive food item, so eating smaller portions not only reduces your caloric intake, it lowers the price of each portion as well.

Low-calorie cooking starts with being able to buy the right cut of meat to suit the purposes of a particular dish. The next step is to use the proper cooking method that improves the flavor and tenderness of the meat, and at the same time keeps calories at a minimum.

All cooking methods are related to a specific type of heat environment and are classified as a dry heat method or a moist heat method. Dry heat cooking methods are used with the more tender cuts of meat that contain little connective tissue. The cooking temperatures are usually moderate to high, and the cooking time brief. Dry heat cooking methods include roasting, broiling, panbroiling, and sautéing. Moist heat cooking methods are used with the less tender cuts of meat that contain a relatively large amount of connective tissue and require long, slow simmering at low temperatures to make them tender. Moist heat cooking methods include simmering, braising, and stewing.

Trying to minimize the "fat calories" in the meat cuts you buy can determine the method of preparation you use, but the proper cooking procedure will ultimately depend upon the tenderness and quality of the meat you buy.

LOW-CALORIE DRY HEAT COOKING METHODS

Roasting

Roasting is the cooking of large, tender cuts of meat with hot, dry air. When roasting takes place in an oven, the procedure is identical to "baking," but through the years, the term "roasted" has come to be applied almost exclusively to meat cookery, while the term "baked" usually describes the method of preparation for breads, vegetables, desserts, and combination dishes.

Originally, all meat was roasted on a spit over an open fire. The intense heat seared and browned the outside surface and sealed in the internal juices. As the roast turned on the spit, excess moisture was allowed to evaporate into the open air, while at the same time, the meat was being basted continually with its own melting fat. Soon after the meat was seared, it was moved farther away from the fire and allowed to slowly develop that natural flavor and aroma that made this simple method of cooking meat so memorable.

Today, most roasts are cooked uncovered in an oven. But the classic method of open-fire cooking I have just described (it is also referred to as barbecuing or open-spit roasting) is still practiced by backyard chefs and outdoorsmen.

Successful roasting, as with other cooking methods, is simply a matter of mastering basic principles and techniques of preparation rather than remembering recipes. Once you've developed the ability to roast a primal cut of beef, for instance, it's easy to apply what you have learned to the roasting of identical cuts of lamb, veal or pork.

BASIC ROASTING TECHNIQUES

1. *Remove the meat from the refrigerator* at least 30 minutes before cooking to allow it to reach room temperature. This will help the meat develop the best possible flavor and help cut the cooking time down somewhat.

2. *Season the roast with herbs or spices.* This is not a necessary step; it is simply a matter of personal taste and preference. Don't flour the meat; it only increases the possibility of scorching and adds unneeded calories as well.

3. *Insert a meat thermometer* into the center of the thickest muscle. Be sure that the bulb end of the thermometer isn't resting in fat or touching a bone. To be able to roast a cut of meat using only the usual time-weight ratio tables takes a great deal of expertise. You will also find that most oven thermostats are too variable to be counted on for accuracy. Most of the recommended temperatures and cooking timetables are too high for our modern cooking equipment, so rely on a good meat thermometer to determine the degree of doneness of meat. Incidentally, I strongly recommend you invest in an expensive (about $9.00) instant-reading thermometer like meat and health inspectors use. Unlike those that you leave in the meat during cooking, these are inserted just long enough to give a reading. They are accurate to within two to three degrees and will give you the temperature of most anything from freezing to boiling.

4. *Place the roast fat side up on a rack* in a shallow-sided pan that is large enough to catch the drippings from the sides of the roast, but not so large that the drippings will evaporate and burn. A shallow-sided roasting pan also prevents steam from building up around the sides of the roast. The rack will hold the meat off the bottom of the pan and prevent it from panfrying in its own drippings.

5. *Add diced aromatic vegetables*—carrots, onions, and celery, if desired. A *mirepoix* gives additional flavor to bland roasts, and often substitutes as a rack to keep the meat off the bottom of the pan.

6. *Preheat the oven to 350° F. and roast the meat* at this constant temperature until the desired degree of doneness is indicated on the meat thermometer. Do not add water, do not baste, and do not cover the pan. Adding liquids or covering the pan will set up a "stewing" condition, and the meat will actually be cooked by moist heat rather than being dry-roasted. After the roast is well sealed, a small amount of water is sometimes added to the bottom of the roasting pan. This is only done if it appears that the carmelized drippings are beginning to evaporate and smoke. In a few instances, very dry or bland roasts are occasionally basted with wine or stock to prevent them from drying out.

7. *Turn the roast* at least once to provide even browning and to prevent dryness. Don't puncture the meat while turning; you'll lose valuable and flavorful juices.

8. *Allow the roast to stand or "rest"* for at least 15-minutes before slicing. This allows the collagen to set. As the heat pressure diminishes, the internal juices redistribute themselves throughout the meat.

STANDING RIB ROAST OF BEEF (NON-SEARING METHOD)

1 five- to eight-pound rib roast   salt and pepper

Press the salt and pepper into the meat. Place roast in a shallow roasting pan, fat side up. Insert a meat thermometer into the center. Be sure that the bulb of the thermometer doesn't touch a bone. Don't baste or add any liquid to the pan. Roast, uncovered, in a 325° F. oven until the thermometer reads 140° for rare, 160° for medium, or 170° F. for well done. This is an average cooking time of 25 minutes per pound at this temperature. Allow the roast to "rest" at least 15 minutes before carving. Standing rib roasts are usually cared horizontally. Place the roast on a serving platter. Hold it steady with a cooking fork. With a slicing knife or carver, slice the meat parallel to the table, starting at the outer edge and slicing toward the bone. Cut down from the top along the edge of the bones to remove each slice.

Makes 4 to 6 servings at 280 calories per 4-ounce serving.

Chef's Cooking Tip:
If, after purchasing a rib roast with the intention of roasting it, you run short of time, simply cut the meat into steaks and broil them. A total cooking time of about 15 minutes is all that's needed!

STANDING RIB ROAST (SEARING METHOD)

1 five- to eight-pound rib roast   salt and pepper

Remove roast from refrigerator to bring to room temperature. Press salt and pepper into the surface of the meat. Insert a meat thermometer into the thickest portion of the roast without the bulb end resting in fat or on a bone. Preheat the oven to 500° F. for at least 15 minutes. Place the roast in the oven in a shallow roasting pan, fat side up. Reduce the heat to 350° F. and cook, uncovered, to the desired degree of doneness; 140° for rare, 160° for medium, and 170° F. for well done. The initial heat should produce enough drippings to prevent smoking or burning in the bottom of the pan. If the drippings do evaporate and begin to burn, a small amount of water can be added to the pan to cool it. Remove the roast from the oven and allow it to "rest" at least 15 minutes before carving.

Makes 4 to 6 servings at 280 calories per 4-ounce serving.

Chef's Cooking Tip:
If the roasting pan is going to be deglazed with stock or wine as the base for "au jus" or pan gravy (*sans* the fat, of course), add ¼ cup diced onion, celery, and carrot during the last half hour of roasting for added flavor.

ROAST TENDERLOIN OF BEEF

1 four- to five-pound whole beef tenderloin
salt and pepper
1 cup diced onion
1 cup diced celery
1 cup diced carrot

Remove the roast from the refrigerator; pat dry with paper toweling. Using a sharp boning knife, remove the excess fat and connective tissue. (For such an expensive cut, you should be able to persuade your butcher to help you with this step.) Season with salt and pepper. Place roast on diced vegetables in a shallow roasting pan. Cook, uncovered, in a hot 450° F. oven about 10 minutes per pound, or until the meat thermometer registers 120° F. for rare. Allow the roast to "rest" in a warm place for 5 to 10 minutes before slicing.

Makes 6 to 8 servings at 260 calories per 4-ounce serving.

Chef's Cooking Tip:
A tenderloin roast takes an extremely short time to cook. The meat is already luxuriously tender, and it is only cooked to make it more palatable and to develop its flavor. Under no circumstance should a tenderloin be overcooked.

BEEF LOIN STRIP ROAST

1 five- to six-pound beef loin strip roast

1 tablespoon crushed peppercorns

Preheat the oven to 550° F. Remove the roast from the refrigerator. Press the crushed peppercorns into the surface of the meat with the heel of the hand. Place the roast on a rack in a shallow open pan and let stand at room temperature for ½ hour before cooking time. Insert a meat thermometer mid-length of roast. Reduce the oven temperature to 400° F. and cook the roast, uncovered, to the desired degree of doneness: 140° for rare, 150° for medium rare. Allow the meat to "rest" for at least 15 minutes in a warm place before slicing.

Makes 6 to 8 servings at 225 calories per 4-ounce serving.

Chef's Cooking Tip:
A boneless loin strip roast is sometime called a New York strip roast or a club roast. It is too tender a cut to ever be cooked beyond the medium-rare stage.

ROAST SIRLOIN OF BEEF

1 five- to six-pound boneless sirloin of beef
1 tablespoon crushed peppercorns

2 cups chopped onion
2 cups chopped celery
2 cups chopped carrots

Preheat oven to 550° F. With the heel of the hand, press the crushed peppercorns into the surface of the meat. Place the roast, fat-side up, on the chopped vegetables in a shallow roasting pan. Allow the roast to come to room temperature. (This helps to cut down on the cooking time.) Insert a meat thermometer into the center of the largest muscle; reduce the oven temperature to 400° F. and cook, uncovered, to the desired degree of doneness; 140° for rare, 150° for medium rare. Allow the roast to "rest" in a warm place for at least 15 minutes before slicing.

Makes 6 to 8 servings at 225 calories per 4-ounce serving.

Chef's Cooking Tip:
If you purchase a sirloin of beef "rolled and tied," it will require more cooking time per pound because of the removal of the bones that would ordinarily conduct heat. The "rolling" procedure increases the denseness of the roast which also contributes to the longer cooking time.

ROAST RACK OF LAMB
À LA FRANÇAISE

Be sure the butcher has removed the backbone of this roast or it will be almost impossible to carve. Also, have him "french" it for you. To *french* means to cut back the meat and fat from the flank end of the bones.

1 rack of lamb, about 3 pounds
1 clove garlic, halved
salt and freshly ground pepper to taste
½ teaspoon ground rosemary
½ teaspoon paprika

Rub roast all over with garlic, then season with remaining ingredients. Cover exposed chop ends with aluminum foil to prevent burning. Place rack with rib ends down on a rack in a shallow roasting pan or skillet. Roast at 475° F. for about 20 minutes for rare.

Makes 3 servings at 250 calories per serving.

Chef's Cooking Tip:
In my opinion, lamb is at its best when cooked rare, but if further cooking is desired, reduce the oven temperature to 350° F. and continue to cook until the desired degree of doneness is reached.

ROLLED ROAST LEG OF LAMB

1 four-pound rolled leg of lamb roast
½ tablespoon whole rosemary
salt and pepper
3 tablespoons lemon juice
1 cup each: onion, celery, and carrot
1 cup dry white wine or vermouth

Rub the lamb all over with rosemary, salt, and pepper. Insert a thermometer into the thickest part of the roast. Place the diced vegetables in the bottom of a shallow roasting pan just large enough to accommodate the roast. Place meat on the vegetables and baste with lemon juice. Preheat oven to 350° F. Cook roast, uncovered, 35 to 40 minutes per pound, or until the thermometer reaches 150° for medium rare or 170° for medium well. Baste occasionally with the wine and pan juices throughout the entire cooking period. Turn the meat a few times for even browning. Allow the roast to stand in a warm place to firm up before slicing.

Makes 4 to 6 servings at 220 calories per 4-ounce serving.

Chef's Cooking Tip:
A rib roast, rolled loin roast, sirloin, or shoulder roast all can be roasted in this manner, but for the dieter, the leg roast is the least fattening.

ROAST LEG OF VEAL

1 four-pound boned and rolled leg of veal
1 teaspoon whole rosemary
salt and pepper
1 cup each: diced onion, celery, and carrot
1 cup dry white wine or vermouth

Rub roast with rosemary, salt, and pepper. Press the seasoning into the surface of the meat with the heel of your hand. Insert a thermometer into the meatiest part of the roast. In a shallow roasting pan add the diced aromatic vegetables; then the roast. Cook in a moderate 350° F. oven, uncovered, about 35 minutes per pound. The meat thermometer should register 170° F. for well done. Baste occasionally with the wine and pan juices. Turn roast at least once for even browning.

Makes 4 to 6 servings at 260 calories per 4-ounce serving.

Chef's Cooking Tip:
The roasted aromatic vegetables, wine, and pan juices provide the base for an excellent low-calorie sauce. After removing the roast, add ¼ cup of tomato sauce or tomato purée to the pan. Simmer pan over medium-high heat until liquid is reduced and thickened. Strain through a food mill or process in a blender and serve.

BONELESS ROAST LOIN OF PORK

2 pounds boneless top loin roast
1 teaspoon freshly ground pepper
⅓ teaspoon whole thyme
⅓ teaspoon garlic powder

When you buy the roast, have the butcher trim away most of the outside fat. Wipe the meat with paper toweling; season with pepper, thyme, and garlic powder. Insert a meat thermometer into the thickest part of the roast.

Place the meat on a rack in a shallow-sided roasting pan and cook, uncovered, in a 350° F. oven for about 30 minutes per pound. The thermometer is very important. When roasting pork, the final thermometer reading should be at least 170° F. for well done. Fresh pork should always be cooked to the well-done stage, but on the other hand, there is no need to dry the meat out by overcooking.

Allow the roast to "rest" in a warm place to firm up for at least 15 minutes after it has been removed from the oven.

Makes 4 servings at 150 calories per 2-ounce cooked serving.

Chef's Cooking Tip:
Lean (and I emphasize lean) pork loin, shoulder or leg roasts are not any more fattening than comparable cuts of beef or lamb, and because pork roast is always cooked well done, a great deal more fat is rendered out during cooking than would be the case with beef or lamb, which are usually cooked rare to medium.

Broiling

Broiling is undoubtedly the most popular method of preparing thick, tender, juicy cuts of meat that are too small to roast. Steaks, chops, and hamburger that are of top quality and well aged are the meat cuts that are usually cooked by this method.

The temperatures used for broiling meat are hot, intense, and direct, and the actual cooking takes place over the radiant glow of hot coals or under the direct heat of a gas or electric broiler.

Bear in mind that I have stressed "thick and tender" as prerequisites for cooking meat in this way. It should be cut no less than 1¼ inches thick. Any thinner and you'll have well-done meat by the time it is crusted. Although there are times when a particular quality of meat would benefit from low-temperature broiling, searing it over medium-high heat, then finishing it off using medium to medium-low temperatures maximizes its flavor and tenderness.

In contrast to roasting, which utilizes moderate to low cooking temperatures to reduce shrinkage, successful broiling is the direct result of intense heat coagulating the surface proteins and forcing the natural juices toward the center of the meat. As excess moisture is evaporated in the hot, dry air, the proteins on the surface carmelize and a brown crust is formed.

The meat is then turned so the second side is exposed to the direct flame The carmelizing process is repeated and the natural juices are sealed between the two charred surfaces. Unless this preliminary searing with intense heat is accomplished, the outside surface will never char. If the meat overcooks as a result, it will be hard, dry, tough, and nutritionally almost worthless.

The cooking time and temperatures used for broiled meats might vary with the kind, grade, and cut, but in general, cooking meat quickly in dry, intense heat develops the best flavor and aroma.

Just before the meat cooked in the broiler is done, turn the heat off and allow it to finish cooking in the trapped convected heat of the broiler alone. This should take from 5 to 10 minutes and gives the juices concentrated in the center of the meat a chance to disperse evenly. I have seen many cooks continue to cook a cut of meat until it was hopelessly ruined, simply because they mistakenly thought the meat was still *raw* in the center.

BASIC BROILING TECHNIQUES

1. *Remove the meat from the refrigerator* one hour before cooking. This will reduce the cooking time and help to prevent the outside surface from becoming too charred before the meat has had a chance to reach the desired degree of doneness.

2. *Season the meat* with freshly ground pepper. When the seasoning is done before broiling, the added flavor will become part of the crust. It's usually best to salt the meat after cooking since salt tends to retard the carmelization of the surface.

3. *Set the oven control* to its highest setting. Allow enough time before cooking for the inside of the broiler to get as hot as possible. Besides not being aged long enough, one of the main reasons why the broiled meat you eat at home lacks the flavor of the meat you eat in restaurants is because commercial ranges and broilers cook at much higher temperatures. The maximum broiling temperature of a home range is 550° F. The broiling temperature of a commercial range is closer to 1000° F.

4. *Adjust the distance of the broiling pan* or rack after the meat is seared to regulate the cooking temperature. Basically all meat cuts are seared over medium-high heat, then finished off using medium to medium-low temperatures. The two most important considerations are the thickness of the meat and the degree of doneness desired. For thin pieces of meat and those to be cooked rare, broil close to the source of heat. For thick pieces of meat and those to be cooked medium to well done, sear the meat a few minutes as close to the flame as practical, then lower the broiling pan to cook the meat to the desired degree of doneness without burning the outside surface.

5. *Broil the meat* until brown on one side. Turn the meat with tongs and finish cooking on the second side, adding additional seasonings to the browned surface, if desired.

6. *Test for doneness* by pressing the meat with your fingers. A rare piece of meat will feel soft. As you continue cooking, it will become progressively more resistant to the touch. Well-done meat will feel very firm.

7. *Allow the meat to "rest"* in the broiler after the meat is turned off for 5 minutes to disperse the juices evenly.

HAMBURGERS

1 pound lean ground round
1 tablespoon minced onion
1 teaspoon diet catsup
⅛ teaspoon each: garlic salt,
　　pepper

TOPPING:
1 tablespoon plain yogurt
1 tablespoon brown spicy
　　mustard

1 tablespoon chopped parsley
1 tablespoon chopped chives

GARNISH:
4 lettuce leaves
4 ripe tomato slices
6 pickle slices

Combine ground round, onion, catsup, and seasonings. Shape into four patties. Broil under moderate heat to the desired degree of doneness. Blend topping ingredients in a cup. Chill. Serve hamburger on a plain toasted bun. Top with chilled topping and garnish with lettuce, tomato, and pickle.

Makes 4 servings at 280 calories per serving.

Chef's Cooking Tip:
Still-frozen hamburger patties can be successfully broiled if the heat is kept low enough to prevent the outside surface from charring before the inside is cooked through.

BROILED LIVER AND ONIONS

1 large onion, thinly sliced
4 tablespoons dry sherry wine
2 tablespoons diet catsup
1 pound baby-beef or calf's liver,
　　sliced ⅜-inch thick

salt and pepper to taste
paprika

Place sliced onion and sherry wine in a medium-size skillet. Cover and cook over medium heat for 5 minutes. Uncover. Add diet catsup and continue to cook over medium-low heat for 30 to 45 minutes. Add a small amount of water, wine, or tomato juice if sauce becomes too thick. Remove from heat; cover. Place liver on a nonstick broiler pan. Broil under moderate heat, about 2 minutes on each side, until just pink in the center. Do not overcook. Remove from heat; season with salt and pepper. Cover liver with sautéed onions and sauce. Garnish with paprika and serve immediately.

Makes 4 servings at 190 calories per serving.

Chef's Cooking Tip:
Watch cooking time carefully. Liver toughens when it is overcooked.

BROILED SALISBURY STEAK

1 pound lean ground round
1 tablespoon diet margarine
½ cup minced onion
2 tablespoons minced green pepper
1 teaspoon freshly chopped parsley
1 teaspoon Worcestershire sauce
salt and pepper to taste

In a small saucepan, steam minced onion and pepper for 2 minutes; drain. Combine ingredients and shape into 4 patties 1 inch thick. Broil under moderate heat to the desired degree of doneness.

Makes 4 servings at 200 calories per serving.

Chef's Cooking Tip:
To maximize the "juiciness" of lean hamburger, don't overcook, overhandle, or freeze. Also, remember that no matter how you like your ground steak cooked, always sear the surface at high heat to seal in the juices before lowering the heat for a medium to well done.

BROILED STEAKS

2 (5-ounce) steaks   salt and pepper to taste

Preheat broiler. Trim steaks of all visible fat. Broil under high heat to sear the surface and seal in the juices. When the first side is browned, season with salt and pepper to taste. Turn and brown on second side. When desired degree of doneness is reached, season second side. Turn off broiler heat and allow steaks to "rest" for a few minutes before serving.

Makes 2 servings at 260 calories per serving.

Chef's Cooking Tip:
A *rare* cooked steak will take about 5 minutes cooking on each side. If you like your steaks medium to well done, move the broiler rack further away from the flame or turn down the heat until the desired degree of doneness is reached *after* the meat is initially seared.

BROILED SIRLOIN TIPS

1½ pounds top sirloin
1 medium-size onion, thinly sliced
1½ cups dry white wine
1 tablespoon red wine vinegar
¼ teaspoon thyme
¼ teaspoon oregano
¼ teaspoon pepper
⅛ teaspoon garlic powder

Cut sirloin into 1-inch cubes. Combine onion, wine, vinegar, thyme, oregano, pepper, and garlic powder. Place meat in a glass bowl. Pour marinade over, then cover and refrigerate for 6 hours or overnight. When ready to serve, drain and broil under high heat until the desired degree of doneness is obtained.

Makes 4 servings at 250 calories per serving.

BROILED LAMB SHISH KABOBS

1½ pounds leg of lamb
salt and pepper
2 minced garlic cloves
2 small bay leaves
1 lemon
8 fresh medium-size mushrooms
4 tomato wedges
4 chunks green pepper
4 chunks yellow onion

Cut lamb into ¾-inch cubes; place them in a glass dish or ceramic bowl. Add minced garlic and bay leaves. Cut lemon into wedges and squeeze juice over lamb. Add wedges to marinade. Mix well; cover and refrigerate several hours. Remove from refrigerator and drain 30 minutes before serving. Alternate lamb, tomato wedges, mushrooms, and green pepper and onion chunks on 4 skewers. Brush with marinade. Broil or barbecue under moderate heat about 12 to 15 minutes, turning and basting frequently. Season to taste.

Makes 4 servings at 340 calories per serving.

Chef's Cooking Tip:
The bamboo skewers you buy in Oriental shops won't char under the broiler if you soak them in water for several hours before using them.

BROILED LIVER

1 pound baby-beef or calves' liver   salt and pepper to taste

Slice liver ⅜-inch thick. Place slices on a nonstick broiler pan. Broil under moderate heat, about 2 minutes on each side for rare, 3 minutes for medium, and 4 minutes for well done. Transfer to a heated serving dish; season with salt and pepper and serve.

Makes 4 servings at 160 calories per serving.

Chef's Cooking Tip:
Freezing the liver just until firm makes slicing easier.

LONDON BROIL

1½ pounds flank steak
¼ cup dry red wine
¼ cup soy sauce
⅛ teaspoon marjoram
⅛ teaspoon crushed peppercorns

Place flank steak in a shallow glass dish and marinate in soy sauce, wine, and seasoning mixture, covered, for one hour or longer; turn occasionally. Broil quickly under high heat about 5 minutes per side. Baste with marinade during cooking. With meat still under broiler to keep warm, turn off heat and allow the steak to "rest" for 5 minutes. To serve, carve in thin slices across the grain.

Makes 6 servings at 220 calories per serving.

Chef's Cooking Tip:
Because of its coarse grain, it helps to score flank steak on both sides in a 1-inch diamond pattern with the tip of a sharp knife before cooking to prevent the ends from curling.

BARBECUED SPARERIBS

4 pounds (2 sides) spareribs
8 peppercorns
3 whole cloves
1 bay leaf
2 cloves garlic, minced
1 can (8-ounce) tomato sauce
½ cup soy sauce
2 teaspoons chile powder

Cut each rack into 3 equal portions. Place in a large pot and barely cover with cold water; season with peppercorns, cloves, bay leaf, and 1 minced garlic clove. Bring to a boil, then reduce heat and simmer for 45 minutes. Drain and cool.

Arrange ribs in a shallow baking dish. Add second garlic clove and remaining ingredients and marinate ribs anywhere from 2 hours to overnight in the refrigerator, turning occasionally to coat ribs evenly.

To finish cooking, arrange ribs on the barbecue over hot coals and cook for 20 to 30 minutes. During last 15 minutes, baste with marinade and continue cooking until ribs are glazed and tender.

Makes 6 servings at 295 calories per serving.

Chef's Cooking Tip:
Besides cooking off most of the fat calories, preliminary parboiling makes for moister, tastier meat than dry heat alone and cuts the barbecue time by one half.

Panbroiling

As a cooking method, panbroiling is basically the same as broiling, except that the cooking is done on a surface unit rather than under a broiler or over a charcoal fire. A hot, dry, open skillet or griddle is used to sear the meat and seal in its internal juices. The meat is cooked by the conducted heat that is transferred from the hot metal surface underneath. No added fats, oils, or liquids are employed in the cooking process, however.

Panbroiling is also faster than broiling and is especially effective for cooking lean or small portions of meat that would dry out and be overcooked if subjected to the intense, direct heat of a broiler. When properly cooked, panbroiled meats are almost always tastier and more flavorful than meats that are broiled or grilled.

BASIC PANBROILING TECHNIQUES

1. *Dry the meat thoroughly* with paper toweling. Be sure to do this even if the meat has been in a liquid marinade. If there is *excess* moisture on the surface of the meat before panbroiling, the liquid will vaporize as it comes in contact with the hot pan, and the meat will not brown properly. With very lean meats and quality steaks that are aged and contain very little water, however, the meat can be briefly dipped in water, broth, or wine, then drained but not dried before being placed in the hot skillet.

2. *Spray a heavy skillet with a food release agent.* I personally prefer either cast-iron or heavy cast-aluminum pans because of their even heat distribution qualities. A heavy nonstick skillet designed for high heat is ideal, of course.

3. *Heat the skillet very hot.* Flick a few drops of water off your fingers into the pan. When the beads of water dance over the surface, the pan is hot enough for panbroiling.

4. *Place the meat in the pan and sear quickly on one side.* It will take from one to five minutes for a crust to form on the bottom surface and to be halfway cooked, depending upon the thickness of the meat. When beads of moisture appear on the surface, turn the meat over with tongs or a spatula and sear the other side.

5. *Do not cover the pan or add any liquids* during the cooking time. Panbroiling is a dry heat method that employs the heat of conduction to cook the food. Water, stock, or wine used to deglaze the pan can be added after the meat is removed.

6. *Remove any excess fat as it accumulates.* This will not be necessary for thin cuts of meat or for meat that is cooked rare. Meat cuts that are thicker than one inch or are to be cooked medium rare to medium must be cooked longer at a reduced temperature to prevent the surface of the meat from burning. The subsequent fat accumulation should be poured off to prevent the meat from being "fried" rather than panbroiled when the temperature is reduced.

7. *Test the meat for doneness* by pressing the surface with your fingers. When the meat stiffens to the touch, it should be cooked to the rare stage. Remember that panbroiled meat takes about half the time to cook than oven-broiled meat.

BEEF CURRY

4 (5-ounce) beef tenderloin steaks
1 tablespoon dry white wine
5 ounces unsweetened pineapple juice
⅛ teaspoon garlic powder
¼ teaspoon curry powder
½ cup pineapple cubes
⅓ cup coconut, shredded and browned
salt and white pepper to taste
freshly chopped parsley

Brown the beef steaks quickly in a dry nonstick skillet over high heat. Remove when medium rare to a warm platter; deglaze skillet with wine. Add remaining ingredients and reduce over high heat to thicken. Return steaks and juices to skillet to warm through. Garnish with chopped parsley or chives.

Makes 4 servings at 300 calories per serving.

BEEF STROGANOFF

1¼ pounds tenderloin of beef
¼ cup dry red wine
2 tablespoons Worcestershire sauce
2 tablespoons diet catsup
1 teaspoon prepared mustard
1 cup sliced mushrooms
½ cup chopped green onions
½ cup beef broth
½ cup plain yogurt
1 tablespoon cornstarch
freshly chopped parsley
paprika

Cut meat into thin pieces about 2 inches long; dry thoroughly with paper toweling. Panbroil in a heavy nonstick skillet over high heat until browned on all sides. Remove to a warm platter. Reduce heat; add dry red wine to deglaze pan. Add Worcestershire sauce, catsup, and mustard and reduce to a thick paste. Add mushrooms, onions, and broth. Cover and simmer for 3 minutes. Stir yogurt and cornstarch together. Uncover skillet and remove from heat. Slowly stir in yogurt; add reserved meat and juices. Return skillet to surface unit and simmer over low heat to heat through, about 3 minutes. Do not boil or yogurt will curdle. Garnish dish with freshly chopped parsley and paprika.

Makes 4 servings at 260 calories per serving.

FILLET OF BEEF ITALIAN

1¼ pounds tenderloin of beef
2 teaspoons olive oil
2 teaspoons vegetable oil
2 garlic cloves, crushed
2 medium-size onions, chopped
1 green pepper, chopped
1 can (16-ounce) Italian-style plum tomatoes
½ cup tomato purée
¼ cup dry vermouth
2 tablespoons tomato paste
2 teaspoons oregano
¼ cup freshly chopped parsley
salt and pepper to taste

Cut meat into thin pieces about 2 inches long. Dry thoroughly with paper toweling and reserve. Combine olive oil, vegetable oil, and garlic in a large saucepan over medium-high heat. When garlic turns golden brown, remove and discard. Add onions; sauté for 3 minutes; add green pepper and sauté 3 minutes longer. Add plum tomatoes, tomato purée, dry vermouth, tomato paste, and whole oregano. Simmer sauce, uncovered, for 10 minutes. Add chopped parsley, salt, and pepper. Meanwhile, panbroil meat in a nonstick skillet over high heat until browned, about 2 minutes. Transfer sauce to skillet and stir with meat to combine flavors. Remove from heat, cover, and allow to stand for 5 minutes before serving.

Makes 4 servings at 270 calories per serving.

MARINATED LONDON BROIL

1¼ pound small flank steak
1 cup dry red wine
½ cup tomato juice
½ cup vinegar
½ teaspoon salt

1 teaspoon crushed peppercorns
1 teaspoon marjoram
1 teaspoon Worcestershire sauce
1 teaspoon chopped parsley

For marinade, combine half of the wine, ½ cup tomato juice, ½ cup vinegar, salt, peppercorns, and marjoram. Place meat in a glass baking dish; pour marinade over meat and cover. Refrigerate 6 hours or overnight. Turn meat occasionally. Remove steak from marinade. Pat dry with paper toweling. Sear steak in a heavy nonstick skillet over high heat for 5 minutes on each side. Reduce heat to medium and cook approximately 10 to 15 minutes longer, or until just rare. Remove meat to a warm platter. Pour off any excess fat. Deglaze pan with Worcestershire sauce and remaining ½ cup red wine. Reduce liquid by one-half over high heat. Add chopped parsley; pour sauce over steak. Carve meat at extreme angle across the grain in thin slices.

Makes 4 servings at 280 calories per serving.

Chef's Cooking Tip:
Flank steak has less than 6 percent fat per pound and is the leanest beef cut you can buy. Cook only to "rare" and carve in thin slices to keep meat tender.

MUSHROOM BURGERS

The chopped mushrooms and onions in these patties add needed moisture and flavor without adding calories, and seasoning vegetables don't blot up melting fat as starch fillers like bread crumbs and rice do.

1 pound lean ground round
¼ cup chopped fresh mushrooms
¼ cup minced onion, cooked

1 teaspoon Worcestershire sauce
½ teaspoon seasoned salt
¼ teaspoon black pepper

Combine ingredients. Shape mixture into 4 patties 1 inch thick. Refrigerate for at least 30 minutes to firm. Sear patties in a heavy nonstick skillet over high heat. Turn once, allowing 5 minutes per side for rare. For medium rare to medium, reduce heat and continue cooking 3 to 5 minutes longer.

Makes 4 servings at 200 calories per serving.

PANBROILED STEAK AU POIVRE

4 (5-ounce) beef tenderloin steaks
1 tablespoon whole black peppercorns
½ cup dry red wine
1 tablespoon Worcestershire sauce
1 tablespoon freshly chopped parsley
1 tablespoon chopped chives

Crush the peppercorns slightly and press them into both sides of the steaks with the heel of the hand. Let the steaks stand at room temperature for 30 minutes. Heat a heavy nonstick skillet over high heat. Sear the steaks on both sides, allowing 5 minutes per side for rare. For medium rare to medium, reduce the heat to moderate and continue to cook an additional 3 to 5 minutes, depending upon the thickness of the steaks. Remove the steaks to a warm platter. Deglaze the pan with the wine and Worcestershire sauce, scraping the pan with a spatula. Allow pan sauce to thicken by reduction, then add the parsley and chives to the sauce. Stir for a few seconds. Pour the sauce over the steaks and serve.

Makes 4 servings at 230 calories per serving.

PANBROILED STEAK DIANE

4 (5-ounce) beef tenderloin steaks
salt and pepper to taste
1 teaspoon "Kitchen Bouquet"
2 tablespoons Worcestershire sauce
2 tablespoons diet catsup
¼ cup dry red wine
1 tablespoon freshly chopped parsley

Season steaks with salt and pepper. Sear steaks in a heavy nonstick skillet over high heat. Turn once, allowing 5 minutes per side for rare. For medium rare to medium, reduce heat to medium and continue cooking 3 to 5 minutes longer, depending upon the thickness of the steaks, until the desired degree of doneness is obtained. Remove steaks to a warm platter. Add the remaining ingredients, except parsley, to the skillet and reduce over high heat until thickened. Pour sauce over steaks and sprinkle with chopped parsley before serving.

Makes 4 servings at 230 calories per serving.

CURRY OF BEEF NOISETTE

1¼ pounds tenderloin of beef

SAUCE:
 2 tablespoons dry sherry
 ¼ cup minced shallots or onion
 ¼ cup diced carrot
 ¼ cup diced celery
 ¼ cup diced apple, seeded and peeled
 ¼ cup diced banana
 1 cup unsweetened pineapple juice
 1 cup chicken broth
 1½ teaspoons curry powder
 ¼ teaspoon mace
 ¼ teaspoon garlic powder
 ⅛ teaspoon ginger
 ⅛ teaspoon cayenne pepper
 salt and white pepper to taste
 2 teaspoons cornstarch
 2 tablespoons cold water

GARNISHES:
 2 tablespoons each: toasted shredded coconut, chopped chives, and diced red apple, unpeeled.

Cut tenderloin into ¼-inch-thick slices. In a large nonstick skillet, brown meat quickly over high heat, about 1 minute per side. Remove beef to a warm platter.

Reduce heat to medium. Add wine, shallots, carrots, and celery; sauté for 3 minutes. Add apple, banana, pineapple juice, chicken broth, and seasonings; simmer, uncovered, for 10 minutes to combine flavors. Return beef and juices to skillet.

Combine cornstarch and cold water; stir into skillet mixture. Cook and stir until sauce is thickened and bubbly. Serve over rice. Garnish with toasted coconut, chives, and diced red apple.

Makes 4 servings at 300 calories per serving.

Sautéing

Sautéing is a dry heat cooking process by which small, tender pieces of meat are quickly tossed or stirred in a nonstick skillet over medium heat. In many respects, it is simply a variation of panbroiling, but in sautéing, the meat cooks faster and at a slightly lower temperature than in panbroiling.

Although all thin cuts of meat can be sautéed, it should be limited to those specific cuts of veal and pork that are too lean to be panbroiled. And don't hesitate to use a food release agent (especially one with butter flavoring added) on your nonstick surfaces. It facilitates browning and gives added flavor of its own.

BASIC SAUTÉING TECHNIQUES

1. *Dry the meat* thoroughly on paper toweling. Excess moisture will inhibit proper browning and searing.

2. *Season the meat* with salt and pepper. Beef and lamb are usually seasoned after the initial searing is accomplished.

3. *Sear the meat* in a heavy, nonstick skillet over medium heat. Be careful not to overcrowd the pan; cook in several batches, if necessary.

4. *Cook the meat* at moderate temperature, uncovered, until tender. Turn or move the meat about to prevent scorching. Do not overcook. The meat is done when it can be pierced easily with the tip of a knife.

5. *Remove the meat* to a warm platter. To serve with a sauce, pour off any accumulated fat, then deglaze the skillet with a liquid (allow about 1 tablespoon per serving) and reduce quickly over high heat until thick. Spoon sauce over meat and serve immediately.

ARMENIAN LAMB

1 teaspoon olive oil
1 teaspoon vegetable oil
1 garlic clove, minced
1 large onion, sliced
1 pound leftover cooked lamb, cubed
2 fresh tomatoes, peeled and cut into eighths

2 packages (10-ounce) frozen French-style green beans
¼ cup chicken stock
½ teaspoon whole oregano
salt and coarse black pepper to taste

Defrost and drain beans; set aside. Heat olive and vegetable oils in a nonstick skillet. Add garlic and onion; stir over medium-high heat for 2 minutes. Add lamb cubes and sauté 2 minutes longer. Add remaining ingredients to skillet. Cover and simmer over low heat for 10 minutes.

Makes 4 servings at 260 calories per serving.

STIR-FRIED BEEF AND BROCCOLI

1 pound top round or flank steak
2 tablespoons soy sauce
2 tablespoons dry white wine
1 teaspoon sugar
1 slice ginger root, shredded
1 tablespoon vegetable oil

¾ cup beef broth
2 tablespoons flour
2 tablespoons curry powder
¼ teaspoon white pepper
2 cups fresh broccoli flowerets
1 medium onion, thinly sliced

Cut meat across the grain on the diagonal into ⅛-inch-thick slices; then cut into thin strips about 2 inches long. Marinate meat in a small glass bowl in a mixture of soy sauce, wine, sugar, and ginger root for 30 minutes; turn meat occasionally.

Heat the oil in large nonstick skillet or wok. Add the broccoli and onions; stir-fry over high heat for 2 minutes; remove vegetables from pan. Add beef strips and marinade to skillet; stir-fry for 2 to 3 minutes. Combine broth, flour, curry powder, and pepper in a small bowl. Stir this mixture into hot pan and continue to stir until bubbly. Return broccoli and onions and cook 1 minute longer to heat through. Serve immediately.

Makes 4 servings at 250 calories per serving.

STIR-FRIED BEEF CURRY WITH RICE

1 cup uncooked long-grain rice
1 pound top round or flank steak
3 tablespoons soy sauce
2 tablespoons dry sherry
2 tablespoons cornstarch
1 teaspoon brown sugar
1 slice ginger root, shredded
4 tablespoons diet catsup

1 teaspoon oyster sauce
4 teaspoons vegetable oil
1 medium onion, quartered
1 medium green pepper, cut into chunks
2 medium tomatoes, cut into wedges
4 teaspoons curry powder

Prepare rice according to package directions; keep warm. Meanwhile, slice meat into 2-inch lengths diagonally against the grain, ⅛ inch thick.

In a medium-size bowl, combine soy sauce, sherry, cornstarch, sugar, and shredded ginger root. Add meat and toss to coat evenly. Marinate 15 to 30 minutes.

In a small bowl, combine diet catsup and oyster sauce; set aside. Heat 2 teaspoons oil in a large nonstick skillet or wok over high heat. Add onion and pepper chunks; stir-fry until vegetables are tender-crisp. Remove and set aside. Wipe out pan.

Add remaining 2 teaspoons oil. Stir in curry powder and heat through. Add meat mixture; stir-fry over high heat 2 to 3 minutes. Add tomato wedges; stir until heated through. Add sautéed vegetables and catsup mixture; heat through. Serve immediately over rice.

Makes 4 servings at 280 calories per serving.

Chef's Cooking Tip:
Fresh ginger root should be stored in the refrigerator. It will stay fresh for two to three weeks. For longer storage, peel and store unused portions of ginger root in a jar filled with dry sherry wine and refrigerate; it will last indefinitely.

STIR-FRIED BEEF AND PEPPERS

1 pound top round or flank steak
1 tablespoon cornstarch
1 tablespoon dry red wine
¼ teaspoon salt
⅛ teaspoon pepper
1 tablespoon vegetable oil
1 medium onion, thinly sliced
1 medium green pepper, thinly sliced
1 medium red pepper, thinly sliced
2 slices fresh ginger root, shredded
¼ teaspoon sugar

Cut the meat across the grain on the diagonal into ⅛-inch-thick slices; then cut into thin slices 1½ inches long. Marinate meat in a small glass bowl in a mixture of cornstarch, red wine, salt, and pepper for 30 minutes; turn meat occasionally.

Heat oil in a large nonstick skillet or wok. Sear and brown the meat over high heat; remove meat and set aside on a warm platter. Add the onion, peppers, and ginger root; stir-fry until tender. Add sugar; return meat to pan; stir-fry to heat through and blend flavors. Correct seasoning by adding a dash of soy sauce or sesame oil to taste. Serve immediately.

Makes 4 servings at 260 calories per serving.

SAUTÉED CREOLE LIVER

1 large onion, sliced
1 green pepper sliced
1 celery rib, sliced
¼ cup dry white wine
1 can (14½-ounce) diced tomatoes in sauce
½ teaspoon oregano
½ teaspoon salt
¼ teaspoon pepper
¼ teaspoon cumin
dash Tabasco sauce
1 pound beef liver, sliced ⅜-inch thick
¼ cup flour
½ teaspoon garlic salt
1 tablespoon vegetable oil

Place sliced onion, pepper, and celery in a large nonstick skillet; add wine; cover and steam over high heat 5 minutes. Uncover; add tomatoes and seasonings and simmer 20 minutes longer. Remove vegetables to a side dish. Wipe out the skillet and add the oil. Sprinkle liver with flour and garlic salt. Brown lightly in oil over medium-high heat, about 2 minutes per side. Add cooked vegetables to skillet to heat through and serve.

Makes 4 servings at 260 calories per serving.

SAUTÉED LIVER AND ONIONS

1 large onion, thinly sliced
¼ cup dry sherry wine
2 tablespoons diet catsup
¼ cup flour
½ teaspoon salt
¼ teaspoon pepper
¼ paprika
⅛ teaspoon garlic powder
1 pound baby beef or calves' liver, sliced ⅜-inch thick
1 tablespoon butter or margarine

Place sliced onion and sherry wine in a medium-size skillet. Cover and steam onion slices over high heat for 5 minutes. Uncover; add diet catsup and continue to cook over medium-low heat for 30 to 45 minutes. Add a small amount of liquid if sauce evaporates too quickly. Meanwhile, heat butter in a large nonstick skillet over medium-high heat. Combine flour, salt, pepper, paprika, and garlic powder. Coat liver lightly; shake off excess. Sauté liver quickly without crowding (in two batches if necessary) for about 2 minutes on each side until just pink in the center. Cover liver with sautéed onions, garnish with paprika and serve.

Makes 4 servings at 270 calories per serving.

STIR-FRIED PORK AND PINEAPPLE

¾ pound lean boneless pork
1 small onion, thinly sliced
1 medium green pepper, thinly sliced
1 medium red pepper, thinly sliced
1 tablespoon vegetable oil
½ cup orange juice
¼ cup soy sauce
1 tablespoon dry sherry
2 teaspoons honey
⅛ teaspoon garlic powder
⅛ teaspoon pepper
2 cups fresh pineapple chunks
4 teaspoons cornstarch
2 tablespoons chicken broth

Cut the pork across the grain on the diagonal into ⅛-inch-thick slices. Clean and slice onion and peppers. Heat oil in a large nonstick skillet or wok. Add sliced pork, onion, and peppers; stir-fry about 3 minutes or until pork is browned. Remove pork mixture from pan; set aside on a warm platter.

Combine orange juice, soy sauce, sherry, honey, garlic powder, and pepper in a small bowl. Pour mixture into pan; add pineapple chunks. Cover and cook 2 minutes. Remove pineapple with a wire ladle. Return pork mixture to skillet. Dissolve cornstarch in broth; stir into pork mixture. Stir-fry until thickened. Add cooked pineapple; stir-fry only long enough to heat through.

Makes 4 servings at 365 calories per serving.

VEAL CACCIATORE

1 pound (8 scallops) milk-fed veal
¼ teaspoon salt
⅛ teaspoon pepper
1 cup sliced mushrooms
½ cup sliced onion
1 cup sliced green pepper
2 cups peeled, seeded, and diced whole tomatoes
¾ cup chicken broth
1 teaspoon whole oregano

Season veal scallops with salt and pepper. Heat a large nonstick skillet over medium heat; brown scallops about 1 minute on each side. Remove from skillet to a warm platter. Add the remaining ingredients to the skillet; reduce heat and simmer until vegetables are tender, about 15 minutes. Return scallops to skillet; heat through and serve.

Makes 4 servings at 220 calories per serving.

VEAL SCALLOPINI

1 pound (8 scallops) milk-fed veal
  salt and pepper to taste
1 teaspoon Worcestershire sauce
2 tablespoons dry sherry wine
2 tablespoons minced onion
1 can (8-ounce) diced tomatoes
  in sauce
1 tablespoon freshly chopped
  parsley
¼ teaspoon whole oregano
¼ teaspoon garlic powder

Season veal scallops with salt and pepper. Heat a large nonstick skillet over medium heat; brown scallops about 1 minute on each side; remove from skillet to a warm platter. Add the remaining ingredients; simmer 5 to 10 minutes to blend flavors and thicken sauce. Return scallops to skillet; heat through and serve.

Makes 4 servings at 220 calories per serving.

LOW-CALORIE MOIST HEAT COOKING METHODS

Simmering

Any cut of meat, no matter how tough it is to begin with, can be made tender and succulent if it is cooked properly. Tender cuts of meat with little connective tissue are usually cooked quickly in dry heat to maximize and retain their tenderness. Tough, relatively lean cuts of meat that contain large amounts of connective tissue, however, require long, slow, moist heat cooking to make them tender. The three basic moist heat methods of cooking these tougher cuts are simmering, braising, and stewing.

In simmering, the cooking is initiated in boiling liquid. Thus the confusion when we refer to particular dishes as being "boiled"—such as *boiled brisket of beef* or *New England boiled dinner*—but which are actually "simmered" at a temperature well below the boiling point. In fact, no meat should ever be boiled. If we cook a piece of meat for too long a time at a high temperature, moist or dry, the connective tissues binding the muscle fibers will completely dissolve and the meat will be stringy and dry.

The initial boiling of the liquid at the start of the cooking process sears the surface of the meat and seals in the valuable juices. It also expels unwanted elements in the meat that would cloud the stock. These elements form a scum on the surface of the liquid during the first ten minutes of cooking and should be skimmed off before the heat is reduced.

"Boiled" meats have a bland flavor and should be served with spicy condiments such as mustard and horseradish to make them more appetizing

BASIC SIMMERING TECHNIQUES

1. *Immerse the meat in boiling water*, stock, or a combination of flavoring liquids. Use enough liquid to completely cover the meat. The high heat will coagulate the surface proteins and help to seal in the juices. Many recipes call for the meat to be covered with cold liquid, which is then slowly brought to a boil. This technique is done when the flavor of the cooking liquid is of prime importance, such as in the famous French *pot au feu*.

2. *Return the cooking liquid to the boil*. Remove the scum and foam that rise to the surface with a soup ladle.

3. *Add seasonings and aromatic vegetables* to the pot. These items are added to give extra flavor to the meat and the broth. Peppercorns, thyme, bay leaf, and parsley stems are the most commonly used seasonings. Onions, carrots, and celery are the usual vegetables to use for flavoring. Try this cooking trick: Cut the onion in half horizontally. Stab each half with a cooking fork and hold it over a gas burner until the inner surface is well charred. You'll be surprised how this technique adds color and aroma to the broth. By the end of the cooking period, these aromatic vegetables will have leached all their nutrients into the cooking liquid and should subsequently be discarded or puréed to thicken the broth.

4. *Simmer the meat* below the boiling point for approximately 2 to 2½ hours, or until tender. The cooking time will be about 15 to 20 minutes per pound. When tender, a cooking fork inserted into the meat can be withdrawn with ease. The pot is usually covered during the simmering process to prevent the liquid from evaporating, but bear in mind that a cover entraps the heat and raises the water temperature. Watch the pot carefully to be sure the cooking liquid doesn't boil at any time during the simmering stage.

5. *Add the garnishing vegetables* that will be served with the meat 15 to 20 minutes before the meat is done. Use a wire strainer basket to lower the vegetables into the broth so they can be removed easily after they are cooked.

BOILED BEEF DINNER

2 pounds lean beef
water to cover
2 cloves
1 onion
1 celery rib
2 carrots
3 parsley stems
3 peppercorns

1 garlic clove, crushed
1 small bay leaf

GARNISHING VEGETABLES:
4 carrots, sliced
1 onion, rutabaga, and turnip, peeled and quartered
6 wedges (1 medium head) cabbage

Place meat in a large saucepan with enough water to cover. Bring slowly to a boil; skim. Cut onion in half horizontally and char over hot flame; stick with cloves and add to stock. Tie whole carrots, celery, and parsley stems together with kitchen twine, then add to stock along with peppercorns, garlic, and bay leaf. Cover and simmer from 2 to 3 hours or until meat is tender. Remove flavoring vegetables. Add sliced carrots and quartered onion, rutabaga, and turnip. Cover and cook 15 minutes. Add cabbage and cook 15 minutes longer, or until vegetables are tender. Remove meat and cut into ½-inch-thick slices. Serve with strained broth and vegetables.

Makes 6 servings at 250 calories per serving.

Braising

Braising is the slow simmering of portion-cut meats or roasts (pot roasts) in a covered pot or roasting pan with a small amount of flavored liquid. The cooking can be done on top of the stove over a low heat or in a slow to moderate oven.

This moist heat method of cooking is used chiefly in the preparation of economical, less tender cuts of meat that require a combination of moist heat and low temperature to tenderize the meat fibers and soften the connective tissue. Although you'll often find tender meats like pork, lamb, and veal being braised, in my opinion they're easier to prepare if they're cut thinly and sautéed quickly the low-calorie way.

Although braising is similar to other methods of moist heat cookery, the meat used in braising is almost always seared and browned well for flavor and appearance before any liquid is added. Traditionally, this browning is done in hot fat or oil and sometimes with flour. (White meats are never browned, but they can be seared to tighten their outside surfaces.) However, you can save hundreds of unwanted calories and still achieve the same taste, texture, and flavor of traditional braises by searing the meat in a hot skillet (as in panbroiling), under the broiler, or in a hot oven.

Another way to save calories is to cook the dish a day in advance; then reheat it, covered, over low heat or in a slow oven before serving. This gives you a chance to remove any excess fat that has congealed on the surface before reheating.

BASIC BRAISING TECHNIQUES

1. *Dry the meat* thoroughly with paper towels. Excess moisture will prevent the meat from browning properly.

2. *Sear and brown the meat* on both sides in a deep heavy skillet or Dutch oven over moderately high heat. This searing process carmelizes the surface proteins, sealing in the natural juices and increases the flavor of the meat.

3. *Remove the meat* from the pan and pour off any accumulated fat. The natural juices and flavor compounds that have carmelized on the bottom of the pan will give added taste and aroma to the cooking liquid.

4. *Add seasoning and a small amount of liquid.* The liquids used (anywhere from 2 tablespoons to 2 cups, depending on the recipe) can be water, wine, vinegar, broth, fruit juice, vegetable juice, marinades, or a combination of these ingredients. Heat the cooking liquid until it reaches a boil. The hot liquid will help seal the meat's surface. Return the meat to the pan, reduce the heat to a low simmer, and cover the utensil tightly. The small amount of liquid generates enough steam to cook the meat. Many cuts of meat that are braised or pot-roasted, however, do not require additional liquids and are cooked by the steam generated by their own internal juices and any added vegetables.

5. *Cook the meat until tender,* anywhere from one to three hours, either on top of the stove or in the oven at 300° F. or 350° F. When I braise a dish on top of the stove, I like to use an asbestos pad between the gas burner and the pan to get the heat down low enough for simmering. This isn't necessary with electric stoves, however.

Watch the pan carefully to be sure that the liquid never boils. Too high a heat will dry the meat out and make it tough and stringy. It's also a good idea to remember that pot roasts, braised dishes and casseroles can overcook just like any other food. Fortunately, with moist heat cooking, you are allowed a little more leeway than with the dry heat methods. Meats that are braised are always cooked well done.

6. *Remove the meat from the pan,* skim the fat off the surface of the liquid, then reduce the liquid over high heat to thicken. Pour this thickened sauce over the meat and serve.

BRAISED BEEF WITH MUSHROOMS

1½ pounds round steak
1 cup chopped onions
1 cup chopped celery
1 cup peeled, seeded, and diced tomatoes
½ cup chopped green pepper
½ cup beef broth
salt and pepper to taste
1 cup sliced fresh mushrooms

Brown meat in a large nonstick skillet or Dutch oven over high heat until both sides are seared and browned, about 5 minutes. Add the remaining ingredients, except mushrooms, and cook slowly on a surface unit or in a moderate to slow oven (325–350° F.), covered, until the meat is tender; add additional amounts of liquid during cooking if necessary. Cooking time will be about 1½ hours. Add sliced mushrooms the last 15 minutes of cooking.

Makes 4 servings at 220 calories per serving.

Chef's Cooking Tip:
To freeze fresh mushrooms for later use, rinse fresh whole mushrooms; drain. Trim ends; drop in hot boiling water for 2 to 3 minutes to blanch. Cool; spread mushrooms on a baking sheet pan and freeze. Store them in tightly sealed plastic bags.

BRAISED LAMB CHOPS

4 lean loin lamb chops
1 tablespoon minced shallots
¼ teaspoon salt
⅛ teaspoon pepper
1 can (4-ounce) mushrooms
1 tablespoon cornstarch
2 tablespoons water

Trim surface fat from chops; brown on both sides in a large nonstick skillet over high heat. Add shallots, salt, pepper, and mushrooms with liquid. Reduce heat; cover tightly and simmer over low heat for 60 minutes or until tender. Mix together cornstarch and water; stir into mixture until it boils and thickens. Serve sauce over chops; garnish with freshly chopped parsley.

Makes 4 servings at 375 calories per serving.

STEAK AU SUISSE

2 pounds beef round steak
1 tablespoon vegetable oil
1 teaspoon salt
½ teaspoon pepper

1 medium onion, diced
¼ cup dry red wine
1 cup brown stock
1 can (16-ounce) diced tomatoes in sauce

Select a lean, thin steak; have the butcher trim the meat of all surface fat and cut into six portions. If you can, have him tenderize the steaks in a meat cuber. This step is worth an extra charge. If not, tenderize them yourself with a meat pounder.

Heat oil in a large nonstick skillet over medium-high heat. Rub steaks with salt and pepper and brown quickly on both sides. Add remaining ingredients; cover and simmer 45 to 60 minutes or until meat is tender.

Makes 6 servings at 250 calories per serving.

Chef's Cooking Tip:
For a thicker sauce, mix 1 tablespoon cornstarch with 2 tablespoons water; stir into pan juices. Cook and stir until thickened and bubbly. Add 5 more calories per serving.

SWEET AND SOUR STUFFED CABBAGE

1 large head green cabbage

STUFFING:
1 pound lean ground round
½ cup minced onion
1 tablespoon diet catsup
1 teaspoon Worcestershire sauce
1 teaspoon chopped parsley
½ teaspoon salt
¼ teaspoon pepper

SAUCE:
¼ cup minced carrot
¼ cup minced onion
¼ cup minced celery
1 small clove garlic, minced
2 cups apricot nectar
¼ cup tomato juice
1 tablespoon cider vinegar
salt and pepper to taste

Core cabbage; simmer in 1 gallon of boiling water about 7 minutes. Drain and remove 8 outer leaves. In a small bowl, combine stuffing ingredients; divide evenly between leaves. Roll leaves up from rib end, folding sides of leaf toward center. Place rolls seam side down in a shallow baking dish. Add 1 cup tomato juice; cover and bake at 325° F. for 1½ hours. Uncover and bake an additional 15 minutes to brown.

Prepare sauce 1 hour before serving. In a small saucepan, steam minced carrot, onion, celery, and garlic with ¼ cup water for 5 minutes. Add remaining ingredients; simmer slowly over low heat to blend flavors and thicken. Serve 2 rolls and 1 ounce of sauce for each person.

Makes 4 servings at 280 calories per serving.

Chef's Cooking Tip:
Prevent scratches on your expensive nonstick skillets and baking pans by placing paper towels between them before storing.

ZESTY POT ROAST WITH ONION SOUP MIX

3 pounds blade-cut chuck roast
1 envelope onion soup mix
2 cups water
4 carrots, sliced
4 celery ribs, sliced
1 large rutabaga, cubed

Place roast in a small roasting pan or Dutch oven. Add onion soup mix; cover. Place pan in a preheated 350° F. oven for 10 minutes to allow meat and soup mix to brown slightly. Uncover; add 2 cups of water to deglaze bottom of pan (this technique saves you the 200 calories in the oil it usually takes to sear and brown a pot roast). Recover; bake for 2 to 2½ hours. Add the cut-up vegetables; continue to bake until the vegetables are tender, about 30 to 40 minutes. Remove the meat and vegetables to a warm platter; pour the pan juices into a small saucepan. Allow the juices to rest a few minutes to allow the fat to come to the surface. Skim off the fat with a small ladle or a bulb baster. Reheat juices (about 1 cup) and reduce over high heat to thicken. Pour sauce over roast and serve.

Makes 6 to 8 servings at 275 calories per 4-ounce serving.

Stewing

Stewing is a moist heat method of cooking uniformly cut pieces of red or white meat in a small amount of liquid. There are two types of stews—"brown stews," prepared by searing and browning the meat before combining it with a liquid, and "white stews," made with the unbrowned white meat of veal or chicken.

Most stews are easy to prepare, but they usually require long, slow simmering on top of a stove or in an oven to cook the less tender cuts of meat and to blend the extracted meat juices with any added seasonings and vegetables into a rich, nutritious sauce.

The cooking techniques used for stewing are almost identical to those used for braising; however, there are some important differences between the two methods: In braising, you are cooking a large cut of meat that has been seared and browned in just enough liquid to produce steam. A braised dish is actually half baked and half steamed, but it is the steam that breaks down the connective tissues and softens the meat fibers to make the meat tender. Stewing is braising meat that has been cut into several pieces and just barely covered with liquid. The meat cuts may or may not be browned, depending on the kind of meat and the requirements of the recipe. A stewed dish takes less time to cook because of the smaller pieces of meat.

You can easily save yourself—and your waistline—about 300 calories by altering your method of preparation and browning the meat in a moderately hot, nonstick Dutch oven or skillet without using oil or fats. That's the way to start reducing calories.

But save even more by draining away any fat rendered out during the browning stage and diligently skim off the fat that comes to the surface of the liquid during cooking with a spoon or a plastic bulb baster. If you succeed in skimming off at least three tablespoons of fat during the cooking process, you can credit yourself with an additional savings of 300 more calories!

A stew can be served thin like soup or it can be thickened after the initial cooking period. Thickening the liquid with a pure starch like arrowroot or cornstarch mixed with water will give you half the calories there would have been if you had thickened the liquid with a similar mixture made with flour. A lower-calorie idea, however, is to remove the lid from the pan about 30 minutes before the stew is finished cooking and let the liquid thicken and reduce by evaporation. Just remember that stews can be ruined by overcooking, just like any other cooked food. Don't try to reduce the sauce to the point that you ruin the quality and flavor of the meat.

BASIC STEWING TECHNIQUES

1. *Cut the meat into uniform pieces*, generally into 1- to 2-inch cubes. Dry the surface of the meat with paper toweling to prevent any excess moisture from inhibiting the browning process.

2. *Brown the meat* slowly in a nonstick Dutch oven or saucepan over moderate heat. Don't use any fat! Just be sure not to crowd the pan or the meat will begin to steam and won't brown. "White stews" using pork, veal, and chicken meat are not browned in this manner. These white meats are usually seared as the hot cooking liquid is poured over them.

3. *Add enough hot liquid to cover the meat.* Heating the liquid beforehand isn't absolutely essential, but it does help to seal in the flavor of white meat, as I've mentioned, and it cuts down on the total cooking time considerably. The cooking liquid may be water, stock, soup, wine, fruit, or vegetable juice, or any combination of these liquids.

4. *Season the meat* with herbs and spices. Keep in mind that what gives a "stew" its authentic national distinctive taste and character is the flavoring of the seasoning rather than its method of preparation.

5. *Cover the pan* tightly to prevent the steam from escaping. If the cooking liquid evaporates and falls below the level of the meat, it will not cook uniformly unless it's turned or stirred as in braising. A covered pan also reduces the cooking time.

6. *Cook the meat* at a low simmer on top of the stove or in a moderate oven until the meat is tender. When the meat can be pierced easily with a knife or cooking fork, it is done. A stew must never boil or be overcooked. As with other simmering dishes cooked on top of the stove, I find an asbestos pan over my gas burner to be absolutely essential for proper heat control. Stewed meat dishes must be cooked with the greatest of care, or the meat will become dry and stringy, or at worst, completely disintegrate.

7. *Add the garnishing vegetables* the last 30 or 40 minutes of cooking time, except peas, which can be put in the last 15 minutes. An alternative method is to parboil the vegetables separately and add them to the stew just before serving. This method doesn't flavor the stew as well as when the vegetables are cooked with the meat, but they will have a nicer appearance and have a firmer texture.

BEEF GOULASH

1 pound lean ground round
½ cup chopped onion
½ cup chopped green pepper
1 can (16-ounce) whole tomatoes, crushed
1 cup tomato purée
⅓ cup water
¾ cup cooked elbow macaroni
½ cup grated Parmesan cheese, divided
salt and pepper to taste

Cook the elbow macaroni according to package directions; rinse under cold water; set aside. Combine meat, onion, and green pepper in a large nonstick skillet. Brown over medium-high heat for 10 minutes, or until meat is browned and vegetables are tender. Drain off fat; add crushed tomatoes, tomato purée, water, cooked macaroni, and ¼ cup Parmesan cheese. Simmer gently for 20 minutes to blend flavors. Pour contents of skillet into a shallow baking dish (if your skillet has a metal handle, it can go directly into the oven). Sprinkle remaining Parmesan cheese over the top; bake, uncovered, in a 350° F. oven about 20 minutes until the sauce bubbles and the cheese has browned.

Makes 3 servings at 250 calories per serving.

Chef's Cooking Tip:
Rinsing cooked pasta under running water is a low-calorie way of removing excess surface starch, and since the pasta won't stick together as readily, there is less temptation to add calorie-laden butter or oil.

BEEF STEW

1 pound stew beef, cut into one-inch chunks
2 tablespoons chopped onions
½ clove garlic, minced
½ cup dry red wine
2 teaspoons Worcestershire sauce
½ teaspoon gravy base (Kitchen Bouquet, Maggie, etc.)
1 can (16-ounce) whole tomatoes
1 cup beef broth
1 teaspoon salt
½ teaspoon marjoram
½ teaspoon pepper
¼ teaspoon thyme
1 medium-size onion, sliced
2 medium-size potatoes, cubed
2 carrots, sliced
2 celery ribs, sliced

Heat a Dutch oven or heavy saucepan over medium-high heat. Add meat and brown on all sides. Stir in chopped onions, garlic, wine, Worcestershire sauce, gravy base; sauté for 2 minutes to deglaze pan. Add tomatoes, broth, and seasonings. Cover and simmer 1½ hours. Add vegetables and simmer 30 to 40 minutes more, or until vegetables are tender.

Makes 4 servings at 310 calories per serving.

LAMB STEW

1½ pounds lamb, cut into 1-inch cubes
1 tablespoon tomato paste
1 bay leaf
½ teaspoon marjoram
½ teaspoon salt
¼ teaspoon pepper
¼ teaspoon garlic powder
¼ teaspoon celery seed
3 cups water
6 small white onions, peeled
2 potatoes, cubed
2 turnips, cubed
2 large carrots, cubed

Brown lamb cubes and tomato paste in a large nonstick skillet or Dutch oven over medium-high heat. Add bay leaf, marjoram, salt, pepper, garlic powder, celery seed, and water. Simmer, covered, for 1 hour. Remove bay leaf. Cool and refrigerate several hours or overnight. Before reheating, skim visible fat from the surface. Add vegetables; simmer, covered, about 45 minutes or until vegetables are tender. Adjust seasoning to taste and serve.

Makes 4 servings at 330 calories per serving.

CHILE CON CARNE

1 pound lean ground round
¾ cup chopped onion
¾ cup chopped green pepper
1 can (16-ounce) whole tomatoes, crushed
1 can (15-ounce) kidney beans, undrained
1 can (8-ounce) tomato purée
1 tablespoon chile powder
½ tablespoon cumin
salt and pepper to taste

Brown the meat, onion, and peppers in a large nonstick skillet over medium-high heat; stir frequently to break up the meat chunks. Drain off fat; add remaining ingredients. Bring mixture to a boil; reduce heat; cover and simmer 1½ to 2 hours, stirring occasionally.

Makes 4 to 6 servings at 150 calories per ¾-cup serving.

Chef's Cooking Tip:
Most prepackaged ground beef contains close to 30% fat! Eliminate over 1,000 calories per pound of meat by purchasing a lean bottom round roast and having it custom-ground to order. Not only do you save the calories, but you also know the kind and grade of beef you're eating.

POULTRY

Poultry is one of the most popular and universally recognized foods in the world, and its versatility in low-calorie cooking is almost endless. A chicken dish, for instance, can range from the most inexpensive, everyday casserole, to an elegant, exotic, international masterpiece.

Time and modern methods change everything, even poultry. Today's birds are tender, easily digested, full of vitamins and minerals, high in protein, and, of course, marvelously low in calories. In fact chicken is lower in calories than any other red or white meat we put on our tables. What's more, poultry is readily available to most of us and usually economical.

What these modern, domesticated birds have gained in leanness, however, they have lost in flavor. And the success of any poultry dish will depend on careful attention to the proper methods of preparation that retain the tenderness of the meat while at the same time preserving what little flavor there is.

POULTRY CLASSIFICATIONS

Of all domesticated poultry marketed today, chicken, turkey, duck, and Rock Cornish game hens are the only ones that are readily available to the American consumer. Other than Cornish hens, which are the smallest member of the chicken family, each variety is classified by weight, age, and fat content. Only *broiler-fryer* chicken, turkey, and duck should be purchased by the diet-conscious cook. These hybrid birds are less fat, and subsequently lower in calories than more mature poultry.

BUYING POULTRY

The kind of bird you purchase and the manner in which it's packaged for sale has a lot to do with the time it takes to prepare it for cooking. "Ready-to-cook" poultry can be purchased fresh or frozen, whole or in parts. Young broiler-fryer chickens are usually purchased fresh. Fryer-roaster turkeys and broiler ducklings, on the other hand, are almost always purchased frozen.

To my mind, buying a whole, *fresh* bird is your best choice by far. For one thing, cut-up poultry parts lose some of their flavorful juices because of the many exposed surfaces. And if the poultry parts are frozen, further flavor is lost in the thawing process. With a whole bird, there is also the added bonus of having the giblets, skin, and bones from which to make soup or stock.

Although I've just recommended buying poultry whole, there are times when it becomes advantageous to buy cut-up poultry. The white meat of chicken and turkey is dryer, cooks faster, and has less calories than the dark meat, and for these reasons, many people prefer to purchase just the white meat poultry parts. Incidentally, turkey breasts may be purchased raw or fully cooked. This really comes in handy when large quantities of cooked, diced, or sliced poultry is needed.

STORING AND HANDLING POULTRY

One of the greatest concerns for chefs in their kitchens is the storing and handling of food after it has been purchased. It should be no less a concern for the home cook. All poultry is highly perishable. Like any kind of meat, it should be refrigerated at all times.

Fresh poultry purchased whole should be left uncut until close to cooking time; the unbroken skin will protect the flesh from exposure to bacteria and possible spoilage. Before refrigerating, take the store wrapping off and remove the giblets and neck from the body cavity. Store them separately from the bird. The giblets are very perishable and should be cooked immediately or frozen for later use.

Rinse the bird inside and out, pat dry with paper toweling, then rewrap loosely with plastic wrap. Place it in the coldest part of your refrigerator and use it within two days. If you have to hold it longer than that time, poach or steam the bird and use the meat in a cold salad or in a cooked poultry recipe

Cut-up fresh poultry is even more susceptible to spoilage than the whole bird because of the many cut surfaces and should be used as soon as possible.

Frozen poultry should be kept in its original wrapper until ready for use. It must also be thawed before cooking. The best way to do this is to let the bird defrost slowly in its original wrapper over a 2- to 3-day period in the refrigerator. For faster defrosting, it can be immersed in cold water—never hot water—with its original wrapper intact. Thawing frozen poultry at room temperature is very risky. I wouldn't recommend it. Never, by the way, refreeze poultry that has been thawed.

Leftover turkey or chicken meat should be removed from the bones after a meal, cooled, then refrigerated as soon as possible. The carcass and bones can then be cracked and used to make a good soup, sauce, or stock.

PREPARING POULTRY FOR COOKING

CLEANING AND TRUSSING

Regardless of how clean your poultry looks when you get it home from the market, it should always be rinsed or soaked in cold water before it is cooked or stored. Get into the habit of flushing the bird inside and out with cold running water. Better to be safe than sorry.

Boiled, poached, or roasted poultry is usually trussed or tied before cooking. Besides enclosing the body cavity to keep the internal juices in for self-basting, securing the legs and wings against the body gives the bird a better overall appearance when served, especially in roasting.

The important reason to truss poultry is to try to equalize the penetration of the heat on the various parts. Because dark leg and thigh meat takes longer to cook than the drier, more delicate white meat of the breasts, trussing the bird protects the breasts while at the same time exposing the dark meat directly to the source of heat.

To truss a bird, measure a piece of butcher's twine two to three feet long. Place the bird breast-side up with the legs pointing away from you. Pull each drumstick forward and low as far as it will go so that the knee of each leg almost touches the wing. Center the string under the extreme tail under the vent and tie the tail in a knot so as to have equal lengths of string on each side.

Cross one drumstick over the other and loop the string in a simple knot over the drumsticks; pull tightly. The drumsticks are now tied to the tail and the cavity opening is sealed shut.

Grasp a length of string in each hand and pull the ends of the drumsticks under the tip of the breastbone. Run each piece of string along each side of the body between the breasts and the inside of the knees, then turn the bird over.

With the bird breast-side down and the legs pointing away from you, bring the strings over the wings. Loop either string around the neck of the bird, then tie the two strings together securely. If there is a neck flap, you can cut it off or tuck it under the string.

CUTTING AND BONING POULTRY

Cut-up poultry and boned poultry are not quite the same thing. Cut-up poultry are whole birds that have been cut into several pieces. Boned poultry are whole birds or poultry parts whose meat is then removed from the bone with a sharp knife.

Most consumers today ignore the economic advantages of buying and cutting up a whole bird and seem content to buy the more expensive cut-up poultry parts. As I've indicated earlier, there are sometimes advantages to buying cut-up poultry. But as a serious diet cook, you'll find it well worth your time to learn how to cut up poultry yourself. The method for cutting and boning varies with each kind of bird—be it Cornish hen, duck, turkey, or chicken. But since chicken is so much more widely used, I shall use it as a sample for the others.

A chicken can be cut into two, four, six, or eight serving pieces, depending on the recipe and the method of cooking used. At about 180 calories for a quarter portion of a 2-pound cooked broiler-fryer, I find it very convenient to cut the chicken into four equal portions and to use the wings and carcass to make soup or stock.

To cut up a chicken, lay the bird on one side, and while grasping the drumstick, cut the skin in a semicircle between the thigh and the body. Turn the bird over and repeat for the second leg. Place the chicken breast-side up with the legs pointing toward you and continue the separation of the legs by cutting from the top until they are only held onto the body by the hip joint. Now grasp each leg at the knee and lift out and up to crack the hip joints from their sockets. Take hold of a drumstick again and flip the chicken over on its breast. Holding the leg in the air, slice through the skin as close to the body as possible to separate the leg from the body. Repeat for the other leg.

Because the meat will shrink from the bone during cooking, it's a good idea to whack off the hip joint knob on the end of each leg. A heavy chef's knife or a cleaver is best for this purpose. Try not to take any meat off with the knob when you do this, however.

One of the greatest advantages of poultry meat for the weight-conscious cook is that the fat is sandwiched between the outer surface of the skin and the meat and can be removed by cutting it out or dissolving it with steam or hot liquid before the meat is combined with other ingredients. Once the legs are separated from the body, trim as much fat off as possible. Fat contains about 9 calories per gram or 270 calories per ounce. Removing the fat from the chicken now is a lot easier than trying to remove it from your waistline later.

To obtain the white meat portions of the bird, pick the chicken up by one wing. Using the wing as a handle, lay the bird on its side with the breastbone away from you. Now position your knife horizontally to the cutting board and place it between the neck and the shoulder. The knife should be pointing directly away from you. With a firm grip on the wing, close to the shoulder, push gently but firmly toward the tail to about a depth of one inch to break one side of the wishbone, which extends between the shoulder and the breastbone. Without removing the knife, tilt the blade back and break one side of the shoulder blade bone, which extends from the shoulder toward the back. These are relatively small bones, and you will be able to hear them snap when they are cut through. When this is accomplished, stop cutting so as not to slice into the breast meat.

With these top two shoulder bones cut, lay the knife blade underneath the neck bone, between the neck and the shoulder closest to the cutting board, and repeat the same procedure for the second breast.

To separate the breasts from the body, retain your grip on the wing and cut the skin on each side of the backbone from the neck to the tail. Now carefully cut the skin covering the breastbone from the neck to the tip of the breastbone. Pin the neck down to the cutting board with the edge of the knife. Grasp the top shoulder with your thumb and pull it back toward the tail, cutting through any rib bones or skin necessary to free the breast from the body. Place the breast, skin-side up, on the cutting board and cut out as much fat as possible.

At this point, you could cut through the shoulder articulation to separate the wings; they can be used as additional servings or put in the stockpot with the carcass to flavor the broth. This cut-up portion of the chicken with the whole wing removed is referred to as a "bone-in half breast." With the rib bones left in, the breast portion will more closely resemble the leg portion in size, and will retain more of its natural juiciness during cooking. With a light 2-pound broiler-fryer, however, the breast meat portions are very small. To equalize the portions to 180 calories each, cut the wing through the "fan" at the elbow joint rather than at the shoulder, leaving the first bone of the wing attached to the breast.

Chicken breasts are the leanest parts of the bird, and for this reason a great many low-calorie recipes utilize them. You can easily go to the market and buy prepackaged "chicken breasts," but as long as you have come this far in cutting up the whole bird, it's only a step further to removing the bones from the "bone-in" breasts.

Lay the breast skin-side up on the cutting board. Grasp the breast portion as before, with the shoulder held by the thumb and first finger. Now roll the breast over the top of your hand to expose the rib cage. The large bone that runs from the shoulder to the rib cage is called the collarbone. At the end of the collarbone, where it meets the rib cage, the cartilage is very white and resembles a knuckle in appearance. While holding the breast firmly at the shoulder, cut through the white cartilage to separate the rib bones from the collarbone. With the cutting edge of the knife, pin the loosened rib cage bones to the cutting board and pull up on the shoulder. Look to see that all of the bones that are not still attached to the shoulder are pulling away. If they're not, simply stop pulling up on the shoulder and reposition the cutting edge of the knife to include them. Turn each breast skin-side down and cut the shoulder blade bone, the collarbone, and the wishbone free from the breast meat, starting in the middle of the breast and working toward the shoulder. Once these three bones are cut free, they can be removed from the shoulder in one piece without detaching the wing joint.

Before cutting up the whole chicken, be sure to read any new recipe carefully for the suggested method of preparation of the cut-up chicken parts. Boned and skinned chicken breasts are called *supremes*. Boned and skinned breasts that still have the first wing joint attached to the shoulder are called *chicken cutlets*. If the recipe calls for supremes or cutlets, then the boning process described above can be done as the breast is removed from the body rather than after its removal.

LOW-CALORIE DRY HEAT COOKING METHODS

Roasting

In today's cooking language, roasting and baking are used interchangeably to describe the preparation of poultry in the dry heat of a closed oven. If the bird is cooked whole, it is referred to as a roast: roast chicken, roast turkey, etc. If it is cut into parts, however, the poultry is said to be baked.

The use of the oven for roasting is an expedient one at best. A true roast is cooked on a spit over an open fire. The skin is seared by the high heat which seals in the natural juices and flavor. If the spit is revolving, the internal juices of the poultry self-baste from the inside, while at the same time allowing the excess moisture to evaporate in the open air.

This type of open-flame roasting is the oldest cooking method known. The characteristic, succulent juiciness associated with poultry roasted on a spit is only partially duplicated in the closed oven. It is important for the oven to be well vented and be hot enough to sear and brown the skin while at the same time absorb the cooking steam that would give the poultry a stewed taste.

The roasting pan should be shallow. This permits the hot air to circulate around the entire bird and roast it evenly. The shallow pan also prevents steam from building up around the sides of the poultry. It is important too, that the roasting pan not be too large for the bird because if the drippings are allowed to spread out over a large surface, they will carmelize and burn. A small amount of water or stock can be added to prevent this, but should take place only after the poultry skin is well sealed by the intense heat. To prevent the bird from being steamed instead of roasted, excess fat and liquid should be removed periodically during the cooking cycle.

The roasted poultry should be placed on a bed of diced aromatic vegetables or on a "V" type rack. This allows the roast to cook *above* the drippings rather than to fry *in* them. The vegetables add flavor to the poultry, while the rack allows the bird to be roasted breast-side down for self-basting.

Roasted poultry should be trussed. It gives the bird a better appearance and prevents the natural juices from escaping from the cavity openings. A properly trussed bird also helps protect the drier white meat of the breasts from being cooked too fast.

BASIC ROASTING TECHNIQUES

1. *Defrost the bird*, without removing it from its original wrapper, in the refrigerator one to two days—depending upon the size of the bird—or under cold water from one to three hours. Refrigerate as soon as it is thawed, or cook immediately.

2. *Rinse the bird* inside and out with cold water before cooking. Drain and pat dry with paper toweling.

3. *Stuff the bird* with the traditional stuffing that has been loosely packed in the neck and vent cavities, or simply salt and pepper the inside cavity and roast the fowl without stuffing. The roasting time will be somewhat reduced, depending upon the size of the bird.

4. *Close the bird* by sealing the cavity opening with a small piece of foil tucked inside the opening or with the traditional skewers and butcher's twine lacing. Also skewer the neck skin to the back.

5. *Truss the bird* with butcher's twine (see trussing) or tuck the drumsticks under the skin band at the tail.

6. *Roast the bird* in a preheated 350° F. oven on a rack set in a low baking pan. Start the fowl breast-side down for even browning and to baste the drier white breast meat with the internal juices. Remember that poultry, like the white meat of veal and pork, is always cooked well done. When the bird is done, a meat thermometer inserted in the center of the inside thigh muscle should register 185° F. If you're using one of the expensive, thin-shafted thermometers like those used by meat and health inspectors, you should get a reading of 170° F. when it is inserted in the thickest part of the

breast. If the bird is stuffed, a thermometer put into the center of the stuffing should register 165° F.

If the skin of the bird becomes overly brown, cover the bird with a loose "tent" of aluminum foil to slow down the browning.

7. *"Rest" the bird* 15 to 20 minutes after roasting in a warm place to allow the juices to set. This also makes carving the bird a lot easier.

ROAST CHICKEN À L'ORANGE

1 (3-pound) broiler-fryer
   salt, pepper, ginger, paprika
1 large orange, quartered
¼ cup dry white wine
1 cup orange juice
1 tablespoon brown sugar

1 teaspoon Worcestershire sauce
½ teaspoon dry mustard
1 tablespoon arrowroot or
   cornstarch
½ cup cold chicken broth

Clean chicken inside and out under cold running water; pat dry with paper toweling. Place orange quarters in cavity. Truss bird with butcher's twine. Season skin with salt, pepper, ginger, and paprika. Place bird on a rack in a shallow pan; roast at 400° F. about 1½ hours or until internal juices run clear. Turn bird frequently during roasting. Do not baste. Remove chicken to a warm platter. Pour off excess fat from roasting pan but do not disturb the "crusties" carmelized on the bottom. Place the pan on top of the stove; deglaze with wine. Add orange juice, brown sugar, Worcestershire sauce, and dry mustard; bring to a boil. Pour sauce into a 2-cup saucepan. Skim any fat from the surface of the sauce with a ladle or bulb baster. Place the saucepan on stove; bring to a boil over medium heat. Combine arrowroot and chicken stock. Slowly pour mixture into the orange sauce; stir until thickened and bubbly. Quarter chicken; baste with orange sauce and serve.

Makes 4 servings at 225 calories per serving.

ROASTED CHICKEN

1 (2½-to-3-pound) broiler-fryer
salt and pepper to taste
paprika

1 cup each: diced onion, carrot, celery

Rinse chicken inside and out; dry with paper toweling. Season inside cavity with salt and pepper. Truss chicken with butcher's twine; season outside skin with salt, pepper and paprika. Place diced aromatic vegetables in a shallow baking pan just large enough to accomodate the trussed bird. Preheat oven to 400° F. for 15 minutes.

Place chicken on its right side and roast for 30 minutes. Turn it on its left side and roast an additional 30 minutes. Place the bird breast side up; finish cooking for another 15 to 30 minutes, or until the chicken is done. If the skin is browning too much, cover the bird with a loose piece of foil. Do not rely entirely on your oven temperature gauge. Most of them are inaccurate. The chicken is done when the internal juices that pour from the vent run clear and are free from any rosiness. The knee joint should be soft to the touch and the drumstick will move easily.

Makes 4 servings at 210 calories per serving.

Chef's Cooking Tip:
The natural tenderness of the broiler-fryer, the high roasting temperature, and the self-basting of the breast meat from the inside make additional basting with fats or liquid unnecessary.

ROAST DUCK

1 (5-pound) frozen duckling, thawed
salt and pepper
1 apple, cored and quartered

1 onion, chopped
2 carrots, chopped
2 celery ribs, chopped

Rinse defrosted duckling inside and out; dry with paper toweling. Remove package of gizzards, neck bone, and extra pockets of fat attached just inside the cavity opening. Season duckling with salt and pepper inside and out. Stuff cavity with cored apple, 1 tablespoon diced onion, and ¼ cup each of the diced carrot and celery. Truss the bird with butcher's twine. Place the remaining aromatic vegetables in the bottom of a shallow baking pan that is just large enough for the duckling.

Preheat the oven to 400° F. for 15 minutes. Roast bird on its right side for 30 minutes. Turn the bird and roast it on its left side an additional 30 minutes. Place breast side up; roast about 30 minutes longer, or until duckling is cooked. Do not cover and do not baste. Remove excess fat and drippings from the bottom of the roasting pan during each turning to prevent steaming. If the skin is browning too much during cooking, cover loosely with a tent of foil. Transfer the duckling to a heated platter; allow the bird to "rest" for 15 to 20 minutes before carving.

Makes 4 servings at 220 calories per serving.

ROAST UNSTUFFED TURKEY

1 (6-to-8-pound) young oven-ready turkey

salt and pepper

Rinse the defrosted turkey inside and out; dry with paper toweling. Salt and pepper inside cavity; truss with butcher's twine. Preheat oven to 350° F. Place turkey breast side down in an open roasting pan using a "V" type rack to support the bird. Roast the turkey 3 to 3½ hours, basting occasionally with water and then the pan juices to prevent the drippings from burning in the bottom of the pan. Place turkey breast-side up after the first 1½ hours of roasting. Insert a meat thermometer into the thickest part of the thigh next to the ribs without touching a bone. The turkey is done when the thermometer registers 180 to 185 degrees. The internal juices that pour from the vent when the bird is tilted should run clear and be free of rosiness. The knee joint will feel soft and the drumstick will move easily. (If you're using a thin-shafted thermometer, the breast meat will register 170° F.). Be sure to plan the roasting time so the cooked bird is allowed to "rest" in a warm place 15 to 20 minutes after it is removed from the oven. The meat retains more juices this way and it makes for easier carving.

Makes 8 servings at 210 calories per 4-ounce serving.

Chef's Cooking Tip:
Inserting aromatic herbs or vegetables into the unstuffed cavity before trussing adds additional flavor and moisture.

ROCK CORNISH HENS

2 (1½-pound) ready-to-cook
   Cornish hens
salt and pepper to taste

1 cup each: diced onion, carrot,
   and celery

Thaw frozen hens; remove the bag of giblets from the cavity. Rinse inside and out; dry with paper toweling. Season inside cavity with salt and pepper.

Truss hens by tying the drumsticks to the tail and bending the wings "akimbo" style so the wing tips are touching the backbone. Place the diced aromatic vegetables in a shallow baking pan just large enough to accommodate the two hens. Preheat the oven to 400° F. Place hens on their right side; roast for 20 minutes. Turn on their left side; roast an additional 20 minutes. Place breast side up to finish roasting, about 10 minutes longer, or until the hens are tender. Do not rely entirely on your oven temperature gauge. The hens are done when the internal juices that pour from the vent after roasting run clear and are free from any rosiness. Do not overcook.

Makes 4 servings at 160 calories per serving.

Chef's Cooking Tip:
A good rule of thumb when roasting poultry is that the smaller the bird is, the higher the roasting temperature. A Cornish hen can be cooked in half the above time if roasted at 475° F., but remember to turn the birds frequently to prevent burning.

Baking

The cooking techniques for modern-day roasting of poultry in a closed oven are rather straightforward and exact. Trussing the bird; a hot, dry oven; and no liquid added are all techniques that make this dry heat method distinguishable from other methods of preparation.

Baking is also a dry heat process, but the poultry is cut up rather than trussed before cooking. If the cut-up bird goes directly into the oven without further preparation, it will look and taste like it was roasted.

There are two distinct advantages to baking poultry parts rather than roasting the bird whole: The first is that you are free to purchase just the parts you prefer—breasts, thighs, turkey legs, etc. For the dieter, this usually means buying the lower-caloried white meat. The second advantage to cut-up poultry is that the cooked portions can be served immediately from the oven. The roasted bird, on the other hand, must rest for at least 15 minutes and then be carved before it is ready to eat.

Because a *mirepoix* (a bed of diced aromatic vegetables) or a cooking rack are not used in baking, the cut-up poultry cooks in its own drippings. For this reason, poultry baked in this manner is sometimes referred to as "oven-fried."

Although technically a dry heat method of cooking, you'll find that many baked poultry recipes incorporate moist heat methods of preparation. Some of these recipes, for instance, call for a dish to be "baked" with a sauce; others have the sauce being made while the poultry cooks. In some the poultry is browned or even cooked completely before adding other ingredients; in some it is not. Then to really confuse you, there are many recipes where the poultry is "moist-baked" in a covered casserole instead of being cooked in an open pan.

Obviously there are many ways to bake poultry. But some baking methods are more expedient than others. When you're in a hurry, baking the cut-up poultry, uncovered, in a 400° F. oven for 25 to 35 minutes works best. But when the meal might conceivably have to wait for an hour or so after being prepared (a buffet or picnic luncheon, for instance) then moist baking in a covered casserole is much preferred.

BASIC BAKING TECHNIQUES

1. *Quarter the bird* and remove all visible fat. Rinse and pat dry with paper toweling. Place cut-up poultry parts on a nonstick shallow baking pan. Season to taste.

2. *Cook the bird* uncovered in a preheated 400° F. oven for 15 minutes. Turn the pieces over and bake 15 minutes longer.

3. *Reduce the oven temperature to 350° F.* Turn skin side up and bake 10 to 20 minutes longer, or until tender. Brush with heated wine, broth, fruit, or vegetable juice, or a prepared sauce during the cooking process, if desired. The poultry is done when the juices that emerge from the knee joint are clear and free from rosiness.

4. *Crisp the skin under the broiler* for a richer color and to glaze.

BARBECUED CHICKEN

1 (2½-pound) broiler-fryer,
   quartered
salt and pepper
1 can (8 ounce) tomato sauce

2 tablespoons honey
2 tablespoons vinegar
1 tablespoon prepared mustard
1 teaspoon liquid smoke

Cut chicken into serving pieces, removing all visible fat. Season with salt and pepper to taste. Combine the remaining ingredients in a small saucepan; bring slowly to a simmer. (There is more than enough sauce; save some for next time.) Place the chicken pieces in a shallow nonstick baking dish or skillet, skin side up; baste lightly with the barbecue sauce. Bake, uncovered, in a preheated 400° F. oven for 1 hour. Baste with the pan juices and sauce every 15 minutes. Be sure that the sauce doesn't scorch.

Makes 4 servings at 225 calories per serving.

Chef's Cooking Tip:
When basting, remove the pan from the oven and shut the door quickly. Keeping the oven door open will drop the oven temperature down 50 degrees and extend the cooking time.

CHICKEN CACCIATORE

1 (2½ pound) broiler-fryer,
   quartered
onion salt, pepper, paprika
1 clove garlic, minced
1 onion, chopped
1 green pepper, chopped
1 can (16-ounce) diced tomatoes
   in sauce

½ cup dry white wine
1 tablespoon freshly chopped
   parsley
½ teaspoon salt
½ teaspoon whole oregano
¼ teaspoon whole thyme or
   rosemary
¼ teaspoon pepper

Preheat oven to 425° F. Season chicken with onion salt, pepper and paprika; place skin side up on a nonstick baking pan. Bake, uncovered, for 15 minutes to crisp skin and dissolve fat. Transfer chicken to a 3-quart Dutch oven. Add remaining ingredients, except mushrooms. Cover and bake at 350° F. for 45 minutes. Uncover. Add sliced mushrooms and cook 15 minutes longer.

Makes 4 servings at 200 calories per serving.

CHICKEN KABOBS TERIYAKI

1½ pounds chicken breasts, skinned and boned
½ cup water
⅓ cup soy sauce
2 tablespoons fresh lemon or lime juice
1 tablespoon vegetable oil
½ teaspoon dry mustard
½ teaspoon ground ginger
⅛ teaspoon ground pepper
4 fresh pineapple chunks (1-inch)
4 green pepper squares
4 onion squares
4 medium-size mushrooms
4 cherry tomatoes

Cut chicken into 1-inch cubes and place in a large shallow dish. Combine water, soy sauce, lemon juice, oil, mustard, ginger and pepper; mix well. Pour over chicken and marinate in refrigerator several hours or overnight, turning pieces occasionally to coat evenly. When ready to cook, alternately thread meat and vegetables onto 4 (8-inch) skewers. Place on a nonstick baking pan. Brush kabobs with remaining marinade and bake in a 450° F. oven about 15 minutes, turning and basting during cooking.

Makes 4 servings at 250 calories per serving.

BAKED CHICKEN PARMESAN

1 (2½-pound) broiler-fryer, quartered
salt and pepper
1 teaspoon onion powder
1 teaspoon garlic powder
1 teaspoon whole oregano
1 teaspoon paprika
¼ cup chicken broth
4 teaspoons freshly grated Parmesan cheese

Quarter chicken, removing all visible fat. Season pieces with salt, pepper, onion powder, garlic powder, oregano, and paprika. Place chicken pieces in a shallow nonstick baking pan; bake skin-side down in a preheated 350° F. oven, uncovered, for 20 minutes. Turn skin-side up; baste with broth; bake 10 minutes longer. Remove the pan from the oven; sprinkle with Parmesan cheese. Return chicken to the oven and bake another 15 to 30 minutes or until the chicken is cooked through and the cheese has browned. The baking pan can be put under the broiler for just a few minutes if you like the chicken dark and crusty.

Makes 4 servings at 160 calories per serving.

Chef's Cooking Tip:
Only freshly-grated Parmesan cheese will do. The canned variety isn't even a good substitute for the real thing. Once you've tried it, you could never use canned Parmesan cheese again.

CHICKEN SAUTÉ SEC

1 (2½-pound) broiler-fryer,
    quartered
pepper
½ cup dry white wine
¼ cup chopped green onions
    (white part only)

1 cup sliced fresh mushrooms
2 tablespoons chopped parsley
⅛ teaspoon thyme
⅛ teaspoon basil
salt and pepper to taste

Wash chicken pieces; pat dry with paper toweling. Season with pepper. Place chicken in a nonstick baking dish or skillet, skin-side down. Bake, uncovered, in a 400° F. oven for 20 minutes. Turn chicken skin-side up and bake 20 minutes longer, or until cooked through. Remove chicken from pan. Place pan on top of the stove and deglaze with wine over high heat. Add onions, mushrooms, parsley, thyme, basil, and additional pepper, if desired. Reduce the wine mixture, stirring constantly, until liquid is evaporated. Spoon mushroom glaze over chicken and serve.

Makes 4 servings at 160 calories per serving.

Chef's Cooking Tip:
If the baking pan is not sufficiently thick, deglaze with wine, then pour the contents into a small saucepan or skillet to reduce and thicken.

HONEY-BAKED DRUMSTICKS

4 large chicken legs
¼ cup orange juice
2 tablespoons honey

2 tablespoons soy sauce
1 teaspoon grated ginger root
1 teaspoon sesame seed

With a sharp knife, cut through knee joint to separate thighs from drumsticks. Arrange in a shallow nonstick baking pan; add remaining ingredients. Cover; marinate in refrigerator 3 to 4 hours; turn occasionally. Remove from refrigerator 30 minutes before baking. Preheat oven to 375° F. Bake with marinade, uncovered, for 50 minutes, or until chicken is done. Turn at least once during baking. Baste occasionally.

Makes 4 servings at 230 calories per serving.

Chef's Cooking Tip:
Honey that is stored in the refrigerator will granulate. To restore it to a liquefied state, place the jar in a water bath over low heat. Remove when the crystals have disappeared.

MEXICAN-STYLE BAKED CHICKEN

1 (2½-pound) broiler-fryer, quartered
¼ cup orange juice
2 tablespoons honey
2 tablespoons dry sherry
1 clove garlic, minced
½ teaspoon cinnamon
¼ teaspoon chile powder
dash cayenne pepper

Arrange chicken in a nonstick baking pan. Add remaining ingredients; cover and marinate in refrigerator 3 to 4 hours. Turn occasionally. Remove from refrigerator 30 minutes before baking. Preheat oven to 375° F. Bake with marinade, uncovered, about 50 minutes, or until chicken is done. Turn and baste occasionally during baking.

Makes 4 servings at 230 calories per serving.

Chef's Cooking Tip:
If properly stored, whole spices will keep almost indefinitely. Therefore, it's safe to buy whole spices in larger quantities than would be advisable for ground or powdered spices.

OVEN-FRIED CHICKEN

2½ pounds chicken parts, skinned
salt and pepper
2 tablespoons flour
1 egg, slightly beaten
1 tablespoon skim milk
1 cup dry breadcrumbs

Pat chicken dry with paper toweling; season with salt and pepper. Dust lightly with flour; discard excess. Stir milk into beaten egg. Dip chicken parts into egg mixture; hold to allow excess run off. Dip into breadcrumbs; pat with back of hand to dislodge excess. Refrigerate for 30 minutes.

Place chicken in a large nonstick baking pan or skillet. Bake, uncovered, in a preheated 375° F. oven for 50 minutes.

Makes 4 servings at 245 calories per serving.

Chef's Cooking Tip:
To prevent both hands from getting wet and sticky, remove the chicken parts from the egg mixture with your right hand and place them in the breadcrumbs, then remove them from the breadcrumbs with your left hand.

OVEN-FRIED CHICKEN BREASTS

2 large chicken breasts, boned, skinned, and halved lengthwise
salt and pepper
2 tablespoons flour
1 egg, slightly beaten
1 tablespoon skim milk
1 cup breadcrumbs

Flatten chicken fillets with a mallet, cleaver, or heavy saucepan to ¼-inch thickness; season with salt and pepper. Dust lightly with flour; discard excess. Combine milk with beaten egg. Dip chicken parts into egg mixture, then into breadcrumbs. Pat with back of hand to dislodge excess; refrigerate for 30 minutes to set. Remove from refrigerator. Place in a large nonstick baking pan or skillet. Preheat oven to 425° F. for 15 minutes. Bake chicken, uncovered, for 10 minutes or until golden.

Makes 4 servings at 150 calories per serving.

Chef's Cooking Tip:
For most dry-heat cooking recipes for poultry, the skin should be left on. It prevents the delicate meat from drying out. It's a simple matter for the conscientious dieter to remove it after cooking.

Broiling

Broiling is yet another dry heat method of preparation that adapts itself beautifully to low-calorie cooking. As in roasting and baking, the heat of the oven is hot and dry, but unlike these dry heat methods, broiled food is further subjected to the radiant heat of an open flame. Thus without careful attention, broiled food can scorch and burn in a manner of seconds.

Broiling poultry the low-calorie way calls for cooking at a moderate temperature so the meat gets cooked before the skin is charred. You'll find, for instance, that a cooking temperature of 350° F. produces a beautifully broiled piece of meat that's moist and succulent on the inside and crisp and golden on the outside. Basting the poultry parts with fats, oils, or liquids isn't necessary. What is necessary, however, is that you turn the meat a few times during cooking to insure even cooking and browning.

If your broiler is scorching the poultry skin before the cooking is completed, try baking the poultry parts in a 400° F. oven for 20 minutes before broiling. In some cases, it's easier to brown and score the poultry under the broiler first and complete the cooking in the oven.

BASIC BROILING TECHNIQUES
1. *Quarter the bird* and remove all visible fat. Rinse and pat dry with paper toweling. Season or marinate to taste, preferably several hours in advance of cooking.

2. *Preheat the broiling oven to 350° F. Coat the surface of the broiler pan with a food release agent or wipe lightly with vegetable oil to prevent sticking. Adjust the pan 5 to 6 inches from the source of heat.*

3. *Place the poultry parts skin-side down on the broiling pan.* Broil at a moderate temperature for 10 minutes.

4. *Turn the poultry parts skin-side up* and continue to broil until the bird is tender and nicely brown. Turn when necessary to prevent scorching.

5. *Remove the poultry parts to a hot platter.* Season with salt and pepper to taste. Serve immediately.

BROILED CHICKEN

1 (2½-pound) broiler-fryer, quartered
salt and pepper, onion powder, garlic powder

2 tablespoons chicken broth or lemon juice

Rinse the chicken parts under cold water; pat dry with paper toweling. Season to taste with salt, pepper, onion powder, and garlic powder. Preheat broiler to 350° F. Place chicken skin side down directly on broiling pan or in an oven-proof nonstick skillet. Broil for 10 minutes, 5 to 6 inches from the source of heat. Turn skin-side up; baste with chicken broth or lemon juice. Continue to broil until chicken is tender and golden, about 40 minutes. Turn and baste several times during cooking to prevent scorching.

Makes 4 servings at 160 calories per serving.

Chef's Cooking Tip:
For best cooking results and to prevent the skin from scorching before the meat is cooked through, bring the chicken to room temperature before baking or broiling.

CHINESE-STYLE BROILED DRUMSTICKS

4 large chicken legs
  salt, pepper, ginger, paprika
2 tablespoons diet margarine

2 tablespoons honey
2 tablespoons soy sauce

In a small bowl, combine margarine, honey, and soy sauce. Season chicken parts with salt, pepper, ginger, and paprika; place in a shallow nonstick ovenproof skillet. Pour marinade over chicken; cover and marinate for at least 1 hour. Drain marinade; reserve. Preheat broiler to 350° F. Place skillet 5 to 6 inches from source of heat; broil skin-side down for 10 minutes. Turn skin side up; baste with reserved marinade and continue to broil until chicken is tender and golden, about 40 minutes. Turn and baste several times during cooking to prevent scorching.

Makes 4 servings at 230 calories per serving.

Chef's Cooking Tip:
For convenience, the chicken can be broiled an hour or two in advance, then wrapped in foil and warmed in a preheated oven when it's time to serve.

MUSTARD BROILED CHICKEN

1 (3-pound) broiler-fryer,
  quartered
  salt and pepper
2 tablespoons chicken broth or
  lemon juice

4 tablespoons Dijon-style or
  brown mustard
4 tablespoons plain breadcrumbs

Rinse the chicken parts under cold water; pat dry with paper toweling. Season to taste with salt and pepper. Preheat broiler to 350° F. Place chicken skin-side down directly on broiling pan or in an ovenproof nonstick skillet. Broil for 10 minutes, 5 to 6 inches from the source of heat. Turn skin-side up; baste with chicken broth or lemon juice; cook 20 minutes longer. Remove chicken parts from broiler. Coat with mustard, then sprinkle with breadcrumbs. Broil, skin-side down for 10 minutes; turn and broil 5 minutes longer, or until browned.

Makes 4 servings at 190 calories per serving.

MARINATED CHICKEN KABOBS

1½ pounds chicken breasts, skinned and boned
2 tablespoons minced onion
2 tablespoons fresh lemon or lime juice
1 tablespoon vegetable oil
1 garlic clove, minced
¼ cup soy sauce
¼ teaspoon ground ginger
⅛ teaspoon pepper
4 fresh pineapple chunks (1-inch)
4 green pepper squares
4 onion squares
4 medium-size mushrooms
4 cherry tomatoes

Cut chicken into 1-inch cubes and place in a large shallow dish. Combine onion, lemon juice, oil, garlic, soy sauce, ginger, and pepper; mix well. Pour over chicken and marinate in refrigerator several hours or overnight. When ready to cook, alternately thread meat and vegetables onto 4 (8-inch) skewers. Place on broiler pan or grill and cook about 4 inches from source of heat, turning and basting with remaining marinade until chicken is tender and lightly browned.

Makes 4 servings at 250 calories per serving.

Sautéing

The simplest and most basic method of sautéing poultry meat is to cut it into bite-size pieces or flatten it to an even thickness and sear it lightly in a large nonstick skillet over medium heat. You won't need any butter or oil if you remember not to overcrowd the pan and not to add any liquid to the pan until the meat has been properly seared. The total cooking time is short—no more than eight minutes.

You can sauté unskinned, disjointed poultry parts in the same manner, but the heat must be lowered after the initial searing takes place and the pan partially or fully covered for part of the cooking period.

The important thing to remember about sautéing poultry the low-calorie way is to keep the heat high enough to sear the cut surfaces in order to seal in the juices and flavor, yet low enough so the meat doesn't toughen.

BASIC SAUTÉING TECHNIQUES

1. *Skin and debone the meat.* Cut into bite-size pieces for stir-fry dishes. To prepare cutlets, flatten the meat slightly with a heavy saucepan or the side of a meat cleaver to an even thickness.

2. *Dry the meat* thoroughly to prevent steaming. This can be done by preparing the meat well in advance of cooking and allowing it to air-dry in the refrigerator.

3. *Season the meat* with salt and pepper. Some recipes will call for a light dusting of flour to add flavor and to facilitate browning.

4. *Sear the meat* without added fats, oils, or liquids in a large nonstick skillet over medium heat. Turn the meat frequently for even and complete searing. Be sure to cook without crowding; cook in several batches, if necessary.

5. *Cook the meat,* uncovered, for six to eight minutes or until completely opaque and cooked through. To test for doneness, tap the meat with your fingers. When cooked through, it should feel springy and resilient. Be careful not to overcook.

6. *Remove the meat* to a warm platter. To serve with a sauce, deglaze the pan over high heat with a small amount of wine or broth. Reduce until thick, then spoon over meat. Serve immediately.

BASQUE CHICKEN

1 (2½-pound) frying chicken, quartered
salt, pepper, paprika
½ cup chicken broth
1 clove garlic, minced
1 onion, diced
1 green pepper, diced
2 celery ribs, diced
2 large tomatoes, peeled, seeded, and diced
2 tablespoons freshly chopped parsley
½ teaspoon thyme

Season chicken parts with salt, pepper, and paprika to taste. Coat the surface of a large nonstick skillet with a food release agent. Place the chicken in the skillet skin-side down and cook slowly over moderate heat until the chicken is browned, about 10 minutes; stir occasionally to prevent sticking. Drain off any accumulated fat. Add minced garlic, diced onion, green pepper, and celery to skillet. Add chicken broth, cover, and simmer over medium-low heat 10 minutes. Uncover; stir in diced tomatoes, parsley, and thyme. Recover; simmer 20 minutes longer. Uncover, baste with pan juices; continue to simmer until sauce is thickened, from 10 to 15 minutes.

Makes 4 servings at 210 calories per serving.

GLAZED CHICKEN

1 (2½-pound) frying chicken, quartered
salt, pepper, paprika

1 cup chicken broth
¼ cup dry white wine

Season chicken parts with salt, pepper, and paprika to taste. Coat the surface of a large nonstick skillet with a food release agent. Place the chicken in the skillet skin-side down and cook slowly over moderate heat until the chicken is browned, about 10 minutes; stir occasionally to prevent sticking. Drain off any accumulated fat. Remove white portions from skillet. Add chicken broth; cover and simmer dark meat portions over low heat for 10 minutes. Return white meat portions to skillet; recover and simmer an additional 30 minutes. Uncover; add the ¼ cup of wine and continue simmering until sauce begins to thicken. Turn chicken parts with a pair of tongs to coat all sides. Remove when sauce is reduced to a thick glaze. Spoon glaze over chicken and serve.

Makes 4 servings at 215 calories per serving.

Chef's Cooking Tip:
Use white pepper rather than black pepper in dishes where black specks would mar appearance, such as puréed soups, sauces, fish, and poultry dishes.

HAWAIIAN CHICKEN

1 (2½-pound) frying chicken, quartered
salt, pepper, paprika
1 cup unsweetened pineapple juice
2 tablespoons soy sauce
½ cup drained pineapple chunks

2 tablespoons diced green pepper
2 tablespoons diced red pepper
2 tablespoons finely chopped chives
1 teaspoon toasted shredded coconut

Season chicken parts with salt, pepper, and paprika to taste. Coat the surface of a large nonstick skillet with a food release agent. Place the chicken in the skillet skin-side down and cook slowly over moderate heat until the chicken is browned, about 10 minutes; stir occasionally to prevent sticking. Drain off fat. Remove white meat portions of chicken from skillet. Add pineapple juice and soy sauce; cover and simmer over low heat for 10 minutes. Return white meat portions to the skillet (the white meat portions take less time to cook). Cover and simmer an additional 30 minutes. Uncover, add the pineapple chunks and diced peppers; continue simmering until the sauce thickens, about 10 minutes. Remove chicken to platter; garnish with chives and coconut; baste with thickened glaze.

Makes 4 servings at 215 calories per serving.

KAUAI CHICKEN

1 pound raw chicken, boned, skinned, and sliced
1 teaspoon salt
¼ teaspoon pepper
1 tablespoon oil
1 small clove garlic, minced
1 medium onion, sliced

1 large green pepper, sliced
2 celery ribs, diagonally sliced
1 cup chicken stock
2 tablespoons soy sauce
2 tablespoons water
2 tablespoons cornstarch
1 large tomato, cut in eighths

In Chinese wok or large skillet, heat oil and add chicken, salt, pepper, and stir-fry for 2 minutes to brown. Add garlic, onion, green pepper, celery, and chicken stock. Cover, lower heat, and simmer for 3 minutes. In a small bowl, combine soy sauce, water, and cornstarch, and add to chicken mixture. Add tomatoes. Cook and stir 2 to 3 minutes until sauce is slightly thickened.

Makes 4 servings at 180 calories per serving.

Chef's Cooking Tip:
To mince garlic, add a small amount of salt to hold the bits together. To crush a garlic clove, smash it with the flat side of a chef's knife on a small piece of wax paper.

SAUTÉED CHICKEN LIVERS

1 pound chicken livers
4 tablespoons flour
   salt and pepper to taste
1 tablespoon butter or margarine

1 tablespoon vegetable oil
2 tablespoons freshly chopped
   parsley

Combine flour, salt, and pepper. Cut livers in half and dredge in seasoned flour; discard excess flour. Melt butter and oil in a large nonstick skillet over moderately high heat. Add chicken livers and sauté gently until browned and crisp on the outside, about 5 minutes. If further cooking is desired, reduce heat to low and cook 1 to 2 minutes longer. Garnish with chopped parsley.

Makes 4 servings at 220 calories per serving.

Chef's Cooking Tip:
Sautéed chicken livers can taste bitter if the green gall, or bile, hasn't been removed properly before packaging. Examine livers for any green or blackish discolorations before cooking.

SAUTÉED CHICKEN CACCIATORE

4 chicken breasts, about 6
   ounces each
1 tablespoon cooking oil
½ cup dry white wine
1 clove garlic, minced
1 onion, sliced
1 green pepper, sliced

1 can (16-ounce) diced tomatoes
   in sauce
½ teaspoon salt
½ teaspoon whole oregano
¼ teaspoon each: pepper, basil,
   fennel seed

Bone the chicken breasts; remove skin. Cut into bite-size pieces. Heat 1 tablespoon oil in a large nonstick skillet or wok over high heat. Add chicken; stir-fry until opaque, then remove to a warm platter.

Reduce heat. Add wine to deglaze pan. Add garlic, onions, peppers. Raise heat and sauté quickly until onions are translucent. Add diced tomatoes in sauce and seasonings; cover and simmer for 2 minutes. Return chicken to skillet. Cover briefly to contain the heat. Uncover and serve.

Makes 4 servings at 240 calories per serving.

Poaching

Poaching is simmering whole or cut-up poultry very gently in water or stock. Its objective is to blend the flavors of the poultry and the cooking liquid together during the cooking process. When the meat is firm, moist, and flavorful, it is removed from the pot and the stock is reserved for soups and sauces. You can serve the poultry meat as is with its own steaming broth and some accompanying vegetables. Or you can remove the meat from the bones and use it for salads or cooked meat recipes. If you're planning to serve it cold, allow the bird to cool in its poaching liquid. If it will be reheated, reduce the initial cooking time somewhat so the additional heat won't overcook it. Poultry dries out and toughens when overcooked, even when cooked by moist heat.

As a low-calorie cook, you can learn to eliminate most of the fat calories from normally fatty birds like duck and goose by poaching them until almost done and finishing them in the oven or broiler to brown and crisp. This procedure also eliminates the constant ladling of the dissolved fat from the bottom of the roasting pan.

BASIC POACHING TECHNIQUES

1. *Truss the bird* with butcher's twine.
2. *Place the bird* in a kettle and add enough hot salted water or hot stock to cover. If you're using a rich-flavored stock, it's not necessary to add additional herbs, spices, or aromatic vegetables to flavor the liquid. But if the stock is bland or you're using plain water, by all means add these various ingredients in any combination that suits your taste.
3. *Simmer the bird* on low heat about 1 hour or until the meat is tender when pierced with a fork. During cooking, skim off any accumulated scum or foam from the surface of the liquid with a soup ladle.
4. *Remove the bird* from the liquid by inserting a sturdy cooking fork between the shoulder bones behind the wings. This provides a strong support for the bird and lessens the chance of its dropping back into the hot liquid and scalding you. With the bird raised out of the liquid in this manner, pierce the knee joint with a skewer or small-bladed knife. If the juices that emerge run clear and are free from rosiness, the bird is done.

POACHED CHICKEN

1 (3-pound) broiler-fryer chicken
1 chopped onion
1 chopped carrot
1 chopped celery rib
   water to cover by 2 inches
3 parsley sprigs
½ teaspoon whole thyme
1 bay leaf
8 crushed peppercorns
salt to taste

Rinse the chicken inside and out under cold water. Truss the bird with butcher's twine. Fill the bottom of a small pot with the chopped vegetables and place the trussed bird in the pot. Wash a 4-inch square of cheesecloth in clear water. Add parsley, thyme, bay leaf, and peppercorns; tie the cheesecloth into a bag with a small piece of twine. Add the water; bring slowly to a simmer, skimming foam and fat from the surface occasionally with a soup ladle. Be careful not to overcook. The chicken is done when the internal juices that flow from the vent and the juices that emerge from the thickest part of the thigh are clear. Remove the chicken when done and strain the stock.

Makes 4 servings at 200 calories per serving.

Chef's Cooking Tip:
For a richer stock, return the skin and bones to the pot; then reduce by one-half before straining.

Stewing

Stewing is the moist heat method of simmering cut-up poultry in a small amount of liquid. A recipe's exact definition depends upon how the meat is prepared before cooking; the vegetables, herbs, and spices added to the dish for flavor; how quickly the meat is cooked; and when and how the cooking liquid is thickened for use as a sauce. To complicate matters, stews, casseroles, and skillet dishes that are *stewed* can be "moist baked" in the oven or simmered on top of the stove.

To say that these various types of stewing recipes are difficult to categorize is certainly an understatement, but the common denominator for all these methods of preparation is the interchange of flavors between the cooking liquid, the meat, and the accompanying vegetables and seasonings.

For the dieter, stewing is a two-part process. The poultry parts are usually seared in a separate skillet or in the oven before being combined with the other ingredients. This technique seals in their juices and flavor but keeps the dissolved fat from the poultry out of the recipe and minimizes the need for calorie-laden starch thickeners.

BASIC STEWING TECHNIQUES

1. *Disjoint the poultry.* Or skin, debone, and cut into bite-size pieces as may be required in the recipe. Dry thoroughly with paper toweling.
2. *Season the poultry* with salt and pepper.
3. *Sear the poultry* either in the oven or on top of the stove to brown and seal in the natural juices and flavor, then combine with the liquid and seasoning.
4. *Cook the poultry* in a covered skillet or Dutch oven, either in the oven or on top of the stove from 20 to 60 minutes, depending on the size and tenderness of the pieces. A stewing hen might take as much as two hours to become tender!
5. *Remove the poultry* to a warm ovenproof dish. Skim any fat off the surface of the cooking liquid. Thicken the liquid by boiling it down quickly over high heat, or you may thicken it with a small amount of arrowroot or cornstarch dissolved in cold water. Pour the thickened sauce over the poultry and serve or place in the oven or broiler to glaze.

CHICKEN WITH ARTICHOKE HEARTS

1 (2½-pound) broiler-fryer, quartered
salt, pepper, paprika
¼ cup dry white wine or vermouth
1 clove garlic, minced
1 large onion, chopped
2 large tomatoes, peeled, seeded, and diced
½ teaspoon each: rosemary, thyme, salt
¼ teaspoon freshly ground pepper
2 cans (4-ounce) artichoke hearts, rinsed and drained
1 tablespoon cornstarch
½ cup plain yogurt

Preheat oven to 425° F. Season chicken with salt, pepper, and paprika. Place skin-side up in a nonstick baking pan; bake uncovered for 15 minutes. Place wine, garlic, and onion in a large skillet or Dutch oven. Cover; simmer over medium heat for 5 minutes. Add tomatoes, rosemary, thyme, salt, pepper, and chicken. Reduce oven heat to 350° F. Cover and bake for 50 minutes. Add drained artichoke hearts and cook 10 minutes longer. Drain, reserving one-half cup liquid. In a small saucepan blend cornstarch and yogurt. Slowly stir reserved liquid into yogurt mixture. Simmer over low heat until heated through, but do not boil or the yogurt will curdle. Spoon sauce over chicken; garnish with chopped parsley or paprika and serve.

Makes 4 servings at 220 calories per serving.

COQ AU VIN

1 (2½-pound) broiler-fryer, quartered
garlic salt, pepper, paprika
1 onion, coarsely chopped
1 cup sliced fresh mushrooms
1 tablespoon tomato paste
¼ teaspoon marjoram, tarragon, or basil
⅛ teaspoon thyme
½ cup dry white wine
1 teaspoon freshly chopped parsley

Preheat oven to 425° F. Season chicken with garlic salt, pepper, and paprika. Place chicken skin-side up on a nonstick baking pan; bake uncovered for 15 minutes. Meanwhile, place remaining ingredients, except parsley, in an ovenproof nonstick skillet or Dutch oven. Add chicken; cover and bake at 350° F. for 45 minutes. Uncover and continue to bake 15 minutes longer to evaporate liquid and thicken sauce.

Makes 4 servings at 200 calories per serving.

CHICKEN MARENGO

1 (2½-pound) broiler-fryer, quartered
onion salt, pepper, paprika
1 onion, thinly sliced
1 celery rib, sliced
1 cup sliced fresh mushrooms
2 cups tomatoes, peeled, seeded, and diced
1 tablespoon tomato paste
½ teaspoon whole basil
⅛ teaspoon thyme
¼ cup dry sherry

Preheat oven to 425° F. Season chicken with onion salt, pepper, and paprika. Place chicken skin-side up on a nonstick baking pan; bake, uncovered, for 15 minutes. Meanwhile, place remaining ingredients in an ovenproof nonstick skillet or Dutch oven. Add chicken. Cover and bake at 350° F. for one hour. Remove chicken, onions, celery, mushrooms, and tomatoes with a sieved spatula to an ovenproof serving dish. Thicken liquid by boiling it down quickly over high heat, stirring constantly to prevent scorching. Spread sauce over chicken and vegetables. Return dish to the oven for 10 minutes to glaze.

Makes 4 servings at 200 calories per serving.

Steaming

Steaming is a moist heat method of preparation that cooks food with or without pressure completely surrounded by steam. The poultry is trussed and placed on a rack in a tightly covered pot over a boiling liquid.

This no-fat, low-calorie method of cooking keeps the meat moist and succulent, and chicken cooked in this manner can be substituted in any boiled or poached poultry recipe.

BASIC STEAMING TECHNIQUES

1. *Rinse the bird* under cold running water. Dry thoroughly with paper toweling.
2. *Truss the bird* with soft white butcher's twine.
3. *Season the bird* inside and out with salt and white pepper.
4. *Bring liquid to a boil* in a small stockpot that is fitted with a rack and a tight-fitting lid. Place trussed bird on the rack well above the liquid. Cover the pot tightly.
5. *Steam the bird* over moderate heat for 40 to 50 minutes, or until the bird is tender.
6. *Remove the bird* and drain carefully. Keep warm; allow the bird to "rest" 10 to 15 minutes before slicing.

STEAMED CHICKEN

1 (3-pound) broiler-fryer chicken
salt and pepper
2 cups water
1 cup dry white wine (optional)
1 lemon wedge

Rinse the chicken inside and out; dry with paper toweling. Season inside cavity with salt and pepper. Truss with butcher's twine. Put remaining ingredients in the bottom of a small stockpot or steamer; bring to a boil. Place trussed chicken on a rack well above the level of the liquid. Cover pot tightly; steam over moderate heat until chicken is tender, about 40 to 50 minutes. The chicken is done when the internal juices that pour from the vent when the bird is upended are clear and free from any rosiness.

Makes 4 servings at 180 calories per serving.

Chef's Cooking Tip:
A 3-pound steamed broiler-fryer will yield about 2½ cups of diced, cooked chicken meat.

STEAMED CORNISH GAME HENS

2 (1½-pound) ready-to-cook
    Cornish hens
2 tablespoons chopped onion

2 parsley sprigs
salt, pepper, thyme
2 sheets aluminum foil

Thaw frozen hens. Remove the bag of giblets from the cavity. Rinse inside and out under cold water; pat dry with paper toweling. Place onion and parsley inside each cavity; season with salt, pepper, and thyme. Wrap each bird securely in foil. Place in baking sheet in a 350° F. oven and steam for one hour. Remove hens from oven. Raise oven heat to 425° F. Carefully cut foil at the top and fold back to expose hens. Return to the oven and cook 10 minutes longer to brown. The hens are done when the internal juices that pour from the vent run clear and are free of any rosiness. Remove hens to a warm platter to "rest." Meanwhile, pour the accumulated juices in the foil packets into a measuring cup. When the fat separates, remove it with a bulb baster. Serve the remaining juices as a sauce or pour juices into a small skillet; add 1 teaspoon minced shallots and ¼ cup wine. Reduce over high heat until the consistency of honey, then brush over hens as a glaze.

Makes 4 servings at 220 calories per serving.

SEAFOOD

If you've been eating too much of the wrong kinds of foods and want to lose those unwanted extra pounds, planning your meals around seafood makes good dieting sense. Seafood is a prime source of protein, vitamins, and minerals, yet it has a lower fat content and fewer calories than either meat or poultry. A lean 4-ounce serving of sole or flounder, for instance, is only 89 calories. Compare that to 450 calories for the same size serving of prime rib of beef—and who ever heard of only a 4-ounce serving of prime rib! Even so-called "fatty" fish like mackerel or salmon is lower in calories than most meats. What's more, fish fats contain a higher proportion of polyunsaturated fatty acids than do the fats of meat or poultry—an important consideration for those concerned about cholesterol.

Although seafood is the best calorie and nutrition bargain you can buy, in recent years some fish and most shellfish have become inordinately expensive and are now considered delicacies. But since you're dieting and thus buying and eating less, such an occasional luxury is more than justified. And when you get the urge to overeat, be sure and make seafood your appetizer and main-course choices; you'll be able to enjoy a greater amount of food without damaging your diet.

Finally, bear in mind that when you're dieting, you still need the same essential nutrients from food as a non-dieter, but you must get them from fewer calories. So, enjoy a wide variety of foods but enjoy them in moderation, and be sure to include nutritionally rich, low-calorie seafoods often.

The edible creatures of the sea are divided into three basic categories. The first group are *fin fish*, both saltwater and freshwater varieties. The second group are *crustaceans* or single-shelled creatures. These include crabs, crayfish, lobsters, prawns, and shrimp. The third group are the *mollusks* that are enclosed by one or two shells. Abalone and conch have only one shell, while clams, oysters, mussels, and scallops have two shells.

The main difference between the crustaceans and mollusks is in terms of mobility. Crustaceans are equipped with legs or claws for walking around, and some have finlike tails that aid them in maneuvering about. The mollusks, on the other hand, have no visible means of propulsion.

Another difference between crustaceans and mollusks is their shell. Crustaceans have relatively thin, segmented shell coverings which usually can be peeled off. Mollusks, in contrast, are enclosed in a tough shell that must be pried or steamed open.

The term "seafood" refers to any edible creature that lives exclusively in water, either saltwater or fresh. Shellfish embraces both crustaceans and mollusks.

BUYING SEAFOOD

FRESH SEAFOOD

Fresh or saltwater fish can be purchased in many different forms; (1) *whole*: just as it comes from the water; (2) *drawn*: with only the entrails removed; (3) *dressed*: with the head, tail, scales, and entrails removed, ready to cook; (4) *filleted*: with the sides of the fish cut lengthwise away from the backbone, practically boneless; and (5) *steaked*: cross-section slices cut from dressed fish.

When you have an occasion to buy or receive fresh fish rather than frozen, cooked, or canned, there are certain characteristics to watch for that will tell your senses just how fresh the fish really is:

IT SHOULD LOOK FRESH: The eyes of fresh fish should be full and clear, almost transparent, not cloudy and sunken. The gills should be bright red, not gray or brownish. The skin should have a shiny, irridescent look. The skin colors should be bold and unfaded.

IT SHOULD FEEL FRESH: The skin should be tight, the fins stiff and the scales firmly attached and shining. The flesh should be firm and close-grained; it should be elastic enough to spring back under finger pressure.

IT SHOULD SMELL FRESH: A fresh fish should always have a pleasant, mild, clean odor—never fishy.

As with whole and drawn fish, packaged fillets and steaks should look, feel, and smell fresh. The flesh should have a fresh-cut appearance, with no evidence of drying or discoloration. The flesh should be firm and spring back to shape when pressed with the fingers. The cut-fish portions should be tightly wrapped in moistureproof material, and any discernible odors through the wrappings should smell fresh and clean.

Shellfish are extremely perishable when purchased alive in the shell. They should be kept refrigerated at temperatures close to freezing until ready for use. The shells of fresh oysters and clams should be tightly closed, or if slightly opened, should close immediately when tapped. If the shells don't close, it indicates that the mollusks are dead and should be discarded. Fresh crabs and lobsters should be alive and active until the very moment of their preparation. Fresh shrimp should look clean and shiny and have a light, mild odor. They are usually sold headless.

FROZEN SEAFOOD

Frozen seafood should be solidly frozen when you buy it. It should be tightly wrapped in a moistureproof material. There should be no signs of swelling, which would indicate that the contents had been thawed and refrozen. If you can see the flesh of the seafood through the wrapping, it should appear clear and without discoloration. Look especially for ice crystals or *freezer burn* on improperly wrapped seafood. Frozen seafood will have little or no odor, but when it begins to thaw there should be no objectionable fishy smell. If there is, return it to the place of purchase immediately—or throw it out.

HOW MUCH SEAFOOD TO BUY

The amount of seafood you need per serving for diet recipes will depend on the market form you select. If the seafood is solid meat without skin and bones like fillets and steaks, allow one-third of a pound per serving. If the seafood is untrimmed, allow one-half pound per serving. Add one-quarter pound per serving for whole or drawn fish.

STORING AND HANDLING SEAFOOD

FRESH SEAFOOD

Very few food items require as much careful attention as fresh fish and shellfish. It is one of the most delicate and perishable of foods and must be kept refrigerated at temperatures close to freezing or packed solidly in crushed ice at all times until being cooked. Try to buy your seafood the same day you intend to prepare it. When you get it home from the market, rinse it under cold running water, then store it, covered, in the coldest section of the refrigerator, preferably on a bed of crushed ice. The ice will help prevent the surface of the fish from drying out. You can keep seafood refrigerated for two days. After that, it will begin to deteriorate rapidly and its flavor and quality will be greatly affected.

FROZEN SEAFOOD

Seafood—even when purchased frozen—will spoil quickly unless it is properly wrapped and stored. Only freshly caught fish or shellfish that has been kept chilled with ice or dry ice immediately after it comes from the water should be frozen. The quality and taste will be preserved if the seafood is wrapped in moisture-vaporproof wrapping, glazed with near-freezing water, or frozen in water to protect it from bacterial and enzyme action, oxidation of the fat or oil, and dehydration during storage.

High-fat-content fish such as bonito, butterfish, herring, mackerel, pompano, lake trout, and salmon become rancid faster than leaner types of fish. Before freezing, they should be dipped in a solution of ascorbic acid (2 tablespoons ascorbic acid to 1 quart of water) for a few minutes to delay rancidity.

Lean fish like cod, flounder, haddock, perch, red snapper, and swordfish should be dipped in a cold brine to firm up the flesh. To prepare the brine, use a preparation of ½ cup salt and 1 quart of water.

All frozen fish and shellfish should be stored at a temperature of at least 0° F. or lower until ready for use. Properly packaged seafood can be frozen without loss of quality up to six months under ideal storage conditions and constant low temperature. High-fat-content fish, being more quickly perishable, should not be stored longer than three months.

Thawing Frozen Seafood

Many forms of fish and shellfish do not necessarily need to be defrosted before cooking. But I think that there are too many variables to contend with when trying to cook seafood from a frozen state and, therefore, recommend that you thaw frozen seafood before cooking. In any case, unthawed seafood must be cooked for a longer period of time and at a much lower temperature than thawed seafood to allow the heat to penetrate the frozen center before the outside surface becomes overcooked.

The best way to thaw frozen seafood is in the refrigerator. When it is allowed to defrost slowly at temperatures just above freezing, very little liquid is lost and the fish or shellfish will stay moist, delicate, and palatable when cooked. Frozen seafood that is defrosted at room temperature, on the other hand, loses most of its moisture and is very susceptible to spoilage.

When fast thawing is necessary, leave the seafood wrapped and place it under cold running water (hot water would cook the seafood) until almost defrosted.

Thawed seafood should be kept as cold as possible until it is cooked. If it is wrapped, leave it in its moistureproof wrappings until cooking time. Once the seafood is thawed, however, it should be used immediately.

One pound of seafood defrosted in the refrigerator usually takes anywhere from 10 to 24 hours to thaw, depending on the size and shape of the package and the temperature it was stored at. Small cuts of fish and shellfish, on the other hand, can usually be defrosted in about 30 minutes in a bath of cold water.

PREPARING SEAFOOD FOR COOKING

CLEANING AND DRESSING FRESH FISH

Although most of us find it convenient and practical to buy fresh and frozen fish at the market ready to be cooked, there are occasions when you'll need to know how to clean and dress a freshly caught fish yourself.

Start out by washing the fish under cold water. Then place it on a cutting board or plank or wood (this job is best done outdoors where the scales can fly at will) and either hold it firmly at the head or pin the tail to the board with an icepick. Working from the tail end, scrape a scaler or the blunt edge of a knife against the grain of the scales until the skin is smooth. If the scales are hard to remove, try soaking the fish in water for a few minutes to help loosen them. Incidentally, if you plan to fillet the fish, the messy scaling and eviscerating can be eliminated.

To gut a fish, carefully slit the skin with the point of a sharp knife along the entire length of the belly from the tail to the head and remove the contents of the abdominal cavity with your knife and fingers. Be sure to scrape any residue of blood or membrane lining from the cavity as they tend to give a bitter taste to the cooked fish.

If you're going to cut up the fish before cooking, you'll want to remove the various sets of fins. With a sharp knife, cut through the flesh along each side of the fin, being careful not to cut through the bones. Then grasp the fin between your fingers and pull out the entire root bones and fin together with a backward or forward motion of the hand.

If you have the opportunity to cook a whole fish, leave the fins, head, and tail intact throughout the cooking process. Not only are these parts easier to remove after the fish is cooked, but because fewer cuts are made in the skin, the fish will be juicier and more palatable when eaten. You can, of course, leave the head and tail on after cooking, serving the fish stuffed or butterflied on a platter with an appropriate garnish for a more natural effect.

To remove the head, simply slice behind the gills from the throat upward to the backbone. If you're cooking a large fish and the backbone is too large to cut through, try placing the head on the edge of a cutting board and breaking the bone at the cut with the palm of your hand.

A dressed fish with the scales and entrails removed can be split lengthwise in two parts, cut crosswise into ¾-inch-thick steaks, filleted, or boned and stuffed whole.

A fillet is one whole side of a fish that has been cut away from the backbone. To fillet a round fish, lay it on its side and with a razor-sharp knife, make an incision down the length of the spine. Then while grasping the fillet in one hand, use short, staccato strokes of a knife point to separate the flesh from the rib bones. Keep folding the fillet back in one piece until it can be lifted off. Turn the fish over and repeat the process on the other side.

Whether or not you skin the fillets depends on the type of fish and how you plan to cook it. Just remember that if you do skin the fillets, there's no need to scale them.

To skin a fillet, place it skin-side down on a cutting board and cut through the flesh to the skin about one-half inch from the tail. Grasp the loose skin with your fingers, turn the knife blade flat, and with the edge of the knife slightly inclined toward the skin, slide it forward with a sawing motion while pulling the fillet backward with the other hand.

CLEANING SHELLFISH

Oysters

Scrub the oyster shells thoroughly with a stiff brush under cold running water. With a heavy pair of gloves or a thick towel as protection, place the oyster on a flat surface, deep side down, and hold it in place with one hand. Then work the point of an oyster knife (a short, stiff-bladed knife with a large wooden or plastic handle) into the hinge between the upper and lower shells, applying steady pressure while at the same time twisting the blade until the oyster relaxes. When the knife penetrates the oyster's shell, cut the muscle close to the flat, upper shell and lift it off. Finally, insert the knife between the muscle and the bottom shell and run it along until the oyster is free, being careful not to spill any of the precious liquor.

Clams

Before starting to clean fresh clams, be sure to give them a preliminary examination and discard any whose shells do not close when tapped.

To remove the sand that is imbedded on and in fresh hard-shell clams, first scrub the shells under cold running water. Then allow them to soak about three hours in a seawater bath or in a brine solution made up of two ounces of salt mixed with one gallon of water. Change the water several times as the sand accumulates on the bottom of the pan.

To open small clams with a knife, hold the shell gently in the palm of one hand. Avoid excessive movements that will cause the clam to tighten its powerful holding muscles. Next, place the cutting edge between the two halves of the shell and exert firm pressure with the fingers against the dull edge of the knife to squeeze the knife and the shell together. Once the shell is penetrated, twist the two halves apart and cut around the clam to sever the strong holding muscle. Large clams can be opened in the same manner described for opening oysters, or they can be opened by placing them in a small amount of boiling water, then covering the pot and allowing them to steam five to ten minutes. The disadvantage of this method, however, is that most of the flavorful clam liquor is lost.

A third method of opening hard-shell clams is to put them in the freezer just long enough for the liquid inside the shells to expand and force the two halves apart.

Shrimp

Raw shrimp—sometimes referred to as "green shrimp" (although they are by no means green in color)—can be cooked before cleaning, or they can be cleaned and then cooked, as you choose. But I would definitely recommend that you cook the shrimp in the shells when you can. Not only do the shells protect the delicate meat from drying out, but they add considerable flavor as well. To avoid toughness when using frozen shrimp, be sure they are thoroughly defrosted before cooking.

To shell fresh shrimp, either before or after cooking, grasp the shell with both thumbs on the inside leg area and remove it as if you were shelling a peanut. Pinch off any legs or body membranes that might remain, using your thumb and forefinger. If you wish to leave the fan-shaped tail intact, hold the tail between the thumb and forefinger of one hand and break off the shell at the base with the other hand.

If the shrimp are large enough (a step not necessary with small or medium-size shrimp), you will want to remove the dark sand vein that runs down the back. Devein shrimp before cooking by loosening the shells halfway along the back and inserting a skewer under the vein to fish it out. Then rinse the shrimp under cold running water to remove any remaining grit or sand. The shrimp are now ready to refrigerate or cook. To devein after cooking, make a shallow lengthwise cut down the back of each shrimp with a sharp knife or use a special deveining tool designed for this purpose and scrape the vein out.

Crabs

True gastronomes will insist that any exoskeletal shellfish like crab or lobster should be killed live by stabbing it to death and cleaning it before cooking. Most cooks, however, usually prefer to kill a crustacean by plunging it into boiling water and cleaning it after it has cooled.

To clean and dress a cooked fresh or frozen hard-shell crab, pull the upper and lower shells apart with both hands. Then rinse and scrape out the intestines, olive-green fat, and the spongy gills from the body cavity under running water. Cut through the center with a large knife or cleaver to separate the two body halves; then cut each body section in half again. Twist or cut off the legs and claws from the body segments, if desired. Crack the legs and claws with the side of the knife or cleaver so the meat can be easily extracted. To serve orders of cracked crab over ice, arrange the body, leg, and claw portions attractively around a small dish filled with low-calorie diet dressing or cocktail sauce over ice.

Lobster

Whether you clean a lobster before or after it is cooked is best determined by its method of preparation: If a lobster is going to be cooked by dry heat, as in broiling or baking, it is cleaned before you cook it. If you're going to use a moist heat method of cooking like boiling or steaming, the cleaning comes after the cooking. Incidentally, don't attempt to recook a lobster that has already been cooked; it will be dry, stringy, and tasteless.

To clean a lobster before cooking, place it on its back and insert the point of a knife between the body and tail shells. This kills the lobster instantly by severing its spinal cord. It also takes nerve! Another quick method is to place the lobster on a cutting board with back or shell-side up. Hold a towel firmly over its head and claws and quickly insert the point of a knife into the center of the small cross on the back of the head. Live lobsters can also be killed before cooking by dropping it head first into boiling water as you would for boiling, but remove it almost immediately when it goes limp, then proceed with the cleaning and cutting.

With a large knife, split the lobster in half lengthwise or cut it in two and open it flat lengthwise without cutting through the back shell. Remove and discard the stomach (the small sand sac just behind the head), the spongy lungs (which lie in the upper body cavity between the meat and the shell), and the intestinal canal which runs from the stomach to the base of the tail. Be sure to save the black coral or *roe* (it turns red when cooked) found in female lobsters. Either keep it in or remove it and use it in a stuffing or sauce. The gray-colored liver or *tomally* which is found between the shell and the body is another delectable morsel. Remove it before cooking to mix with the stuffing or leave it in and spoon it out afterward.

COOKING SEAFOOD

Seafood is probably the easiest food you can cook. It is a naturally tender, delicate meat that needs to be treated gently and cooked lightly. You can serve moist, tender seafood entrées every time if you remember that all seafood cooks very quickly and needs only a small amount of heat to coagulate the protein in its muscle fibers and to soften the thin sheets of connective tissue that lie between them. But when seafood is overcooked, the softened tissues begin breaking down and the flavorful juices and nutrients are subsequently squeezed out.

This precise moment of doneness varies, not only with the method of preparation used, but with the size, shape, and temperature of the seafood at the time of cooking. For this reason, temperature-time ratio tables and recipes should only be taken as a general guide to seafood cookery, and in actual practice the skills and knowledge of the cook must be relied upon. Seafood is cooked when it loses its watery, translucent look and becomes completely opaque and the flesh is just beginning to flake when probed with a fork.

Although certain varieties of seafood lend themselves better to either dry or moist heat cookery, given the same approximate thickness and cut, most fish are enough alike that the methods for cooking one will work just as well with any other. The same is true for shellfish. The basic methods for cooking low-calorie seafood dishes are broiling, baking, sautéing, simmering, poaching, and steaming.

LOW-CALORIE DRY HEAT COOKING METHODS

Broiling

Broiling, which includes grilling and barbecuing, is a dry heat method of cooking fish fillets and steaks over or under an intense direct heat source. In classic cookery, broiled fish is always protected from the heat with either bastings of fat or with coatings of flour or breadcrumbs. In low-calorie preparation, however, basting fats and coatings are seldom used, not only because of their obviously high calorie count, but because they tend to seal in and absorb the inner fat of the fish that could be dissolved and eliminated, resulting in an even greater calorie savings. Basting is essential, but the broiling method can be made low calorie if wines, broths, and fruit juices are used as the basting liquid instead of the customary melted fats.

The easiest way to broil thin fish fillets and steaks is to sprinkle the top and bottom surfaces of the fish with seasonings and place them in a shallow preheated nonstick baking pan with just enough liquid added to keep the fish moist during cooking. In this way, the seafood is broiled by direct heat from the top and poached by moist heat from the cooking liquid. The seafood browns, but it doesn't lose any of its natural juices and flavor.

The actual cooking time for broiled fish depends upon the intensity of the heat and the thickness and temperature of the fillets or steaks. But in general, the average cooking time for a home broiler will range from five to ten minutes for a fish cut of three-quarter-inch thickness.

Just remember that because of the absence of protective fats or coatings, most standard recipes and timetables cannot be relied upon when you are preparing low-calorie fish items. When broiling fish, start testing for doneness after the first three minutes. The fish is done when the flesh is completely opaque and the meat is just beginning to flake when tested with a fork.

BASIC BROILING TECHNIQUES
1. *Preheat the broiler* ten minutes before cooking.
2. *Wash the fish* quickly in acidulated water (one tablespoon lemon juice to each quart of water) and pat dry with paper toweling.
3. *Season the fish* with salt, pepper, and paprika. In a shallow nonstick pan or skillet, arrange the fish in a single layer; sprinkle lightly with lemon juice and pour about one-fourth cup of liquid (wine, water, skim milk, etc.) into the pan.
4. *Broil the fish* close to the heat. The actual distance of the broiler pan from the flame depends on the thickness of the fish; the thinner the fish, the closer it should be to the source of heat.
5. *Baste the fish* occasionally with the pan juices. Do not attempt to turn the fish. Cook only long enough for the color to turn opaque.

BROILED FISH FILLETS OR STEAKS

1½ pounds thawed fish fillets or steaks, ¾-inch thick
salt and pepper
2 tablespoons diet margarine
2 tablespoons lemon juice
¼ cup dry white wine or water

Dry the fish with paper toweling; season with salt and pepper to taste. Brush the inside of an ovenproof nonstick skillet or baking dish with 1 tablespoon diet margarine. Place the fish in the pan; brush the top of the fish with the remaining margarine. Add lemon juice and wine.

Broil under moderate heat, 3 to 4 inches from source of heat until fish is golden brown and completely opaque, about 8 to 10 minutes. Do not turn fillets or steaks during broiling. Baste occasionally with juices to keep fish moist.

Makes 4 servings at 160 calories per serving.

Chef's Cooking Tip:
An excellent pan sauce can be made by removing the fish to a warm platter and reducing the pan juices down quickly over high heat. Minced shallots or green onions, herbs, and spices can be added for extra flavor.

BROILED LOBSTER TAILS

4 (7-ounce) rock lobster tails   4 tablespoons diet margarine

To broil lobster tails in the shell, "butterfly" them by cutting through the top shell with a sharp, heavy French knife. Don't cut all the way through the meat. Spread the shell open with the thumbs so the lobster tails will lie flat during broiling.

Set broiler heat at 350° F. Place lobster tails meat side up in a nonstick skillet or on a rack in broiler pan. Broil 4 to 5 inches from source of heat until lobster is completely opaque, about 15 minutes. Baste frequently with melted margarine.

Makes 4 servings at 220 calories per serving.

Chef's Cooking Tip:
South African, Australian, and New Zealand lobster tails have a better texture and flavor than their Northern Hemisphere cousins. This is due to the fact that they live in colder water and subsequently have more fat.

SEAFOOD SHISH KABOBS

8 large shrimps   8 chunks fresh pineapple
8 large scallops   4 mandarin orange sections
4 chunks rock lobster   ½ cup unsweetened pineapple
4 tomato wedges   juice
4 chunks green pepper   1 lemon
4 chunks onion

Thread assorted seafood chunks, fruits, and vegetables onto bamboo or metal skewers in desired combinations. Place kabobs in a nonstick skillet or baking pan. Place 5 to 6 inches from source of heat; broil under moderate heat until seafood is opaque throughout. Baste kabobs with a mixture of pineapple juice and lemon occasionally during cooking.

Makes 4 servings at 150 calories per serving.

Chef's Cooking Tip:
Mushrooms, tangerine sections, celery strips, grapefruit sections, and melon balls are just a few of the other fruits and vegetables that can be used in combination with seafood.

Baking

The easiest way to cook whole fish or thick-cut fish fillets and steaks is to bake them like a roast, uncovered, without liquid, in a moderately hot to hot oven. This dry heat method of fish cookery is especially adaptable to the cooking of fat fish which retain their moisture and need very little basting to help them brown. The lean, low-fat fish used extensively in low-calorie cooking can also be baked, but they require extra basting and added moisture to prevent them from drying out. For this reason, lean fish are often baked in a sauce or poaching liquid to produce moist "au gratin" dishes.

Seasonings, basting liquids, and marinades are a few of the ingredients in a recipe that can be altered to provide taste and flavor variations to baked fish. Sprinkling the pale surface of fish with paprika instead of basting with butter, for instance, is a low-calorie technique that encourages browning and adds color without adding unwanted calories.

Bake fish in a 350° F. to 400° F. oven, depending on its size, weight, and thickness (the lighter the fish, the hotter the oven) for approximately ten minutes per pound, or until the flesh is just beginning to flake when tested with a fork and when the color is opaque throughout.

BASIC BAKING TECHNIQUES

WHOLE FISH

1. *Scale the fish* and trim the fins close to the body so they won't char. Whenever possible, bake a whole fish with the head, tail, and fins intact in order to minimize the moisture and flavor losses.

2. *Wash the fish* quickly in acidulated water (one tablespoon lemon juice to each quart of water) and pat dry with paper toweling.

3. *Stuff the fish,* or bake it unstuffed. In low-calorie cooking, a flavorful garden vegetable stuffing is the recommended choice. Sew or skewer the cavity closed before baking.

4. *Bake the fish* in a moderate, preheated 350° F. oven, allowing approximately ten minutes per pound. Do not try to turn the fish while baking. To make the transfer of the fish to a serving platter after cooking, bake it on a sheet of heavy aluminum foil that has been coated with a food release agent.

5. *Baste the fish* frequently with dry white wine or lemon juice. Test for doneness with a fork or test with a thermometer by inserting it into the thickest part of the flesh. The fish is cooked when the internal temperature registered on the thermometer reads 145° to 150° F.

FISH FILLETS OR STEAKS

1. *Preheat oven* to 350° to 450° F., depending on the thickness of the fish cuts.

2. *Season the fish* on both sides with salt, pepper, and paprika. Place fish on spray-coated aluminum foil or in nonstick skillets or baking pans.

3. *Baste the fish* with dry white wine or lemon juice.

4. *Bake the fish,* uncovered, 10 to 25 minutes, or until it flakes easily when tested with a fork and is opaque throughout.

BAKED FISH FILLETS OR STEAKS

1½ pounds thawed fish fillets
   or steaks
1 tablespoon diet margarine,
   melted
1 tablespoon dry white wine

1 tablespoon fresh lemon juice
1 tablespoon minced onion
1 teaspoon paprika
salt and pepper

Rinse and dry fish with paper toweling. Place fish in a shallow nonstick baking dish. Combine the remaining ingredients and pour over fish. Bake, uncovered, in a moderate 350° F. oven for 20 to 30 minutes; baste several times during cooking until the fish is fork-tender and completely opaque.

Makes 4 servings at 155 calories per serving.

Chef's Cooking Tip:
Most cooks seem to favor salting a fish before cooking to improve its flavor.

BAKED FRESH SALMON STEAKS

4 (6-ounce) salmon steaks
4 thin onion slices
4 thin lemon slices
4 tablespoons fresh lemon juice

½ teaspoon paprika
¼ teaspoon garlic powder
   freshly chopped parsley

Place each salmon steak on an onion and lemon slice in a shallow baking dish. Combine lemon juice, paprika, and garlic powder and brush over fish. Bake, uncovered, in a preheated 350° F. oven for 20 to 30 minutes, or until fish is completely opaque.

Makes 4 servings at 240 calories per serving.

BAKED FISH CREOLE

1½ pounds fish fillets
2 tablespoons lemon juice
salt and pepper
¼ cup minced green onion
(white part only)
2 tablespoons chopped
green pepper
1 can (6-ounce) sliced
mushrooms, drained
½ cup dry sherry or white wine
½ teaspoon dill weed
½ cup stuffed green olives
1 tablespoon cornstarch
¼ cup water

If fillets are frozen, defrost before cooking. Dry fillets with paper toweling; baste with lemon juice, then season with salt and pepper. Sprinkle fillets with minced onion; roll up jelly-roll fashion. Secure with a toothpick; place the rolls in a nonstick baking pan; cover with mushrooms, green pepper, wine, dill weed, and sliced olives.

Bake, uncovered, in a 350° F. oven 20 to 30 minutes, or until fish flakes easily with a fork. Remove fillets to a warm platter. Blend the cornstarch and water; stir into baking dish. Simmer for 3 minutes until sauce is thickened and bubbly. Pour sauce over fillets and serve.

Makes 4 servings at 180 calories per serving.

BAKED FISH FILLETS ITALIANO

1½ pounds fish fillets, thawed
½ teaspoon whole oregano
1 teaspoon paprika
1 tablespoon diet margarine
1 minced garlic clove
½ cup chopped green onion
(white part only)
½ cup chopped celery
½ cup chopped green pepper
¼ cup tomato juice
1 cup peeled and diced, fresh or
canned tomatoes
salt and pepper

Dry fish fillets with paper toweling. Season with oregano; roll fillets up jelly-roll fashion; secure each fillet with a toothpick. Dust with paprika; arrange fish in a small shallow baking pan. Melt the margarine in a saucepan over medium heat; add the garlic, green onion, celery, and green pepper. Sauté over medium heat for 2 minutes. Add remaining ingredients and mix well. Add the sauce to the baking pan with the fish fillets; bake for 20 minutes in a preheated 350° F. oven until fillets are opaque throughout. Remove fillets carefully to individual serving plates. Serve ¼ cup sauce over each fillet. If the sauce is too runny, strain it through a sieve before serving.

Makes 4 servings at 190 calories per serving.

BAKED FISH FILLETS IN TOMATO SAUCE

1½ pounds fish fillets
   salt and pepper
1 small onion, chopped
1 small green pepper, chopped
1 can (14½-ounce) diced tomato
   in purée

½ teaspoon basil
½ teaspoon salt
⅛ teaspoon pepper

Thaw fillets if frozen; dry with paper toweling; season to taste with salt and pepper. Combine onion and pepper with ¼ cup water in a small saucepan. Cover; steam vegetables over moderate heat for 5 minutes. Drain. Add diced tomatoes and seasonings. Bring to a boil, stirring occasionally. Reduce heat and simmer, uncovered, for 10 minutes. Arrange fillets in a large nonstick skillet or baking dish. Spoon sauce over fish; bake, uncovered, in a 350° F. oven 20 to 30 minutes, or until fish flakes easily with a fork.

Makes 4 servings at 150 calories per serving.

Chef's Cooking Tip:
If a recipe calls for tomato purée, but you're out of it, try substituting equal parts of tomato sauce or one-third the amount of tomato paste mixed with water. Read the labels on the cans, however, and take into consideration any added seasonings and their effect on the recipe.

LOW-CALORIE BAKED FLOUNDER

1½ pounds flounder fillets
1 tablespoon diet margarine
¼ cup sliced green onion
   (white part only)
½ cup fresh mushrooms,
   chopped

1 teaspoon lemon juice
3 tablespoons dry white wine
1 tablespoon chopped parsley
   salt and pepper

Thaw fillets if frozen; dry with paper toweling. Season fillets with salt and pepper and place in a large ovenproof nonstick skillet or baking dish. Melt diet margarine in a small skillet over medium heat; add remaining ingredients. Sauté until mixture is thick and almost all of the liquid has evaporated, about 15 minutes. Preheat oven to 375° F. Pour vegetable mixture over fish; bake for 20 to 30 minutes or until fish flakes and is completely opaque throughout. Remove to platter and serve.

Makes 4 servings at 160 calories per serving.

Chef's Cooking Tip:
A *butterflied* fillet is both sides of a fish without bone but still connected by the skin of the fish's belly.

BAKED HALIBUT STEAKS

1½ pounds halibut steaks
1 large onion, thinly sliced
2 large tomatoes, peeled, seeded and diced
¼ pound fresh mushrooms, chopped
¼ cup green pepper, chopped
3 tablespoons fresh parsley, chopped
3 tablespoons pimento, chopped
3 tablespoons fresh lemon juice
6 ounces dry white wine
¼ teaspoon dill weed
salt and pepper
paprika

Place halibut steaks on sliced onion in a large ovenproof nonstick skillet or baking dish. Add remaining ingredients over fish; bake, uncovered, in a 350° F. oven for 20 to 30 minutes, or until fish flakes easily and is opaque throughout.

Makes 4 servings at 220 calories per serving.

Chef's Cooking Tip:
For best results, all fish, except frozen breaded fillets, should be thawed before cooking. Thawing for about 12 hours in the refrigerator is the best method, both for flavor and for safety.

BAKED WHOLE RED SNAPPER

1 (3-pound) red snapper
⅓ cup lemon juice
  water
  salt and pepper
2 large tomatoes, peeled, seeded, and diced
2 large onions, diced
½ teaspoon dill weed
½ cup dry white wine
2 tablespoons diet margarine
  freshly chopped parsley

Place dressed fish in a shallow baking dish. Add lemon juice and enough water to cover. Marinate, covered, in the refrigerator 2 to 4 hours. Remove from refrigerator one half hour before cooking. Drain, reserving ½ cup of marinade. Season fish inside and out with salt and pepper. Lay fish on diced vegetables in a large baking dish. Add dill weed, wine, margarine and reserved marinade liquid. Cover tightly; bake in a moderate 350° F. oven for about 1 hour, or until fish flakes easily. Garnish with freshly chopped parsley.

Makes 4 servings at 160 calories per serving.

Chef's Cooking Tip:
For true dry-heat baking, cook uncovered at 350° F., but baste frequently with pan juices.

BAKED FILLET OF SOLE

¼ cup dry sherry
1 cup sliced fresh mushrooms
1½ pounds sole fillets
  salt and pepper
1 medium onion, sliced
⅓ cup skim milk
1 tablespoon lemon juice
1 teaspoon Worcestershire sauce
1 teaspoon imitation butter flavoring
paprika

Heat dry sherry in a small nonstick skillet; add mushrooms; cover for 3 minutes; uncover and sauté over high heat until liquid is evaporated. Rinse and dry sole fillets with paper toweling. Place in a large ovenproof nonstick skillet or baking pan. Season with salt and pepper; add sliced onions and mushrooms. Mix milk, lemon juice, Worcestershire sauce, and imitation butter flavoring in a small bowl; pour over fillets. Bake, uncovered, in a moderate 350° F. oven for 20 to 25 minutes, basting several times during cooking until fish is completely opaque.

Makes 4 servings at 160 calories per serving.

Chef's Cooking Tip:
For unsurpassed taste and texture, buy English or Dover sole.

FILLET OF SOLE BONNE FEMME

1½ pounds sole fillets
  salt and pepper
2 tablespoons minced shallots
2 tablespoons freshly chopped parsley

1 cup minced mushrooms
½ cup dry vermouth or wine
juice of 1 lemon
¼ teaspoon thyme

Dry sole fillets and season on both sides with salt and pepper; set aside. Combine remaining ingredients in a shallow baking dish. Fold fillets crosswise, smooth side in, and arrange on top of vegetables. Heat dish on top of range until liquid is just boiling. Remove to a preheated 350° F. oven and bake, uncovered, for 10 to 12 minutes, or until fillets are completely opaque. Transfer fillets to a heated serving platter with a slotted spoon. Drain mushroom mixture and add to fillets. Spoon prepared fish sauce over fillets, garnish with a dash of paprika or a sprinkling of parsley. Serve immediately.

SAUCE
½ cup skim milk
½ cup bottled clam juice
⅛ teaspoon turmeric

2 tablespoons cold water
1 tablespoon cornstarch
  salt and white pepper to taste

In a small heavy saucepan, combine milk, clam juice and turmeric. Bring just to the boil. Dissolve cornstarch in cold water; stir slowly into liquid and cook, stirring until sauce returns to the boil. Season to taste with salt and white pepper and serve.

Makes 4 servings at 175 calories per serving.

FILLET OF SOLE DUGLERE

1½ pounds sole fillets
¼ cup scallions, green and white portions
1 clove garlic, minced
2 medium-size tomatoes, peeled and diced
2 tablespoons freshly chopped parsley

¼ teaspoon salt
⅛ teaspoon pepper
½ cup dry white wine
½ cup bottled clam juice or water

Dry sole fillets with paper toweling. Season lightly with salt and white pepper; set aside. Combine remaining ingredients in a shallow baking dish. Arrange fish on top of vegetables, either rolled or folded, smooth side in. Heat dish on top of range until liquid is just boiling. Remove to oven and bake in a preheated 350° F. oven for 10 to 12 minutes, or until fillets are completely opaque. Transfer fillets to a heated serving platter with a slotted spoon. Garnish with a dash of paprika or a sprinkling of chopped parsley and serve.

Makes 4 servings at 165 calories per serving.

BAKED TROUT AU GRATIN

4 (5- to 6-ounce) pan-dressed trout
salt
2 tablespoons lemon juice
1 clove garlic, minced
½ cup dry white wine
½ cup water
2 tablespoons minced shallots
2 tablespoons chopped parsley
2 tablespoons dry bread crumbs
paprika

Preheat oven to 400° F. Thaw fish if frozen; rinse inside and out; pat dry with paper toweling. Season with salt, pepper, and lemon juice. Place fish in a large nonstick baking pan. Add minced garlic, wine, water, and shallots. Bake, uncovered, for 15 minutes; baste occasionally with pan juices. Remove pan from oven. Sprinkle with remaining ingredients. Reheat in oven or under broiler about 2 minutes to brown bread crumbs and serve.

Makes 4 servings at 200 calories per serving.

Chef's Cooking Tip:
Pan-size trout are usually served with the head and tail intact, but they can be removed before cooking, if desired.

BAKED TROUT IN WINE SAUCE

4 (5- to 6-ounce) pan-dressed trout
salt and pepper
2 tablespoons minced shallots
½ teaspoon dill weed
1 tablespoon lemon juice
½ cup dry white wine
½ cup water

Thaw fish if frozen. Rinse inside and out; pat dry with paper toweling. Season with salt and pepper to taste. Place fish in a large nonstick baking dish. Add remaining ingredients and bake, uncovered, at 400° F. for 20 minutes, or until fish is opaque throughout and its flesh flakes easily with a fork. Remove fish to a warm platter. Place baking dish on top of the stove and reduce cooking liquid over high heat to thicken. Pour thickened sauce over trout and serve immediately.

Makes 4 servings at 190 calories per serving.

Chef's Cooking Tip:
To prevent whole, steaked, or filleted fish from sticking to the bottom of a baking dish or skillet during baking, coat the surface, nonstick, glass or metal alike, with a food release agent.

Sautéing

In fish cookery, fish cooked *à la meunière*, which means "in the manner of the miller's wife," is the best example of a basic sauté. The fish is dusted with flour, then quickly sautéed until golden brown. The cooking is done in a matter of minutes, leaving the skin crisp and golden while the flesh remains tender and moist. Very simple indeed!

The important points to remember about sautéing fish are: (1) the fish must be free of excess moisture (thus the light dusting of flour); (2) the pan must be large enough to accommodate the fish without crowding; and (3) the oil must be hot enough at all times during the cooking process. Unless all these basic rules are adhered to, the surface of the fish will not be seared and the internal juices will leak out. If this happens, the fish will steam in their own juices, rather than brown and subsequently stick to the bottom of the pan.

What has always made sautéed fish recipes so prohibitive, of course, has been the amount of high-calorie fats and oils used for searing. By using nonstick cookware, the amount of oil can be cut in half—and so can the calories.

BASIC SAUTÉING TECHNIQUES
1. *Wash the fish* in acidulated water (one tablespoon lemon juice to each quart of water): pat dry thoroughly with paper toweling.
2. *Season the fish* with salt and pepper.
3. *Coat the fish* lightly and evenly with flour.
4. *Sauté the fish* over medium heat in a nonstick skillet with one to two tablespoons oil or a combination of oil and butter until a light golden brown on one side. Turn fish carefully and continue to cook until golden brown on the second side, or until the fish is completely opaque. Do not overcook.
5. *Remove the fish* to a warm platter. Garnish with chopped parsley, lemon wedges, and additional seasonings, if desired.

SAUTÉED FILLET OF SOLE À LA MEUNIÈRE

1½ pounds fillets of sole
salt and pepper
2 tablespoons flour
paprika
1 tablespoon cooking oil
1 tablespoon diet margarine
½ teaspoon fresh lemon juice
½ teaspoon freshly chopped parsley

If frozen, thaw fish completely; pat dry before cooking. Season fillets with salt and pepper. Dust with flour; discard excess. Sprinkle with paprika. Heat oil in a large nonstick skillet; add fillets. Saute quickly over medium-high heat until golden brown. Remove fillets to a warm platter. Add margarine to skillet; allow to brown slightly. Add lemon juice and blend into juices. Pour sauce over fillets. Garnish with chopped parsley and serve.

Makes 4 servings at 210 calories per serving.

Chef's Cooking Tip:
To insure proper browning, be sure that the fillets are at room temperature before they are placed in the hot skillet. Chilled fillets will cool the skillet and the fish will steam in their own juices.

SAUTÉED FILLET OF SOLE À L'ANGLAISE

1½ pounds fillets of sole
   salt and pepper
2 tablespoons flour
1 egg, slightly beaten

1 tablespoon skim milk or water
1 cup dry white cracker crumbs
2 tablespoons cooking oil

   If frozen, thaw completely; pat dry before cooking. Season with salt and pepper. Dust with flour and discard excess. Stir milk gently into slightly beaten egg. Dip each fillet into egg mixture; drain, then roll into crumbs to coat evenly on all sides. Pat with back of hand to dislodge excess crumbs. Carefully place coated fillets on a rack to dry at room temperature for 15 minutes before cooking. Heat oil in nonstick skillet; add fillets without crowding. Sauté over medium-high heat until golden brown on one side, about 4 minutes. Turn carefully and sauté about 4 minutes longer.

Makes 4 servings at 365 calories per serving.

Chef's Cooking Tip:
   In French cuisine, breaded foods are considered English style, or *à l'anglaise.*

SAUTÉED FILLET OF SOLE

1½ pounds fillets of sole
   salt and pepper
2 tablespoons flour

paprika
1 tablespoon cooking oil

   If frozen, thaw completely; pat dry before cooking. Season fillets with salt and pepper. Dust with flour; discard excess. Sprinkle with paprika. Heat oil in a large nonstick skillet; add fillets. Sauté quickly over moderate-high heat until golden brown. Serve immediately.

Makes 4 servings at 195 calories per serving.

Chef's Cooking Tip:
   Cooking oil is used to coat the skillet because of its higher smoking point in comparison to butter or margarine; thus the fish can be cooked at a high enough temperature to seal in the juices without danger of burning or sticking.

STIR-FRIED SHRIMP WITH SNOW PEAS

INGREDIENTS:
- 2 tablespoons cooking oil
- ¼ teaspoon salt
- 1 whole garlic clove, peeled and halved
- 1 pound medium-size shrimp, peeled and deveined
- 1 package (10-ounce) frozen pea pods, partially thawed
- 2 celery ribs, thinly sliced
- ½ cup water chestnuts, thinly sliced

SAUCE:
- 1 teaspoon grated fresh ginger root
- 1 teaspoon cornstarch
- 2 tablespoons soy sauce
- 1 tablespoon dry sherry
- ⅓ cup cold chicken broth

In a small bowl, combine sauce ingredients; set aside. Heat 1 tablespoon oil in a large nonstick skillet or wok over high heat; add salt. Add garlic and shrimp. Stir-fry for about 2 minutes, or until shrimp becomes opaque and firm. Remove shrimp to a platter; discard garlic clove. Reheat pan. Add remaining tablespoon oil, then vegetables. Stir-fry vegetables for 2 minutes. Return shrimp to pan. Restir sauce and pour into pan slowly, stirring constantly until liquid thickens and clears, about 1 minute. Serve immediately.

Makes 4 servings at 185 calories per serving.

STIR-FRIED SWEET AND SOUR SHRIMP

INGREDIENTS:
- 2 tablespoons cooking oil
- 1 pound medium-size shrimp, peeled and deveined
- 1 can (8¼-ounce) pineapple slices, drained
- 1 large onion
- 1 large green pepper
- 1 celery rib

SAUCE:
- 1 cup unsweetened pineapple juice
- ¼ cup brown sugar
- ¼ cup cider vinegar
- 2 tablespoons tomato sauce
- 1 teaspoon grated fresh ginger root

THICKENER:
- 1 tablespoon cornstarch
- 2 tablespoons soy sauce

In a small bowl, combine cornstarch and soy sauce; set aside. Cut pineapple, onion, celery, and pepper in uniform-size pieces. Heat oil in a large nonstick skillet or wok over high heat. Add shrimp and vegetables and stir-fry for 2 minutes. Add sauce ingredients; bring to a boil. Restir cornstarch mixture and pour slowly into skillet. Stir constantly until liquid thickens and clears. Serve immediately.

Makes 4 servings at 245 calories per serving.

LOW-CALORIE MOIST HEAT COOKING METHODS

Boiling

Boiling is a moist heat method of cooking fish completely submerged in liquid. And although we never think of it as such, it is actually a low temperature method of cookery—the boiling point of water never exceeding 212°F. (or 100°C.) except when under pressure.

Where fish are concerned, the terms boiling, simmering, and poaching are practically synonymous. They are all methods of cooking fish in liquid *below* the boiling point. The only major difference among them lies in the amount of liquid used and the cooking temperature. As cooking processes, however, simmering and poaching are technically only various stages of boiling.

Fish submerged in a *large* amount of water or "court bouillon" and simmered just below the boiling point is said to be boiled. This method is usually used to cook large whole fish, fish chunks, thick steaks, and shellfish. After cooking, the liquid is usually discarded.

On the other hand, fish barely immersed in a *small* amount of liquid, covered, and slowly simmered on top of the stove or in the oven is poached fish. This method is used for small fish fillets and steaks. After cooking, the liquid is almost always reduced over a high flame. The resulting *fumet* can be blended with skim milk to make a sauce or it can be reduced further over high heat to make an emulsified glaze.

BASIC BOILING TECHNIQUES

1. *Make a court bouillon* in a fish poacher. A court bouillon is made with water, dry white wine, vinegar or lemon juice, aromatic vegetables, herbs, and seasonings. Bring the poaching liquid to a boil; simmer for at least 15 minutes, then allow to cool.

2. *Clean the fish* under cold running water; dry thoroughly.

3. *Wrap the fish* in a piece of wetted cheesecloth, leaving the ends long enough to use as handles so that the fish can be removed from the hot liquid without it separating.

4. *Lower the fish into the cool liquid.* If the fish is not covered with the court bouillon, add a little more water. Bring the liquid back to a boil, immediately reduce the heat to a simmer, then cover and cook for 5 to 8 minutes per pound. There is an exception to this step: If the fish is cut into chunks or thick steaks, bring the court bouillon to a boil *before* lowering the fish into it. This, in effect, sears the cut surfaces and helps the fish retain its natural flavor.

5. *Remove the fish* from the simmering liquid; allow to drain. Place on a warm platter. Carefully remove the cheesecloth from the upper surface. Remove the skin; with a thin, sharp knife, scrape away the darkened fatty flesh that lies directly under the skin. Carefully turn the fish over and repeat for the other side.

6. *Garnish the fish* with parsley, watercress, lime or lemon wedges. Serve immediately. To serve cold, wrap the fish in a cheesecloth that has been dampened in the court bouillon, or wrap it with clear plastic wrap and refrigerate until needed.

BOILED LOBSTER TAILS

4 (7-ounce) lobster tails
1 gallon water
1 tablespoon salt

½ cup dry white wine
½ lemon

Combine water, wine, salt, and lemon wedges in a large kettle. Bring liquid to a boil. Drop lobster tails into kettle, either thawed or frozen. When liquid reboils, reduce heat and allow lobster to simmer, uncovered, until opaque throughout. This will take from 5 to 8 minutes. Drain. When cool enough to handle, cut down each side of the thin underside membrane with kitchen shears and remove membrane. To remove meat, insert thumb and fork between shell and meat at the heavy end of the tail. Pull firmly, separating shell and meat in one place. Serve hot or cold with appropriate low-calorie sauce.

Makes 4 servings at 185 calories per serving.

BOILED SALMON

1 (3-pound) salmon
3 quarts water
½ cup vinegar
2 onions, chopped
2 carrots, chopped
1 celery rib, chopped

8 parsley stems
8 peppercorns
3 cloves
1 bay leaf
1 tablespoon salt
⅛ teaspoon thyme

Wrap cleaned salmon in a piece of wetted cheesecloth. In a fish poacher or large Dutch oven, add all the ingredients to make a court bouillon. Bring water to boiling; reduce heat. Simmer, uncovered, for 1 hour. Add more water if necessary to cover fish. Gently lower salmon into the court bouillon. Simmer covered until fish flakes easily with a fork, about 20 minutes. Remove salmon; drain. Remove skin and bones. Garnish with parsley sprigs and lemon slices and serve.

Makes 4 servings at 240 calories per serving.

BOILED SHRIMP

1 tablespoon pickling spice
6 peppercorns, crushed
1 lemon wedge
2 quarts water

½ cup dry white wine
1 tablespoon salt
1½ pounds raw shrimp

Tie pickling spice, peppercorns, and lemon wedge in a 5-inch square of wetted cheesecloth. Combine with remaining ingredients, except shrimp, in a large saucepan; bring to a rapid boil. Add shrimp; return water to the simmer, and simmer about 5 minutes, or until opaque throughout. Don't overcook.

Makes 4 servings at 180 calories per serving.

Chef's Cooking Tip:
Frozen shrimp in the shell (also called "green shrimp") should be thawed slowly in the refrigerator; rinse quickly under cold running water before using.

Poaching

As I have partially outlined in the previous chapter, poaching is a variation of boiling. It is a moist heat method of simmering small fish fillets and steaks in a small amount of liquid—usually a combination of water or stock with wine, vinegar, lemon juice, aromatic vegetables, herbs, and seasonings. This poaching liquid is called a court bouillon and is almost always reduced after the fish is removed to make a flavorful low-calorie sauce.

To poach fish, combine the poaching liquid called for in the recipe and any flavoring ingredients in a shallow, wide skillet. Bring the liquid to a boil and cook for a half hour. Lower the heat, place the fillets or steaks in the court bouillon, return the liquid to a simmer and continue to cook, covered, until the flesh is opaque throughout and begins to flake easily when tested with a fork, usually five to ten minutes.

To prevent delicate-fleshed fish like flounder or sole from breaking apart, they are usually poached in a minimum amount of liquid and are technically poached from the bottom and steamed from the top at the same time. Spray one side of a sheet of waxed paper or parchment cut to fit the skillet with noncaloric cookware spray and place it, sprayed side down, on the surface of the fish. Be sure to cut a small vent hole in the center of the poaching paper to allow excess steam to escape.

The important thing to remember is that the liquid must never boil after the fish is in the liquid or it will cook too quickly and fall apart.

BASIC POACHING TECHNIQUES

1. *Place fish in skillet* that has been coated with a noncaloric cookware spray. Season with salt and pepper.

2. *Add poaching liquid to the skillet,* using just enough liquid to barely cover the fish; then bring the liquid to a simmer. The poaching liquid may be plain or salted water, nonfat milk, or a *court bouillon* (literally, a short stock). In many recipes, a court bouillon is made in the skillet before the fish is added. A simple court bouillon is made with water, wine, vinegar, or lemon juice with aromatic vegetables, herbs, and seasoning being added for further flavoring. Use two tablespoons wine to each one-half cup of water. Add whatever ingredients the recipe calls for and boil, uncovered, for one-half hour. When the court bouillon is ready, place the fish in the skillet, add more water if necessary to keep the liquid above the fish, and readjust the heat so the poaching liquid is just simmering.

3. *Cover the skillet* and let the fish poach for five to ten minutes, or until it flakes easily with a fork.

4. *Remove the fish from the skillet* and place on a warm platter. Reduce the poaching liquid over a high flame by two-thirds.

5. *Strain reduced liquid from skillet* over the fish. Garnish with parsley, paprika, and lemon wedges. Serve immediately.

BASIC POACHED FISH

1½ pounds fish fillets
1 tablespoon diet margarine
¼ cup minced onion
¼ cup dry white wine
½ cup water
1 tablespoon lemon juice
½ teaspoon salt
⅛ teaspoon pepper
⅛ teaspoon dill weed

Melt diet margarine in a large nonstick skillet over medium heat; add minced onion and sauté for 3 minutes. Place fillets carefully in skillet; add the remaining ingredients. Cover lightly with foil or parchment paper, and simmer over low heat until fish is fork tender and completely opaque, about 10 minutes. Baste fillets occasionally with pan juices. Do not turn fillets during cooking. Remove fillets to a warm serving platter. Reduce pan juices over high heat and spoon over fish.

Makes 4 servings at 160 calories per serving.

LOBSTER EN CASSEROLE

1½ pounds lobster tail
1 cup tomato juice
1 green pepper, chopped
1 onion, chopped
2 celery ribs, chopped
1 cup sliced zucchini
3 ripe tomatoes, peeled, seeded and chopped
1 can (4 ounce) drained mushrooms
1 teaspoon salt
½ teaspoon each: pepper, oregano, and garlic powder
1 tablespoon cornstarch
2 tablespoons water

Combine lobster, tomato juice, green pepper, onion, celery, zucchini, mushrooms, salt, pepper, oregano, and garlic powder in a large nonstick skillet or Dutch oven. Cover lightly; simmer over medium heat until vegetables are tender and lobster meat is cooked, about 8 to 10 minutes. Stir occasionally. Add chopped tomatoes; cover and simmer until heated through. Blend cornstarch and water in a small dish. Stir into heated casserole and cook until thickened and bubbly.

Makes 6 servings at 150 calories per serving.

Chef's Cooking Tip:
If you have lobster or other seafoods already cooked, you can make the casserole ahead of time and add the seafood the last 5 minutes of cooking to heat through.

POACHED HALIBUT STEAKS

4 (6-ounce) halibut steaks
1 small onion, peeled and sliced
1 tablespoon fresh lemon juice
1 tablespoon freshly chopped parsley
½ cup dry white wine
½ cup water
½ teaspoon tarragon
salt and pepper to taste

Place halibut steaks in nonstick skillet. Add remaining ingredients and bring to a boil. Cover skillet and simmer over low heat for about 10 minutes until completely opaque.

Makes 4 servings at 160 calories per serving.

DELICIOUS PICKLED SALMON

1¼ pounds salmon steaks or fillets
2 small onions, thinly sliced
1 teaspoon salt
1 teaspoon whole pickling spice
½ teaspoon crushed peppercorns
¾ cup red wine vinegar
½ cup water
1 tablespoon sugar

Place the salmon slices in the bottom of a small glass casserole dish; add remaining ingredients. Cover tightly and refrigerate several hours or overnight. Remove salmon from marinade to a large nonstick skillet. Strain marinade into a small saucepan and bring to a boil. Pour over salmon, cover lightly and poach fish gently for 10 to 15 minutes.

To serve hot: Remove salmon from skillet and garnish with parsley sprigs, watercress, or lemon wedges.

To serve cold: Remove skillet from range before salmon is completely cooked and allow fish to cool in its own liquid. The texture of cooked salmon changes considerably when it is refrigerated.

Makes 4 servings at 205 calories per serving.

SCOTCH SALMON

4 (6-ounce) salmon steaks
1 onion, chopped
1 carrot, chopped
1 celery rib, chopped
2 tablespoons diet margarine
1 cup water
½ cup dry white wine
4 peppercorns, crushed
2 cloves
1 bay leave
1 teaspoon salt

In a 10-inch nonstick skillet, sauté chopped onions, carrots, and celery over medium heat in diet margarine for 3 minutes. Add remaining ingredients, except salmon; cover and simmer 5 minutes. Carefully place salmon steaks in skillet. Cover and simmer for 8 to 10 minutes, or until fish flakes easily with a fork. Transfer salmon carefully to a heated platter and serve. To serve cold, chill the salmon in the stock.

Makes 4 servings at 225 calories per serving.

POACHED BAY SCALLOPS

2 packages (10-ounce) frozen bay scallops, thawed
2 ounces dry white wine
2 ounces clam broth (canned or bottled)
2 tablespoons lemon juice
2 parsley stems
2 cloves
1 bay leaf
4 peppercorns, crushed
salt to taste
paprika

Combine wine, clam broth, lemon juice, parsley stems, cloves, bay leaf, and peppercorns in a large nonstick skillet; bring to a boil. Add scallops and any thawing liquid; add salt to taste. If necessary add just enough water to barely cover the scallops. Cover; bring back to boil, then reduce heat and simmer about 5 minutes, or until scallops lose their transparency. Remove the scallops to a warm platter. Reduce the poaching liquid over high heat until reduced by two-thirds. Strain sauce over scallops and serve hot or allow to cool in broth, then cover and refrigerate.

Makes 4 servings at 150 calories per serving.

Chef's Cooking Tip:
Because scallops are so tender, they should be cooked quickly so the delicate flavor is sealed in by the higher heat.

POACHED FILLET OF SOLE

1½ pounds fillet of sole
¼ cup diced onion
¼ cup diced celery
1 small bay leaf
1 tablespoon lemon juice
1 tablespoon vinegar
1 teaspoon salt
4 peppercorns, crushed
freshly chopped parsley

Place all ingredients except fillets and parsley in a small saucepan; add 1 cup water and simmer 15 minutes or longer to blend flavors. Arrange fillets in a large nonstick skillet. Strain the court bouillon over the fillets; simmer, covered lightly with foil or parchment paper, until the fish is opaque. Remove carefully from skillet; garnish with chopped parsley and serve.

Makes 4 servings at 160 calories per serving.

POACHED FILLET OF SOLE IN MILK

1½ pounds fillet of sole or flounder
½ cup skim milk
½ teaspoon butter-flavored salt
1 tablespoon diet margarine
1 small bay leaf
¼ cup green onion, sliced

Thaw fish fillets; pat dry with paper toweling. Combine milk, butter-flavored salt, margarine, and bay leaf in a large nonstick skillet; bring to a boil. Gently place fish fillets in the skillet; sprinkle with sliced onions. Cover and simmer for 5 minutes, or until opaque.

Makes 4 servings at 160 calories per serving.

Steaming
Steaming—used extensively in Chinese cookery—is a quick cooking, moist heat method of preparing fish in a tightly covered utensil over boiling water. Although not as popular a cooking method as poaching, it is, nevertheless, one of the best ways to capture the natural taste and flavor of delicate, lean fish. It is also ideally suited to low-calorie cooking because the gentle heat leaves the fish (and especially shellfish) so moist and tender that the thick sauces or bastings of fat so often accompanying fish entrées become unnecessary. I doubt if there is any seafood dish (at least I haven't found it) that surpasses the taste and succulence of a Maine lobster steamed over boiling seawater. Any steamed fish, of course, can be served hot or cold, and you'll find steaming to be an excellent method for reheating any cooked fish.

To steam fish and shellfish, bring a small amount of water to a boil in the bottom of a steam cooker. Place the seafood on the steamer rack (spray the rack with a food release agent to prevent sticking), cover it tightly and steam for one minute for each ounce of weight. If you don't have a steam cooker, a wok or any heavy deep saucepan that can be fitted with a rack to prevent the seafood from touching the water will do. Just be sure that the pan is covered tightly—and don't overcook!

BASIC STEAMING TECHNIQUES
1. *Coat steamer insert,* rack, or pan with a food release agent.
2. *Place the fish on the insert pan*; season to taste.
3. *Add water to pan* below the level of the insert; bring to a boil.
4. *Place the insert over the boiling water*; cover tightly and steam fish about five to ten minutes (one minute per ounce) or until fish flakes easily when tested with a fork. The water should remain boiling the entire time.
5. *Serve the fish hot* sprinkled with lemon or lime juice, or allow to cool and use cold in recipes calling for cooked fish.

STEAMED FISH FILLETS

1 pound fish fillets
1 tablespoon diet margarine
1 large onion, sliced
½ teaspoon paprika
½ teaspoon salt
½ cup dry white wine

If fish fillets are frozen, defrost thoroughly. Melt diet margarine in a large nonstick skillet. Add onion, paprika and salt; sauté over medium heat for 3 minutes. Add wine; cover and simmer 3 minutes longer. Uncover; carefully place fish fillets on onion slices. Cover and simmer over low heat for about 8 minutes, or until fish is completely opaque. Carefully remove fillets to a warm platter and cover with onion slices. Reduce pan juices quickly over high heat and spoon over fish.

Makes 3 servings at 170 calories per serving.

STEAMED FISH FILLETS OR STEAKS (THICK CUTS)

1½ pounds thawed fish fillets or steaks
3 cups boiling water
salt and pepper

Coat the surface of a steamer rack with a food release agent. Place the fish fillets or steaks on the rack; season to taste with salt and pepper. Place rack in a pan over rapidly boiling water; cover tightly. Let fish steam about 10 minutes, or until fish flakes easily with a fork. Be sure that the fish does not touch the boiling water.

Makes 4 servings at 140 calories per serving.

STEAMED ROCK COD

1 (3-pound) whole rock cod
2 cups dry white wine
2 cups water
1 onion, chopped
2 celery ribs, chopped
1 bay leaf
6 peppercorns, crushed
½ teaspoon dill weed
½ teaspoon salt

Clean and dress fish. With a sharp knife, make two or three diagonal cuts on both sides of fish, through the skin and flesh, but not quite down to the backbone. Place the remaining ingredients in a fish steamer; bring to a boil. Wrap fish in cheesecloth. Place on a rack over boiling court bouillon. Cover and simmer from 15 to 20 minutes, or until fish is firm and opaque and flakes easily to a fork. Garnish with parsley and lemon slices. Serve hot, or allow to cool, then cover and refrigerate in court bouillon.

Makes 4 servings at 140 calories per serving.

STEAMED HALIBUT STEAKS IN FOIL

4 (6-ounce) halibut steaks
4 thin slices onion
4 tablespoons fresh lemon juice
1 tablespoon butter or margarine
½ teaspoon dill weed
salt and pepper to taste
paprika

Thaw steaks if frozen. Cut 4 pieces of heavy-duty aluminum foil, 12 by 12 inches each. Place a slice of onion on each piece of foil. Top each with a halibut steak and season with the remaining ingredients. Fold the foil over the fish and seal each package well by folding over and over, creasing each time, until foil rests firmly on fish. There must be no openings for juices or steam to escape. Place packages in a preheated 450° F. oven for 10 to 15 minutes, or until opaque. Serve immediately.

Makes 4 servings at 160 calories per serving.

Chef's Cooking Tip:
To prevent fish or other foods from sticking to foil, either spray the foil with a food release agent or place vegetables in direct contact with foil and food.

STEAMED LOBSTER TAILS

4 (7-ounce) lobster tails, thawed
1 cup water
1 teaspoon salt
2 tablespoons diet margarine
dash paprika

Place tails on cutting board, shell side up. With the point of a large French knife, stab the tail to the cutting board at the base of the fanned tail; cut down and cut the top shell in half lengthwise without cutting into the meat. Spread the shells apart. Loosen the meat from the bottom membrane with your thumb; pull the meat through the top shell, leaving the meat attached to the shell at the tail. Close the shell halves and lay the meat on top. The shell will act as a rack to keep the meat out of the liquid for proper steaming.

Place the tails upright in a deep skillet. Add the water and salt. Cover and steam over medium-high heat until the meat is opaque, about 10 minutes. Don't overcook or lobster will toughen.

Remove the cover from skillet, brush lobster with margarine; sprinkle with paprika. Place skillet under broiler for 1 minute to brown surface. Remove from broiler and serve.

Makes 4 servings at 220 calories per serving.

STEAMED RAINBOW TROUT IN FOIL

4 rainbow trout, with heads left on
4 thin slices onion
    salt and pepper
½ cup chopped green onions
½ cup freshly chopped parsley
1 teaspoon tarragon
4 tablespoons fresh lemon juice
1 tablespoon butter or margarine
½ cup dry white wine

Thaw trout if frozen. Rinse under cold water and pat dry with paper toweling. Season the inside of each trout with salt and pepper. Combine the green onions, parsley, and tarragon. Place an equal amount of this mixture inside each trout. Cut 4 pieces of heavy-duty aluminum foil, 12 by 16 inches each. On each piece of foil place a slice of onion. Top each with a trout, then season each with lemon juice, butter or margarine, and wine. Wrap in foil by folding over and over, creasing each time, until foil rests firmly on fish. Place packages in a preheated 450° F. oven for 10 to 15 minutes, or until flesh is opaque. Serve immediately.

Makes 4 servings at 280 calories per serving.

Chef's Cooking Tip:
Other aromatic vegetables, herbs, or spices can be added for variation: mushrooms, carrots, celery, green peppers, thyme, and dry vermouth are just some of the alternatives.

VEGETABLES

The importance of fresh vegetables in our diets is so well documented it would be difficult to find any American who is not aware of it. And yet it's ironic, when you consider the year-round availability of most every variety of produce, that year after year we are deriving a smaller percentage of our total food energy from this vital category of food.

Vegetables should certainly be the mainstay of our diet, for they possess all the essential nutrients—proteins, carbohydrates, fats, vitamins, and minerals—needed by the human body. For the dieter, they also have the benefit of being filling as well as relatively low in calories.

But no matter how fresh or nutritious vegetables are before they are prepared, it's the ingredients and cooking techniques used in cooking them that ultimately determines their final flavor, nutritional, and caloric value.

VEGETABLE CLASSIFICATION

The preparation and cooking of vegetables as food is universal. Their varieties are endless and their versatility unique. They are served in all parts of the meal, from appetizer to dessert, or used as a garnishment for other foods. And while the names and appearance of vegetables found throughout the world may differ, you'll find that most can be cooked by the basic methods outlined in this chapter. All that's required is to learn the particular characteristics of the various categories of vegetables and apply the proper cooking techniques to them.

Vegetables are the edible parts of plants and can be classified as such—roots, stems, leaves, flowers, or seeds. They can also be categorized according to seasons—*summer* or warm-season vegetables and *winter* or cool-season vegetables. From a cook's standpoint, however, I prefer to classify them as they are marketed or processed for storage—*fresh, frozen, canned,* or *dried.*

Fresh, frozen, and canned vegetables are classified by color: green, red, yellow, and white. Dried vegetables are divided into legumes and cereal grains.

FRESH VEGETABLES

Green Vegetables

Like other types of vegetation, the green color in vegetables is due to a pigment called chlorophyll. Chlorophyll, however, becomes very unstable in alkali or acid solutions when heated. Alkali intensifies the green color in vegetables, but it has an adverse affect on their nutrients and texture. If acid is present (most vegetables contain a high percentage of organic acid which dissolves in the cooking water), the green gradually changes to an unattractive olive green.

Red Vegetables

The red color in vegetables (beets, red cabbage, etc.) is due to a class of water-soluble pigments called anthocyanins, and the affect of alkali or acid on these pigments is just the opposite to that of green vegetables when heat is applied. The presence of acid intensifies the red color, while an alkali solution will turn the vegetables a blue-gray or, if present long enough, will bleach the color out entirely.

Yellow Vegetables

Yellow vegetables (carrots, corn, squash, sweet potatoes, rutabagas, etc.) obtain their yellow-orange color from a pigment called carotin. Unlike chlorophyll and anthocyanin, carotin is not affected by alkali when heated, thus yellow vegetables will keep their natural color unless overcooked.

White Vegetables

White vegetables (white cabbage, white onions, turnips, cauliflower, etc.) contain crystalline compound substances called flavones. Although colorless, white vegetables will turn brownish gray to yellow when cooked in hard, alkaline water or if overcooked. A small amount of acid (usually vinegar or lemon juice) should be added to the cooking water to counteract the alkalinity and keep the vegetables white.

FROZEN VEGETABLES

The freezing process captures the ripeness of fresh vegetables and preserves and extends their food value and flavors. It also makes an infinite variety of off-season vegetables available to us the year around. Using frozen vegetables is also convenient: Since they are partially cooked as part of the freezing process they are usually ready to serve in less than ten minutes. And although we usually pay more for convenience foods, frozen vegetables can be economical to use if you don't attempt to buy more than you can properly store or try to cook more than you need for any one meal.

CANNED VEGETABLES

Canned vegetables are convenient to store and easy to cook. They are precooked and, therefore, quick to heat and serve. Along with frozen, they give us the variety of vegetables in our diet necessary for good nutrition when fresh vegetables are not available.

Canned vegetables are always of high quality because they are harvested and processed at their peak of freshness. Unfortunately, the high temperatures used in the canning process alter their flavor, texture, and appearance to such a degree, that they seldom compare favorably with their fresh counterparts when both are properly prepared.

When canned vegetables are used as a side dish, rely on imitation butter flavoring (no calories!) and appropriate seasonings to bring out their full flavor and taste.

Canned vegetables are nutritious when they are heated and served in the liquid in which they were packed. They are also more economical than fresh or frozen at certain times of the year.

DRIED VEGETABLES

Dried beans, peas, and lentils are known as legumes. They are all fruits of leguminous plants—that is, they are attached to the stem of the plant within pods. This type of vegetable is highly nutritious, and along with cereal grains, is the predominant source of protein for most of the world's people. Although a traditional staple in Europe, Africa, South America, and the Middle Eastern countries, dried legumes are not used to any great extent in American vegetable cookery. They are used primarily in soup-making and casseroles.

Cereal grains are the dried fruits of grasses. They include rice, barley, wheat, rye, and corn. In America, however, rice, barley, and corn are the only grains used as vegetables.

By themselves, legumes and cereal grains are considered low-quality protein foods. This is because they are each deficient in one or more of the "essential" amino acids needed by our bodies to synthesize protein. It's only when we combine legumes and cereal grains together in one meal or prepare them in combination with other high-quality protein foods, such as nuts, seeds, or dairy products, that we produce a food of high nutritional quality.

BUYING VEGETABLES

If you're a home gardener, you know that vegetables taken straight from the garden to the kitchen have a texture and taste that is far superior to that of vegetables sold commercially. But in our industrialized society, most of us must be content with buying our produce at local supermarkets rather than growing our own.

In order to select the freshest products possible, you'll need to become more knowledgeable about vegetables and their seasons. You'll also want to learn the best possible ways to store, prepare, and cook them.

For quality and flavor, fresh vegetables have no equal. Our use of processed vegetables (frozen, canned, or dried), however, permits us to enjoy vegetables out of season and have them readily available when we need them. They are also convenient to use and cook in less time than fresh because they are prepared and partially or fully cooked as part of the freezing and canning process.

BUYING FRESH VEGETABLES

Good, nutritious, low-calorie meals start with buying the freshest vegetables possible. Here are some general buying tips: Choose firm, crisp, fresh-looking products that are free of blemishes. Greens should be crisp, bright-colored, and without insect injury. Buy vegetables that are a good weight for their size and those that have a normal shape; misshapen vegetables are usually poor in quality and are generally difficult to prepare.

It is usually best to choose the smaller sizes; they will be the youngest and the most tender. And don't buy more than you need. Look for signs of maturity. Although quality and appearance don't always go hand in hand, some vegetables will reveal their age by flowering, seeding or sprouting. Learning more about the various vegetables will enable you to recognize these signs of deterioration and help you select fresher products.

But probably your best overall chance of getting vegetables of high quality and flavor is to buy them in season when the supply is plentiful.

Generally, vegetables are freshest and lowest in price when they are in season. Remember that frozen or canned vegetables are always preferable to old or wilted fresh vegetables.

Artichokes

Select artichokes with leaves that are closely packed and a bright green color. Avoid those with spreading leaves; it is a sign of aging and the edible portions will be tough, dry, and bitter. The brown spots sometimes found on the outer leaves indicate age, bruising, or frost, but as long as they don't penetrate the inside of the artichoke, the quality will be unaffected.

There is no relationship between size and flavor. Buy one medium artichoke per person. Do not wash artichokes until ready to use them. Wrap them in clear plastic wrap and store in the refrigerator. They will hold in good condition about seven days.

Asparagus

Choose asparagus with tightly closed, compact, green or purplish tips, and firm straight stalks that are green for at least two-thirds of their length. Only the green portion of fresh asparagus is tender; the tough white portion is left on to help the stalks retain their flavor and freshness. Avoid angular or flat stalks or stalks with tips that are opened or decayed. Asparagus with wilted stalks or loose tips are apt to be tough and stringy. Reject warm asparagus. Store in a plastic bag in the refrigerator and use as soon as possible.

Beans

Look for crisp, bright-appearing beans of good green or yellow color. They should have a velvety feel and be reasonably well shaped. Choose long, straight pods that snap crisply and easily when broken. Avoid beans that are limp, bruised, or broken.

Frozen beans are an acceptable substitute for fresh, but canned beans should be avoided. Use the canned variety strictly for marinated salads. Beans are subject to damage if stored at too low a temperature. Keep them cold and humid and use as soon as possible.

Beets

Early beets are often sold in bunches with the tops attached, while late-crop beets are sold with the tops removed. Ironically, beets were originally raised for their top leaves rather than their roots. Today, of course, they are cultivated chiefly as a root vegetable and also as a source of sugar. If the tops of early beets are fresh and reasonably unblemished, you can cook and eat them in the same manner as fresh spinach.

Broccoli

Broccoli and cauliflower are closely related. Look for firm, plump, tender stalks and firm, compact clusters of tightly-closed buds, showing no signs of flowering. Avoid buying broccoli with buds that are loose, yellow, or wilted; these are signs of overmaturity. Also, avoid broccoli with soft, slippery spots on the buds—these are signs of decay. Store in the refrigerator in a plastic bag for a few days only. Broccoli is very perishable, so use as soon as possible.

Brussels Sprouts

Brussels sprouts are like miniature cabbages. They should be firm, compact, fresh, and very green. Avoid sprouts with loose, yellowish or yellowish-green leaves. Soft or puffy sprouts lack quality and flavor. Store, unwashed, in a plastic bag in the refrigerator. Use within two days. Keep in mind that this marvelous vegetable is often rendered unpalatable by overcooking. Cook them until just tender, 10 to 15 minutes at the most.

Cabbage

There are three varieties of cabbage available year-around: smooth-leaved green cabbage, crinkly-leaved savory green cabbage, and red cabbage. Whether buying the green or red variety, squeeze the head to make sure it is reasonably firm and hard. Look for heads that are bright in color and heavy for their size. The outer leaves should show no signs of wilting, yellowing, or decay. Look especially for insect damage. Worm injury on the outside leaves usually indicates worm injury on the inside.

Chinese cabbage is one of those less-familiar vegetables that is often overlooked, yet it is very versatile and superb in salads and coleslaw. It also lacks the strong flavor of true cabbage. By the way, don't buy packaged coleslaw simply because it's convenient. You are paying a high price for food with very little nutritive value. Instead, buy a head of cabbage and shred it yourself, it's cheaper, tastier, and better for you.

Carrots

Almost but not all carrots sold today are topped (the green tops are removed) and packed in plastic bags. In many ways this practice is quite advantageous, since the tops continue to draw nutrients and moisture from the roots as long as they are left on. But untopped carrots are your guarantee that they have been shipped fresh rather than stored.

Choose young, firm, fresh-looking carrots with long slender rootlets. In general, the smaller the carrots, the more mild-flavored they will be. Mature, full-size carrots usually have been stored for a period of time and have a more pronounced flavor and a much coarser texture. Avoid carrots that have large green "sunburned" areas at the top. Wilted, flabby, soft, cracked or shriveled carrots, and black stem ends indicate age. To store, remove tops if attached and keep in the refrigerator for up to four weeks.

Cauliflower

Cauliflower is a variety of the common cabbage and is available the year around. Cauliflower of good quality will have a white or creamy-white compact head with tight flowerets that are free of discolored brown or black spots. The outer jacket leaves should be green and crisp. Ignore any small green leaflets extending through the head or "curd"; it only mars the appearance, not the quality. Also, avoid cauliflower that is yellowish or spread open. It indicates aging and overmaturity. To store, sprinkle leaves with water and refrigerate in a plastic bag for up to a week.

Celeriac

Celeriac, which is often referred to as celery root or knob celery, is grown for its turniplike base instead of for its stalk. It is not—as some people think—the root of regular stalk celery. Fresh celeriac should be clean, firm, and healthy-looking. Choose those that have small roots, since large ones tend to become woody and hard. Avoid celeriac that have sprouts on the top of the root; it indicates overmaturity. To store, trim roots and tops and refrigerate. This less-familiar vegetable is surprisingly good in stews and soup or used in salads in place of cooked potatoes.

Celery

Choose celery with rigid, crisp stalks with good heart formation and fresh green leaves. Avoid stalks that are blemished, soft, or have wilted leaves. Also avoid celery that shows brown discoloration along the stalk or at the base. I like to buy celery uncut and unwrapped; they are likely to be fresher and the leaves are delicious for flavoring soups, stews, and salads. Celery stores well if kept cold and moist. Place in a plastic bag, close tightly, and refrigerate up to two weeks.

Corn

To be good, fresh corn must be absolutely fresh or fresh frozen. The sugar in fresh corn begins to lose its delicate sweet flavor and converts to a starch almost immediately after it is harvested, and unless it is kept cold and moist from the time it is picked, in a short time it will have tasteless kernels rather than ones that are sweet and flavorful.

If you can't buy corn shortly after it has been picked in the fields, then buy the freshest corn possible at your market. Choose corn with fresh green husks and cobs that are filled with plump, milky kernels. Avoid ears that have already been husked. Store, unhusked, in the refrigerator and use as soon as possible.

Cucumbers

Choose firm, well-shaped cucumbers that are not too large in diameter and have a bright green color. Many distributors wax the outside skins of cucumbers to give them a better appearance and preserve their freshness. However, this treatment oftentimes makes it difficult to judge the true quality of the vegetable. Avoid soft, withered cucumbers or those that have dark, sunken spots indicating decay and overmaturity. Cucumbers will keep in the refrigerator one to two weeks.

Eggplant

The best quality eggplants are firm, heavy for their size, with uniformly dark, shiny, smooth skin, and absolutely unblemished. Avoid eggplants that are spongy, wrinkled, and those with dark spots on the surface; they are all evidence of decay. In general, the smaller eggplants that are picked just before reaching their full growth are best. Store in the warmest part of the refrigerator and use as soon as possible.

Lettuce

There are four main varieties of lettuce marketed today: iceberg, butterhead, romaine, and leaf. Each variety, of course, has its own special quality characteristics. In general, lettuce should be clean, crisp, tender, and fresh-looking with a good bright color—medium to light green. You'll also find some varieties with red or red tinted leaves. Avoid lettuce with wilted or rust-colored stains in the inner leaves or any discoloration or soft decay. Store whole heads in plastic bags in the refrigerator up to one week. Cut-up salad greens that have been washed and drained will keep fresh and crisp up to three weeks if they are stored as close to 34° F. as possible in tightly closed plastic bags or in air-tight containers. But take care that the temperature is not too low, for lettuce freezes easily and becomes translucent and wilted.

Mushrooms

Mushrooms are a fungus which we eat as a vegetable. In buying mushrooms, size and color do not matter. For best quality look for mushrooms with closed caps. This indicates that they are newly picked. Wide-open caps are a sign of overmaturity. Generally, fresh mushrooms have short stems. If mature or slightly aged mushrooms haven't deteriorated too much, they can be chopped and sautéed or used as a stuffing or as a flavoring agent in stews, soups, or casserole dishes. Canned mushrooms have little taste compared to fresh ones. Store mushrooms, covered, in their original containers in a brown bag left open to allow air to circulate.

Okra

Look for pods that are young, tender, fresh, clean with a bright green color. The pods should be free of blemishes with flexible tips. Avoid those that are dull, dry, shriveled, or discolored.

Okra is grown and marketed primarily in the South and used extensively in Creole dishes. Both smooth and ridged are grown, and you'll find them of various lengths up to eight inches. Store in a plastic bag in the refrigerator for up to two weeks.

Onions, Dry

Choose hard, firm onions with small dry necks and crackling-dry, papery outer skins. Avoid misshaped onions, those with wet or very soft necks, sprouting onions, or those with green sunburn spots or other blemishes. Keep dry onions in a cool, dry place at low humidity.

Onions, Green

Good quality green onions—which include chives, leeks, and shallots—should have crisp, green tops. (Shallots are usually topped). Leeks and green onions should have crisp stems that are white for two or three inches from the root. Avoid onions with yellowing or wilted tops or with spongy, fibrous stems. Store in plastic bags in the refrigerator.

Peas

There are two frozen vegetables I find to be of extraordinary taste and quality: frozen peas and frozen corn. The reason for this is simple; the natural sugar in both vegetables begins to change to a starch almost immediately upon their being picked. This process is hastened if the vegetable is not chilled quickly after harvesting. With modern flash-freezing processes, the natural flavor and taste of these two vegetables is fairly well preserved. However, really fresh peas picked at the right stage and shelled just before serving have no equal in flavor and are well worth the effort.

Peppers, Sweet

Although most of the sweet peppers (often called bell peppers because of their shape) are sold when green, those that are allowed to ripen fully turn a bright red color and develop a more mellow and much sweeter flavor.

Peppers should be fresh, firm, thick-fleshed and have a bright green or red color. Immature peppers are usually pale-colored, soft, and pliable, while older ones will be dull-colored with cut or punctures through the walls. Store in the refrigerator, unwashed and unwrapped; use within a few days.

Potatoes

There are two basic types of white potatoes: the *long type*, which generally have mealy interiors and are best for baking or mashing, and and *round type*, which have firm, waxy interiors and are best for boiling or roasting.

Potatoes of any kind or size should be firm, well-shaped, and smooth with shallow eyes and free from blemishes, sunburn, and decay. Avoid potatoes with large areas of green, sprouted skins, cuts and bruises, or any signs of decay. Store potatoes in a cool dark place for two to three weeks.

Rice

There are three familiar categories of rice—white, brown, and wild rice, although the latter is not considered a true rice but a native American grain that grows wild in the north-central states of Minnesota and Wisconsin. Wild rice has an interesting taste and texture and is best when combined with other foods.

There are several types of white rice—short-grain, medium- or round-grain, and long-grain. Nutritionally they are all alike, but differ in size, texture, and flavor. Short-grain rice cooks up tender and moist, but it tends to be sticky. It is the preferred type of rice for sauces and puddings. Long-grain rice is best for use in soups, molds, and stuffings, or as a cooked vegetable where it is desirable for the grains to be separate and dry. Long-grain Carolina rice has become a standard in this country and is very likely the best all-around long-grained rice in the world.

Brown rice is unmilled whole-grain rice with its bran coat and husk remaining on the kernel. It has more nutritional value than white rice (white rice is natural brown rice with the outside covering removed) but requires about twice the cooking time to make it tender.

Spinach

Fresh spinach is both a favorite vegetable and a salad green. Look for leaves that are large, fresh-looking, and crisp with a good, dark-green color. Avoid spinach with leaves that are discolored, wilted, or bruised. Wash spinach carefully to remove sand and grit particles. Store lightly covered in the refrigerator and use as soon as possible.

Squash

There are two general groups of squash: "summer" squash and "winter" squash. These loose classifications actually refer more to the cooking process employed for these vegetables rather than to their seasonal availability. (Some form of summer or winter squash is available year-round.)

Summer squash varieties include yellow crookneck, straightneck, Italian zucchini, and patty pan. They are harvested while still immature and when the entire squash is soft and edible. Look for those that are fresh-looking, shiny, and heavy for their size. Generally, they are best when small to medium in size.

Winter squash varieties include acorn, banana, buttercup, butternut, hubbard, turban, and spaghetti squash. They are harvested when fully mature, their skin and seeds being hard and inedible. Winter squash should be heavy for its size with tough, hard rinds. Avoid those with soft or wet spots or moldy areas on the rind. They are all signs of decay.

Tomatoes

The best-tasting tomatoes you can buy are the hand-picked "home-grown" or locally farm-grown varieties. These tomatoes will always be flavorful and succulent because they are allowed to mature and ripen completely before being picked—and the longer tomatoes remain on the vine, the better they will taste.

Some tomatoes are picked early, when they begin to turn from green to pink. These varieties develop a flavor and juiciness almost as good as the vine-ripened ones, but they must not be chilled before maturing or they will not ripen properly.

The poorest quality tomatoes are those that are picked green. These tomatoes will redden completely, but they will not attain good taste or texture. There is no foolproof formula for buying or knowing which tomatoes are best. But next time you're buying tomatoes, try smelling them: vine-ripened tomatoes have a fresh, clean tomato odor; machine-harvested tomatoes picked green are odorless.

Look for firm, plump tomatoes that are unblemished and reasonably ripe, and don't be repelled by slight deformities or irregular shapes. Vine-ripened tomatoes are seldom perfect in shape, but they more than make up for it in flavor and aroma. Unless tomatoes are going to be used the same day you purchase them, it is best to buy them less than fully ripe and let them ripen at room temperature in your home away from direct sunlight. Avoid overripe and bruised tomatoes and those with soft spots or surface mold. Store ripe tomatoes in the refrigerator; use within two to three days.

Turnips and Rutabagas

There are white-skinned and yellow-skinned varieties of both these cool-weather vegetables. Generally, turnips are small to medium in size with a purple-collared white skin, while rutabagas are cream or yellow colored with tan or purple crowns and are usually larger.

Buy smooth, firm turnips and rutabagas that are heavy for their size. Avoid those that are soft or shriveled or show too many leaf scars around the top. Store both vegetables in the refrigerator until needed.

BUYING FROZEN, CANNED, AND DRIED VEGETABLES

When buying frozen vegetables, be sure the package contents are frozen solid. Never buy frozen vegetables you suspect have been totally or even partially defrosted. Frozen vegetables deteriorate quickly once they are thawed.

Avoid limp, stained, or sweating packages and those that are torn or damaged in any way. As a waistline-watcher, avoid vegetables that are seasoned in butter or cooked in a sauce. To obtain the maximum food value and flavor from frozen vegetables, buy them as little cut up as possible, cook them as soon as they are thawed, and serve them without delay.

Select canned vegetables by grade when possible. Grade A, or Fancy and Grade B, or Choice are the best quality. While all canned vegetables are packed in liquid, the ratio of solid food to liquid varies among the various grades, can sizes, and brand names, and for this reason it becomes difficult, without expensive trial and error, to determine which brand or can size is the best buy. Nor is price a reliable criterion. Quite often your best buy will be the lower priced private brands rather than the higher priced advertised brands.

When buying canned vegetables, never—and I mean never—consider buying swollen or dented cans. Even if the store was giving them away, you would still be gambling with your health and safety.

Most dried legumes (beans, peas, lentils, etc.) can be purchased in see-through packages or in bulk. Select those that are even in size (the smaller ones cook faster) and have a bright, uniform color. A fading color indicates overmaturity. Avoid legumes that are discolored or broken, and if purchased in bulk, there should be no foreign materials, such as small stones, stems, or leaves, mixed in. Packaged beans require little or no examination before cooking. A pound of dried beans will provide approximately eight servings.

The food value of cereal grains (rice, wheat, barley, etc.) is destroyed by refining. When possible, buy them whole, unseasoned, and unmilled.

STORING VEGETABLES

Most fresh vegetables require refrigeration to preserve their food value and flavor and can be stored an average of three to five days. They should be cleaned and trimmed as soon as they come from the market and placed in plastic bags or in the crisper section of your refrigerator until needed. Less perishable vegetables, such as potatoes and dry onions, keep best out of the refrigerator and should be stored in a well-ventilated, dry, cool area.

Frozen vegetables can be stored from 6 to 12 months at a constant low temperature of 0°F. or below and should be kept frozen solid right up to cooking time. If necessary, thaw frozen vegetables in the refrigerator. Never refreeze frozen vegetables once they are thawed, however. Cook them immediately and refrigerate.

Store canned vegetables in a cool, dry place where they are not exposed to sunlight. If stored longer than three months, it's a good idea to invert the cans on the shelf to redistribute their contents.

Dried vegetables do not require the same storage care as other types of vegetables. They keep almost indefinitely and can be stored at room temperature in their original packaging or in plastic containers or glass jars. Be sure to keep all containers tightly covered to keep out dust, moisture, and insects. Whole grains can also be stored in this manner.

PREPARING VEGETABLES FOR COOKING

FRESH VEGETABLES

All fresh vegetables you bring into your home must be thoroughly trimmed, briefly washed, and dried before cooking. But to assure cleanliness in vegetables, particularly of the bud, head, and fruit groups that may be infested, exceptionally dirty, or covered with chemical residues, it is often necessary to soak them briefly or to give them a preliminary blanching in advance of cooking. Vegetables may also be blanched to rid them of strong flavors (cabbage), so they may be peeled easily (tomatoes), to maintain their whiteness (cauliflower), to rid them of excess moisture (eggplant), and to cut down on the cooking time (green beans). Ideally, these preparations should be done close to the time of cooking. Destruction of nutrients begins and progresses rapidly once vegetables are cut and exposed to air. Also, many nutrients are soluble in water, which means they are leached away if the vegetables are soaking or cooked in a large amount of water for too long a time. Remember that fresh vegetables will always retain more of their food value and flavor if they are not washed or cut until you are ready to use them. When you must prepare vegetables in advance of cooking, cover them with a clean damp towel or place them in plastic bags and put them in the refrigerator until ready for use.

To insure uniform cooking, vegetables should be cut to the same size and shape. They are also cut for aesthetic reasons: vegetables should not only taste good, they should be visually appetizing as well. In addition, the manner in which vegetables are cut is important for the sake of both flavor and texture. When the primary need is for flavoring, as in sauces, the vegetables are minced. When texture is important, as in soups, stews, and side dishes, then the vegetables are chopped, diced, sliced, or julienned. Ultimately, the method of cutting will be determined by the cooking method employed and the characteristics of the vegetables to be cooked.

Indispensable to preparing vegetables by hand is a sharp, high quality French or chef's knife. They're expensive, costing perhaps twenty-five to thirty dollars, but cheap, lightweight knives make the job of cutting vegetables harder than it has to be. Buy one good knife, care for it properly, and it should last you a lifetime. I use a large 10-inch knife exclusively, but for the average home cook, I recommend having two knives—one 6 inches long for small jobs like mincing, and one 10 inches long for heavy-duty work.

TO CHOP VEGETABLES means to cut them more or less finely into uneven bits. The finest chopped vegetables are said to be minced. To "chop," hold the knife firmly in one hand, the other hand resting on top of the blade near the tip with the fingers extended. This slight pressure on top of the knife helps you achieve a rocking or "staccato" up and down motion and lets the weight of the knife at the handle do all the work. You'll find this method to be much faster than if both ends of the blade are lifted off the board.

TO DICE VEGETABLES means to cut them into cubes ranging from one-eighth to one-half inch in size. To obtain a uniform dice, first cut the vegetables lengthwise into equal-size strips. Then bundle the strips together and cut them crosswise into uniform cubes.

TO SLICE VEGETABLES means to cut relatively thin, broad pieces averaging one to one and a half inches long, one-half to one inch wide and one-fourth inch thick. For slicing, hold the knife in the same manner as for dicing, but the other hand must be placed on the food so that the fingertips are tucked underneath, and the middle section of the first two fingers act as a guide to the up and down motion of the knife blade. Keep the blade pressed against your fingers as you're cutting. Unless you are using a serrated-edge blade (they're really great for soft vegetables like tomatoes), try putting pressure on the forward motion of the knife only, rather than using a sawing, back and forth stroke.

TO JULIENNE VEGETABLES means to cut them into thin, long strips. First cut the vegetables into one-eighth inch slices. Then stack two or three slices together and cut them, either with the grain or crosswise, into one-eighth-inch matchstick pieces. When leafy greens or cabbage are cut in julienne, the result is known as shredding.

FROZEN AND CANNED VEGETABLES

One of the big advantages of using frozen vegetables is that the preparation work necessary for fresh market or garden vegetables—trimming, washing, drying, and cutting—has been done by the food processor before the vegetables were frozen. In addition, all frozen vegetables are blanched as part of the freezing process and therefore require less cooking time than fresh vegetables.

In general, frozen vegetables are cooked without thawing. There are some important exceptions, however, so follow the manufacturer's cooking instructions on the package.

Canned vegetables require no special preparation. They are fully cooked and simply need to be reheated. To derive the maximum food value and flavor from canned vegetables, gently heat and serve them in their own liquid.

DRIED LEGUMES

Before dried vegetables can be cooked, they must be soaked in water to replace the moisture lost in the drying process. Lentils and split peas, however, are preprocessed and do not necessarily require soaking.

To prepare dried legumes for cooking, first rinse them under cold water and examine them for small stones or debris. Then soak them for several hours or overnight at room temperature, using three to four times as much water as beans. The amount of time necessary for soaking will largely depend on the dryness of the bean and the hardness and temperature of the water. Remove any beans that float.

An alternative quick-soaking method of preparing dried beans and other legumes is to cover them with water and immediately bring to a boil. Reduce the heat to low, allow to simmer 2 minutes, then remove from the heat and let the blanched vegetables soak, tightly covered, for one to two hours. Using the quick-soaking method is the same as soaking for 10 to 15 hours at room temperature. To test whether legumes have sufficiently soaked, break a bean in two; if the color is uniform throughout, and if you can easily slice each half crosswise into halves, they are ready to be cooked. Tiny bubbles on the surface of the soaking liquid indicate that the legumes have been soaked too long. They can still be cooked, however.

COOKING VEGETABLES

From a nutritional standpoint, we derive the greatest benefit from vegetables when they are eaten raw. But many vegetables need to be cooked to be edible, while others are cooked to intensify a particular flavor or to bring about a desired taste. Vegetables play an important role in any low-calorie regimen, mainly because they are higher in bulk and lower in calories than most other foods and because they are rich in important vitamins and minerals. Unfortunately, vegetables are so often abused—by the growers and food processors as well as in our kitchen—that the best flavor and most of the nutrients are destroyed before they ever reach our tables. Low-calorie vegetable cookery is simply a matter of understanding the differences between the various types of vegetables and how each is affected by dry or moist heats.

Most vegetables, like meats, are cooked according to a few basic methods. Some types of vegetables, however, can be adversely affected by improper cooking procedures. Generally, the methods and cooking techniques that preserve the maximum flavor and color in vegetables is most apt to preserve the greatest amount of nutrients.

COOKING FRESH VEGETABLES

Theoretically, green vegetables should be cooked uncovered so that the volatile plant acids that adversely affect their color can escape into the air. In the presence of heat, these acids react chemically with the green color pigment, gradually changing it to an unattractive olive-green. Cooking in an uncovered pot greatly minimizes these color changes.

In practice, however, most green vegetables cooked in a covered utensil retain their natural color fairly well if cooked quickly, with only a small amount of liquid, and overcooking is avoided. This is especially true for frozen green vegetables, because they are already partially cooked.

In contrast to green vegetables, red vegetables benefit from their own acid content and turn redder and more attractive-looking when additional diluted acids such as lemon juice, apple juice, vinegar, wine, or tart apples are added to the cooking liquid. Red vegetables should be cooked with a small amount of liquid in a covered utensil. An exception is red cabbage, which should be cooked partly uncovered for part of the cooking time to allow undesirable sulfurous odors to escape from the pan.

Yellow vegetables are the least susceptible to color change in the presence of heat and little affected by either acid or alkali in the cooking liquid. Nevertheless, like all vegetables, they will lose their color intensity and most of their food value if overcooked. Yellow vegetables cook best by moist heat. They should be cooked, covered, in very little liquid for the shortest time required to make them tender and served immediately.

COOKING FROZEN VEGETABLES

Keep in mind when cooking frozen vegetables that they are pre-processed and therefore require much less cooking time than do fresh market or garden vegetables. Generally, frozen vegetables are cooked, covered, in the least possible amount of liquid. Leaf vegetables can be defrosted, but all other varieties of frozen vegetables are not defrosted before cooking.

COOKING CANNED VEGETABLES

All canned vegetables are fully cooked and need only to be heated through before serving. Although some of the nutrients in canned vegetables are destroyed by the high temperatures used in canning, they still provide at least some of the food value of fresh and infinitely more when fresh vegetables are improperly handled or overcooked.

The liquid in which vegetables are packed contain water-soluble vitamins and minerals and some of the flavor of the canned solids and should not be discarded.

For a small amount of liquid, the vegetable can simply be heated and served in its own juice. But if there is too much liquid, it should be cooked down rapidly by at least half before the vegetable is added with other ingredients.

COOKING DRIED LEGUMES

The methods for preparing and cooking dried legumes are basically the same for all varieties, with the exception of split peas and lentils which are preprocessed and do not necessarily require a soaking period. Their cooking times are variable, however, and depend on the variety of legume, its size, age, its intended use, and the locality in which it was grown. Even the mineral content of the cooking liquid affects the cooking time of dried vegetables, so it's a good idea to test them for tenderness near the end of the cooking period to prevent overcooking.

Prepare the legumes for cooking (see the section on preparation) by rinsing and then soaking in three to four times as much water as beans, several hours or overnight. I have found beans to be more digestible if the soaking liquid is discarded and fresh water added before cooking. The amount of time necessary to soak legumes can be shortened if they are covered with cold water by at least one inch, brought to a boil and cooked rapidly for two minutes. They should then be removed from the heat and allowed to soak one to two hours, tightly covered, at room temperature.

To cook, bring the beans and liquid to a boil, reduce the heat to a simmer, then cover and cook gently until tender. Add more water during the cooking period if necessary to prevent sticking. The important point to remember when cooking dried legumes is to always keep the heat at a very low temperature. Legumes toughen when subjected to high cooking temperatures for too long a time. To avoid this, always use a heavy-bottomed pot or an asbestos pad under a regular saucepan.

Legumes usually require about two to three hours to cook; pre-processed split peas and lentils need less cooking time to make them tender. Remember that legumes generally double in size when cooked, so leave room in the pot for expansion: one cup of a dried legume (approximately one-half pound) will yield two to two and a half cups, or about four servings.

Dried legumes and whole grains, which would otherwise require a long cooking period, can be prepared quickly and conveniently in a pressure cooker. They gain in flavor, texture, and digestibility when prepared in this way. A pressure cooker is really simple and safe to use. Just remember not to fill it more than half full with food and water. And although it adds unwanted calories, it's a good idea when cooking legumes and whole grains in a pressure cooker to add a tablespoon of cooking oil to the liquid. This helps prevent the contents of the pot from foaming up during cooking and possibly clogging the steam escape valve.

The cooking time for dried vegetables cooked under pressure varies with the age and type of food, the amount of soaking time, and the hardness of the cooking liquid. Cooked at 15 pounds pressure, hard beans such as Great Northerns and kidney beans require 10 to 15 minutes cooking time to become tender. Soft beans such as lima beans, navy beans, split peas, and lentils can be prepared in under 10 minutes.

LOW-CALORIE DRY HEAT COOKING METHODS

Broiling

Tender vegetables with a high moisture content, such as eggplant, mushrooms, tomatoes, and summer squash, can be successfully broiled. Broiled vegetables cook quickly and need careful attention to prevent scorching. Unless they are thinly sliced, they should be partially cooked, then lightly coated with oil, grated cheese, or crumbs before being exposed to the intense heat. Broiling gives vegetables an excellent flavor and an appealing appearance.

BASIC BROILING TECHNIQUES

1. *Scrub the vegetables* and remove any blemish marks. Slice one-fourth inch thick. Thicker slices should be partially cooked before being exposed to the fire.

2. *Coat the vegetables* lightly with oil, cheese, or crumbs. Place slices in a shallow nonstick baking pan.

3. *Cook the vegetables* under moderate heat four to five inches from the flame for three to five minutes, or until browned.

BROILED MUSHROOMS

1 cup mushrooms
1 tablespoon diet margarine
1 tablespoon lemon juice

dash garlic salt
dash onion salt
pepper to taste

Wash and drain mushrooms quickly; cut off stems. Place mushrooms in an 8-inch ovenproof skillet. Mix together margarine and lemon juice and brush over mushrooms. Sprinkle with remaining seasonings. Set broiler for 350°F. and cook mushrooms about 10 minutes, shaking pan frequently.

Makes 2 servings at 35 calories per serving.

Chef's Cooking Tip:
When buying fresh mushrooms, look for those with tightly closed caps. There should be no gaps between the stem and the cap. This indicates that the mushrooms are fresh and tender, and there will be less tendency for the mushrooms to soak up excess water.

BROILED ONION

2 medium-size Spanish onions
1 tablespoon diet margarine

salt and pepper to taste

Cut both ends from onion and rinse under hot water to remove paperlike skin. Cut onions in half crosswise. Place halves on a nonstick baking sheetpan or in an overproof skillet. Brush with margarine. Broil under low flame until onions are tender, 8 to 10 minutes. Season to taste before serving.

Makes 4 servings at 52 calories per serving.

BROILED ZUCCHINI

4 medium-size zucchini
1 tablespoon diet margarine

salt and pepper to taste

Wash zucchini and trim stem and blossom ends. Blanch zucchini in a saucepan of boiling water 5 minutes. Remove from pan and cut in half lengthwise. Place halves cut-side up on a baking sheetpan. Brush with diet margarine and season with salt and pepper. Broil under moderate flame until browned.

Makes 4 servings at 35 calories per serving.

BROILED EGGPLANT PARMIGIANA

1 medium-size eggplant cut into four ½-inch slices
½ cup freshly grated Parmesan cheese
½ teaspoon garlic salt
½ teaspoon onion salt
¼ teaspoon pepper
paprika

Place sliced eggplant on a nonstick baking sheetpan. Top each with Parmesan cheese, garlic salt, onion salt, pepper, and paprika. Cover the sheetpan tightly with aluminum foil, then place in a 350° F. oven for 30 minutes, or until tender. Uncover and transfer sheetpan to a broiler. Broil for just a few minutes or until cheese is golden brown.

Makes 4 servings at 75 calories per serving.

Chef's Cooking Tip:
Because of its high moisture content, eggplant is one of the few vegetables that can be successfully broiled. Combining the methods of broiling and baking eliminates the need to baste with high-calorie oils or fats.

HERBED BROILED TOMATOES

1 large ripe tomato
1 tablespoon soft breadcrumbs
1 tablespoon diet margarine
½ tablespoon chopped parsley
¼ teaspoon dried basil leaves
salt and pepper to taste

Remove core. Cut tomato in half crosswise. Blend ingredients and spread over each half. Broil cut-side up under moderate heat until tomato halves are golden brown and tender, about 5 minutes.

Makes 2 servings at 56 calories per serving.

BAKING

We generally think of baking to mean the dry heat cooking of vegetables in their skins. A baked potato is the classic example, but other firm-fleshed vegetables, such as eggplant, squash, beets, onions, and tomatoes, are also frequently cooked in this manner. Baking vegetables whole in their skins is very good from a nutritional standpoint. It is also very convenient. The vegetables are simply scrubbed, then laid on a rack or placed on a baking pan (the cooking time can be reduced if the vegetables are halved before baking) and cooked until just tender.

Many vegetables, however, are cut into pieces or sliced and moist baked in a casserole. In this method, a small amount of liquid is added and the baking dish covered for all or part of the cooking time. Casseroles are always cooked at a moderate temperature, which enables you to bake your entrée, vegetable, and sometimes even the dessert all at one time.

BASIC BAKING TECHNIQUES

DRY HEAT

1. *Scrub the vegetables* and remove any blemish marks; do not peel.
2. *Bake the vegetables* in a medium-high oven (375° to 425° F.) until tender. Large round vegetables, such as eggplant, tomatoes, and squash, are usually cut into halves before cooking. The cut surfaces should be basted occasionally to prevent drying.

MOIST HEAT

1. *Scrub the vegetables* and remove any blemish marks. Scrap and cut the vegetables into even-size pieces, if you wish, but they are nutritionally better if unpeeled and cooked whole. If you do peel and cut the vegetables, do so just before cooking. This prevents discoloration and results in the least possible loss of vitamins.
2. *Place the vegetables in a casserole dish* without crowding. Add just enough boiling liquid to cover the bottom of the casserole.
3. *Bake the vegetables* in a moderate oven (350° to 375° F.) until tender. Turn the vegetables in the casserole at least once. The casserole should be covered tightly for all or part of the cooking time, depending on whether a brown-crusted surface is desired.

BAKED ACORN SQUASH

2 small acorn squash
4 tablespoons unsweetened apple juice
½ teaspoon cinnamon

Put the whole squashes in a 350° F. oven about 20 minutes until they are soft enough to cut with a large knife. Cut each squash in half and scoop out the seeds. Arrange the halves on a baking sheetpan or shallow roasting pan. Cut a small slice off the bottom of each half if necessary to make the squash sit upright. Fill each half with 1 tablespoon of the apple juice. Add a pinch of cinnamon. Bake, uncovered, about 10 to 20 minutes until squash is tender.

Makes 4 servings at 40 calories per serving.

AMERICAN INDIAN PEPPERS

3 large bell peppers
¼ teaspoon French salad-dressing mix

dash garlic salt

Place peppers on a baking sheet pan and bake in a preheated 450° F. oven approximately 20 minutes, turning occasionally. Remove from oven and place in a covered saucepan for 10 minutes. Peel skin; cut into strips. Sprinkle with salad dressing mix, then allow to stand, covered, several minutes until flavors blend. Uncover and serve.

Makes 4 servings at 19 calories per serving.

Chef's Cooking Tip:
Peppers can also be peeled under the broiler or directly over a flame. Char on all sides, then hold under cold running water to steam peppers and loosen skin.

BAKED ASPARAGUS PARMESAN

16 stalks fresh asparagus
salt and pepper to taste

4 teaspoons freshly grated Parmesan cheese

Trim asparagus to the same length, peel the remaining stalks slightly with a vegetable peeler. Rinse the stalks in cold water and lay them in the bottom of a flat baking dish. Season with salt, pepper, and Parmesan cheese. Cover dish tightly and bake in a 350° F. oven 20 to 25 minutes, or until asparagus is tender.

Makes 4 servings at 36 calories per serving.

BAKED SUMMER SQUASH

1 pound summer squash
1 cup water

butter-flavored salt to taste
cinnamon

Wash squash and cut off stem and blossom ends. Parboil in water for 5 minutes. Drain squash and put in a small baking dish. Bake in a moderate 350° F. oven about 15 minutes. Garnish with butter-flavored salt and cinnamon.

Makes 4 servings at 25 calories per serving.

BAKED POTATOES

Potatoes by themselves are not fattening. It's the added butter, cheese, and sour cream that are the real culprits. Learn to use low-calorie substitutes like diet margarine and yogurt, and keep this little trick in mind: Bake potatoes slowly in the oven for about 2 hours and the small amount of sugar in them will carmelize and flavor the potato almost as well as butter, without adding calories.

2 large russet potatoes   salt and pepper to taste

Scrub potatoes with a stiff brush. Bake in a preheated 375° F. oven for about 2 hours, or until they can be pierced easily with a knife. Be sure to prick the potatoes in several places to let the steam escape during baking.

Makes 4 servings at 80 calories per serving.

Chef's Cooking Tip:
To reheat leftover baked potatoes, dip them in water and return to the oven (350° F.) for 15 to 20 minutes.

BAKED TOMATOES ITALIANO

12 ripe tomato slices
8 thin onion slices
¼ cup low-calorie Italian dressing
2 tablespoons freshly grated Parmesan cheese

½ teaspoon whole oregano or basil
salt and pepper

Arrange tomato and onion slices in alternating layers in a 9 by 9-inch baking dish. Pour Italian dressing over tomatoes. Sprinkle with Parmesan cheese and seasonings. Cover tightly; bake in a 400° F. oven about 20 minutes, or until onions are tender and tomatoes are heated through.

Makes 4 servings at 50 calories per serving.

Chef's Cooking Tip:
Salvage those last bits of cheese. Collect them in a plastic bag in your freezer, then grate them frozen in a food processor. Use to top casseroles, hot vegetables, or chilled salads.

BAKED CORN ON THE COB

4 ears of corn
4 tablespoons diet margarine

½ cup water
salt and pepper to taste

Clean corn by removing husks and silk. Place each ear on a sheet of heavy aluminum foil. Baste each ear with margarine. Add water; season to taste. Wrap each ear securely and bake in a preheated 425° F. oven for ½ hour, or over hot coals on a barbecue for 15 minutes. Turn several times during cooking.

Makes 4 servings at 120 calories per serving.

Chef's Cooking Tip:
Fresh corn requires very little cooking. While most vegetables become softer with longer cooking, corn becomes firmer and toughens when overcooked.

RATATOUILLE

1 large red onion, chopped
2 medium-size green peppers, chopped
1 clove garlic, minced
3 medium-size ripe tomatoes, peeled, seeded, and diced
1 small eggplant, diced
1 small zucchini, diced

¼ cup tomato purée
1 tablespoon freshly chopped parsley
½ teaspoon whole oregano
½ teaspoon salt
¼ teaspoon crushed peppercorns
1 tablespoon freshly grated Parmesan cheese

Place onion, green pepper, and garlic in a Dutch oven and steam with a quarter cup of water or chicken broth for 5 minutes. Add diced tomatoes, eggplant, zucchini, tomato purée, and seasonings. Stir vegetables thoroughly to blend flavors. Cover and bake in a preheated 375° F. oven for 20 minutes. Uncover; sprinkle with Parmesan cheese and bake an additional 20 minutes or until the vegetables are tender.

Makes 6 servings at 50 calories per serving.

Chef's Cooking Tip:
This dish becomes extraordinary if it is allowed to cool and reheated.

BAKED STUFFED POTATOES

3 medium-size baking potatoes
1/3 cup scalded skim milk
3 tablespoons nonfat dry milk powder
2 tablespoons chopped chives
1/2 teaspoon imitation butter-flavored salt
1/8 teaspoon pepper
2 tablespoons butter or margarine
paprika

Wash, scrub, and dry potatoes. Puncture ends with a fork or cooking nail; bake at 400° F. for 1½ hours. Cut lengthwise and scoop out insides without breaking the shells. Mash the pulp with milk, milk powder, chives, butter-flavored salt, and pepper. Pile mixture back into shells. Dot with butter and sprinkle with paprika. Bake 10 minutes more or until just golden.

Makes 6 servings at 100 calories per serving.

BAKED TOMATO PARMESAN

2 whole tomatoes
4 tablespoons freshly grated Parmesan cheese

Immerse tomatoes in boiling water about 3 minutes to remove skins. Cut tomatoes in half, lengthwise through the stem, then lay halves cut-side down on a nonstick baking sheetpan or skillet. Sprinkle with Parmesan cheese and bake in a 400° F. oven until cheese is golden brown, about 15 minutes.

Makes 4 servings at 43 calories per serving.

BAKED ZUCCHINI ITALIAN

2 cups sliced zucchini
1/2 teaspoon oregano
1/4 teaspoon garlic powder
1 dozen cherry tomatoes, halved
salt to taste
1/2 cup freshly grated Parmesan cheese

In a 2-quart saucepan, bring 1 quart salted water to a boil. Add zucchini, oregano, and garlic powder. Reduce heat. Cover and simmer for 10 minutes, or until tender. Drain. Stir in cherry tomato halves and arrange vegetables in a shallow ovenproof baking dish. Season with salt to taste and sprinkle with Parmesan cheese. Bake at 350° F. for 15 to 20 minutes.

Makes 4 servings at 70 calories per serving.

Chef's Cooking Tip:
In dishes cooked by microwave, it's advisable to increase the amount of seasoning used to compensate for the shorter cooking time.

Sautéing and Oriental Stir-Frying

Sautéing and Oriental stir-frying are similar methods of cooking cut-up vegetables quickly with a minimum amount of fat and liquid. Vegetables cooked by these methods retain most of their important food value and are eaten with enthusiasm because of their delicious, just-cooked texture and flavor. In comparison, panfrying and French-frying are cooking techniques that require a large amount of fat and should never be considered for low-calorie cooking. When using either of these two methods, don't forget to coat all your cooking surfaces liberally with a food release agent—even nonstick surfaces; it reduces the amount of fat needed for sautéing and stir-frying by one-half! I especially like to use a nonstick spray that has imitation-butter flavor added; it adds greatly to the flavor of the food without adding calories. The only basic difference between the two methods is that stir-fried vegetables are generally cooked more quickly over a higher heat than is required for sautéed vegetables.

To sauté, heat one tablespoon of butter, margarine, or oil for each pound of vegetables in a heavy skillet with a tight-fitting lid. Add the prepared vegetables and lightly stir them over moderate heat until they are well coated. For a basic sauté, the skillet is covered and the cooking continued over low heat without any added liquid. The vegetables will cook largely in their own juices. Be sure to shake the skillet occasionally to prevent sticking.

To stir-fry, heat one tablespoon of oil (peanut oil for Oriental recipes) for each pound of vegetables in a large skillet or wok. Add the prepared vegetables and stir them over high heat until they are well coated and shiny, about 30 seconds. Then add a small amount of hot liquid; cover, reduce the heat and simmer for just a few minutes, depending on the vegetable. Uncover and stir-fry until the liquid evaporates, or thicken the sauce immediately with a mixture of one teaspoon cornstarch dissolved in two tablespoons water.

BASIC SAUTÉING TECHNIQUES

1. *Wash the vegetables.* Cut into even-size pieces.
2. *Heat a small amount of fat* (one tablespoon for each pound of vegetables) in a heavy skillet with a tight-fitting lid.
3. *Cook and stir the vegetables* over moderate heat until well coated. The small amount of fat sears the cut surfaces and seals in the vegetable's natural juices and flavor.

4. *Cover the vegetables,* reduce the heat to low and simmer until just tender, from five to eight minutes. Keep the heat low and shake the pan frequently to prevent sticking.

BASIC STIR-FRYING TECHNIQUES

1. *Wash the vegetables.* Slice diagonally into slivers. This shortens the cooking time by exposing a greater part of the vegetable to the heat.

2. *Heat a Chinese wok or large skillet over high heat.* Add a small amount of fat (one tablespoon per pound of vegetables is sufficient for low-calorie cooking). Heat for 15 seconds.

3. *Add the vegetables,* stir-fry until well coated. The hot fat will seal the moisture and flavor inside the vegetables.

4. *Add a small amount of boiling liquid,* ⅓ to ½ cup. Add additional seasonings. Cover the pan, reduce the heat to medium and simmer the vegetables until crisp-tender, from three to five minutes. Your eye, however, is the best judge of the exact moment when the vegetables should be removed from the pan. If several vegetables are cooked together, those needing a longer cooking time should be added to the pan first. If thickening is desired, blend one teaspoon cornstarch with two tablespoons cold water to make a paste—only 11 calories for the whole dish!) Stir mixture into pan until sauce thickens and vegetables are well coated. Turn into serving dish and serve immediately.

BEAN SPROUTS AND MUSHROOMS SAUTÉ

1 tablespoon oil
1 cup sliced fresh mushrooms
¼ cup sliced green onions

¾ pound fresh bean sprouts
salt and pepper to taste

Rinse bean sprouts in cold water; drain thoroughly. Heat oil in a large nonstick skillet over high heat. Add sliced mushrooms and onions. Sauté, uncovered, for 3 minutes, stirring constantly. Add bean sprouts and sauté until sprouts are just heated through. Season with salt and pepper and serve immediately.

Makes 4 servings at 88 calories per serving.

Chef's Cooking Tip:
When buying fresh mushrooms, look for ones that are creamy white in color and have tightly closed caps. Store them unwashed in the refrigerator in uncovered containers. Use them within 5 days.

SAUTEED GARDEN VEGETABLES

3 large ripe tomatoes
½ pound fresh green beans, trimmed
1 tablespoon oil
1 onion, thinly sliced
1 celery rib, sliced
½ pound zucchini squash, sliced
1 teaspoon imitation-butter flavoring
½ teaspoon whole basil
salt and pepper to taste

In a large saucepan, bring a large quantity of water to a boil. Core tomatoes and place them in water for 3 minutes. Remove and cool under cold running water. Peel off skin and slice into thin wedges. Place beans in water. Add 1 teaspoon of salt and blanch, uncovered, about 10 minutes, or until just undercooked. Drain. Heat oil in a large nonstick skillet. Saute onions and celery for 5 minutes. Add tomatoes, beans, zucchini, and seasonings to skillet. Stir vegetables until heated through. Serve immediately.

Makes 4 servings at 50 calories per serving.

SAUTÉED MUSHROOMS WITH TOMATOES

1 pound freshly sliced mushrooms
¾ cup dry sherry wine
1 tablespoon lemon juice
salt and pepper to taste
1 ripe tomato, peeled, seeded, and diced

Slice mushrooms and place them in a large nonstick skillet with remaining ingredients. Set over high heat and steam, covered, for 3 minutes. Uncover and sauté until liquid is almost absorbed.

Makes 4 servings at 16 calories per serving.

Chef's Cooking Tip:
Mushrooms need proper ventilation or they will become moist and sticky and turn brown. Store them in the container in which they were purchased or put them into a brown paper bag, not a plastic one.

SAUTÉED CABBAGE

1 small (1½-pound) head cabbage
1 tablespoon oil
½ teaspoon salt
½ teaspoon sugar

Core cabbage and remove tough outer leaves. Cut lengthwise through core into 1-inch-wide wedges; then cut wedges into thirds. Separate leaves (you should have about 5 firmly packed cups) and rinse under cold running water. Drain. Heat oil in a large nonstick skillet over medium-high heat. Add cabbage and sauté quickly to coat leaves with oil. Saute for 2 minutes. Add salt and sugar. Cook and additional 1 to 2 minutes, or until leaves are bright colored and wilted. Serve immediately.

Makes 6 servings at 52 calories per serving.

Chef's Cooking Tip:
There are four kinds of green cabbages regularly sold in the United States: 1) Danish or Hollander, 2) domestic, 3) pointed, and 4) Savoy. These various varieties can be used interchangeably in cooking, but the older and firmer Danish "winter" cabbage will take slightly longer to cook.

SPINACH IN RED WINE

¼ cup chicken or beef stock
¼ pound sliced fresh mushrooms
1 clove garlic, minced
¼ cup dry red wine
½ teaspoon dry mustard
1 package (10-ounce) chopped frozen spinach, cooked and drained
salt and pepper to taste

Heat the stock in a skillet and sauté mushrooms and garlic for 5 minutes. Stir the dry mustard into the ¼ cup of wine and add to skillet. Stir in the cooked spinach, cover, and simmer until heated through.

Makes 4 servings at 20 calories per serving.

Chef's Cooking Tip:
Remember, when cooking fresh vegetables, use a minimum amount of liquid and a minimum amount of time. Cook vegetables only until crisp-tender to retain their nutritional value.

SAUTÉED ZUCCHINI AND CHEESE

3 tablespoons chicken broth
½ teaspoon garlic powder
1¼ pounds zucchini, sliced
salt and pepper to taste
2 tablespoons freshly grated Parmesan cheese

Dissolve garlic powder in broth. Heat broth in a large nonstick skillet. Add zucchini, cover, and cook over moderate heat for 5 minutes. Uncover and sauté over high heat an additional 5 minutes, or until vegetables are tender. Stir frequently. Season to taste with salt and pepper. Sprinkle with Parmesan cheese just before serving.

Makes 6 servings at 25 calories per serving.

Chef's Cooking Tip:
Because of its high water content, presalting zucchini will draw out water and prevent sautéed dish from browning properly. For this reason, season with salt just before serving.

ZUCCHINI PROVENÇALE

4 tablespoons chicken broth
1 cup thinly sliced onion
1 clove minced garlic
2 pounds thinly sliced zucchini
1 green pepper, cut in strips
1 cup diced tomatoes
½ teaspoon whole oregano
salt and pepper to taste

Sauté onions and garlic in broth until tender but not browned. Add the zucchini and green pepper strips; sauté for 5 minutes. Mix in the tomatoes and seasoning. Cover and cook over low heat 10 to 15 minutes, stirring occasionally.

Makes 6 servings at 16 calories per serving.

Chef's Cooking Tip:
When the price of tomatoes is high, diced sweet red peppers are a good color and flavor substitute.

SAUTÉED ZUCCHINI AND ONIONS

1 teaspoon cooking oil
1 cup sliced onion
2 cups chicken broth
4 cups sliced zucchini

¼ teaspoon whole thyme
⅛ teaspoon dill weed
salt and pepper to taste

In a large nonstick skillet, heat oil and sauté sliced onions for 5 minutes over moderate heat. Add chicken broth, sliced zucchini, and seasonings. Simmer, uncovered, for 15 minutes, stirring occasionally.

Makes 4 servings at 25 calories per serving.

Boiling

I think that it would be safe to say that more homemakers cook vegetables by boiling them in water than by any other method—if for no other reason than they are following the directions written on the back of a frozen package. There is nothing inherently wrong with this method of vegetable cookery, however. In fact, it is the best way to cook the various strong-flavored vegetables of the cabbage and onion family and other vegetables that react adversely to intense heat or a long period of cooking. But the amount of water used and the cooking times needed will vary for each kind of vegetable, their freshness, their age, their size, and the way they are prepared for cooking.

Essentially, the object of cooking vegetables is to make them palatable without destroying their characteristic color, flavor, and texture. To accomplish this, a good general rule is to always cook vegetables quickly with as little cooking water as possible. In general, the cooking techniques which retain the quality and flavor in vegetables are most apt to preserve their nutritional values as well.

To retain the nutritional qualities in vegetables, prepare them just before cooking. Vegetables lose much of their nutritional value when exposed to air or allowed to soak in water for any length of time prior to cooking. Cook them quickly, covered, as nearly without water as possible until tender, and serve immediately.

To retain the natural color, flavor, and texture in vegetables, gradually add the prepared vegetables to a large amount of rapidly boiling salted water and continue to cook, uncovered, at a gentle boil until the desired degree of doneness is obtained. The more water you use, the more quickly it will return to the boiling point after the vegetables have been added, and the more colorful and flavorful they will be. Drain and serve immediately, or cool; then reheat briefly in hot water. Do not attempt to keep boiled vegetables warm for any length of time before serving, or their color, texture, and taste will rapidly deteriorate.

CAULIFLOWER A L'ITALIENNE

2 small heads cauliflower
2 quarts water
1 tablespoon lemon juice
1 tablespoon chopped onion
2 tablespoons chopped green pepper
⅛ teaspoon garlic powder
⅛ teaspoon whole basil
salt to taste
1 cup halved cherry tomatoes

Separate heads into cauliflowerets. Cook in boiling water with lemon juice until tender, about 5 minutes. While cauliflower is cooking, sauté onion, green pepper, salt, and garlic powder with ¼ cup of the boiling water in a small nonstick skillet about 5 minutes. Add cherry tomatoes and whole basil to cauliflowerets just long enough to heat through. Drain. Combine cauliflower and cherry tomatoes with the skillet mixture and serve.

Makes 6 servings at 40 calories per serving.

Chef's Cooking Tip:
To retain the color of white vegetables, do not overcook, do not cover the pot. Cook them in just enough liquid to submerge them, and add a little lemon juice or vinegar to the cooking liquid to neutralize the alkaline content of the water.

BOILED CAULIFLOWER WITH PARSLEY

1 large head of cauliflower (about 2 pounds)
½ cup chicken broth
1 teaspoon lemon juice
1 tablespoon freshly chopped parsley

Wash cauliflower thoroughly. Remove outer green leaves and cut into flowerets. Put broth and lemon juice in a saucepan; bring to a boil. Add flowerets, cover and cook about 5 minutes until crisp-tender. Drain and garnish with chopped parsley.

Makes 4 servings at 16 calories per serving.

Chef's Cooking Tip:
If you want to rid cauliflower of its strong flavor, cook it rapidly until just tender. Be sure to leave the pot uncovered so the sulfur compounds are released in the air.

BOILED POTATOES

4 medium new potatoes　　　1 teaspoon salt
2 cups water

Bring water and salt to a boil in a 1-quart saucepan. Cut potatoes in half. Add to boiling water and cook, covered, over medium heat until they are tender and can be easily pierced with a knife, about 15 to 20 minutes. Drain. Shake the pan for a few minutes over a low heat to further dry potatoes.

Makes 4 servings at 70 calories per serving.

Chef's Cooking Tip:
For variations, sprinkle the cooked and drained potatoes with freshly chopped parsley or dill weed before serving.

FRESH BOILED ARTICHOKES

4 medium-size artichokes　　　1 small chopped onion
4 lemon slices　　　2 chopped celery ribs
1 chopped carrot

Cut off stem and tough outside leaves. With a sharp knife or scissors, cut off the sharp points on each leaf. Wash under cold running water; drain well. Coarsely chop carrot, onion, and celery and use them as a base in a large saucepan or Dutch oven. Lay the lemon slices on the base of vegetables; then place an artichoke on each slice. If the saucepan is too big to allow the artichokes to fit snugly, then tie the lemon slices on the bottom of the artichokes with cotton twine.

Fill the pan with hot water. Boil about 30 minutes or until you can easily pull out one of the lower leaves. Remove chokes from the water; drain well by turning them upside down.

Makes 4 servings at 36 calories per serving.

Chef's Cooking Tip:
To maximize the vitamin and nutritive value of fresh vegetables, don't allow them to soak in water before cooking or to remain in the cooking liquid after cooking. Vitamins and minerals are soluble and will therefore be lost in the liquid.

FRESH BROCCOLI WITH LEMON

1 pound fresh broccoli
1 gallon water

½ teaspoon salt
¼ teaspoon nutmeg

Soak broccoli in cold water a few minutes to clean. Cut off tough ends and discard dark green leaves. Bring water to a vigorous boil; add salt and nutmeg and cook from 10 to 15 minutes until stalks are tender. Do not cover. Drain and serve, or plunge in cold water to stop the cooking process and reheat just before serving. Garnish with lemon wedges.

Makes 4 servings at 25 calories per serving.

Chef's Cooking Tip:
If using frozen broccoli, use two 10-ounce packages. Follow the same directions, but remember that frozen broccoli is partially cooked, so cut the cooking time almost in half. Watch the flowerettes—not the stems—because they will cook much faster. This isn't the most nutritious way to cook broccoli, but it does give it a bright green color.

HOT BOILED ASPARAGUS SPEARS

12 fresh asparagus spears
½ teaspoon salt

1 gallon boiling water

Peel, trim, and wash asparagus thoroughly. Bring water to a vigorous boil; add salt. Add asparagus spears and boil gently, uncovered, about 10 minutes. Test for doneness by lifting a stalk out of the water. It should droop at both ends. As a final test, insert a knife blade in the butt-end of one of the spears. It should enter easily. Don't overcook.

Makes 4 servings at 16 calories per serving.

Chef's Cooking Tip:
If using frozen asparagus, remember that the freezing process partially cooks the vegetable. Use the cooking method above, but reduce the cooking time almost in half. Again, don't overcook.

GREEN BEANS AND STEWED TOMATOES

1 can (16-ounce) cut green beans
1 can (10-ounce) stewed tomatoes
¼ cup minced onion
½ teaspoon butter-flavored salt
¼ teaspoon pepper

Drain beans. Combine with remaining ingredients and simmer, uncovered, 10 to 15 minutes.

Makes 6 servings at 30 calories per serving.

HOT SWEET AND SOUR BEETS

1 can (16-ounce) sliced beets
2 tablespoons cider vinegar
1 tablespoon sugar
1 clove garlic, minced
4 whole cloves
1 teaspoon pickling spice

Drain liquid from beets into a small saucepan. Tie garlic, cloves, and pickling spice in a square of cheesecloth or put into a stainless steel tea strainer. Add the vinegar and sugar to the beet liquid. Add the spice bag. Bring the liquid to a boil. Remove liquid from heat, add the sliced beets and chill. Reheat to serve.

Makes 4 servings at 55 calories per serving.

Chef's Cooking Tip:
In contrast to green vegetables which are generally cooked uncovered, red vegetables are cooked covered so that they benefit from their own acid content.

SWEET PEAS MANDARIN

1 package (10-ounce) frozen green peas
1 can (5-ounce) water chestnuts, drained and sliced
½ cup mandarin orange segments
salt and pepper to taste

Cook peas according to package directions. Stir in orange segments and water chestnuts. Heat through and serve.

Makes 4 servings at 40 calories per serving.

HUNGARIAN BRUSSELS SPROUTS

1 pound (40 small) Brussels
    sprouts, blanched
2 cups canned whole tomatoes
1 medium diced green pepper
1 small bay leaf
1 teaspoon caraway seeds
½ teaspoon paprika
    salt and pepper to taste

Buy small, hard, bright-green sprouts. Trim off stem ends. Speed their cooking by cutting an "X" into the stem end or slice them in half lengthwise. Fast cooking is essential. Like cabbage, if sprouts are overcooked, they will become strong-tasting and bitter. Soak sprouts in cold water for ten minutes; drain. Blanch in rapidly boiling water for 3 to 5 minutes, then cool quickly in cold water to stop the cooking process and to set the color. Drain and crush the whole tomatoes. Place tomatoes and remaining ingredients in a large nonstick skillet; simmer for 10 minutes. Add the Brussels sprouts and heat thoroughly, taking care not to overcook. The center of the sprouts should still be crunchy.

Makes 4 servings at 36 calories per serving.

JULIENNE OF BEANS WITH TOMATO

1 pound snap beans, julienned
½ cup chopped white tips of green
    onion
1 minced clove garlic
1 tablespoon diced green pepper
1 tablespoon diced celery
1 ripe tomato, peeled, seeded,
    and diced
salt and pepper to taste
⅓ cup chicken broth

Wash beans; trim ends. Julienne into thin strips. Blanch in a large amount of boiling water, uncovered, about 10 to 15 minutes. Chill in cold water immediately to stop the cooking process and to set the color. Combine the remaining ingredients, except the tomato, in a large nonstick skillet and sauté for about 10 minutes. Add the diced tomato and cooked beans and heat through.

Makes 4 servings at 40 calories per serving.

Chef's Cooking Tip:
To retain more of a vegetable's nutrients, wash it before it is cut rather than after.

MASHED POTATOES

3 medium new potatoes
¼ cup skim milk, warmed

1 tablespoon diet margarine
salt and pepper to taste

Fill a 1-quart saucepan halfway with water. Add a teaspoon of salt; bring to a boil. Meanwhile, pare and quarter potatoes. Add to saucepan. Cover and boil until tender when pierced with a knife, about 20 minutes. Drain. Shake pan for a few minutes over low heat to further dry potatoes; mash. Add warmed milk, diet margarine, and seasoning a little at a time, beating each addition until the proper consistency is reached. Adjust seasoning to taste. Garnish with paprika or freshly chopped parsley.

Makes 2 servings at 92 calories per serving.

Chef's Cooking Tip:
The type of potato you buy is determined by the way you want to cook them; For boiling potatoes, buy Irish Cobblers, Red Pontiacs, or White Roses. For baking potatoes, buy Cherokees or Russet Burbanks (Idaho).

SWEET AND SOUR CUT GREEN BEANS

1 package (20-ounce) frozen cut green beans
3 cups water
3 whole cloves

¼ cup vinegar
2 tablespoons sugar
dash of salt and pepper

Bring the water to a rapid boil; add the beans and cloves; cook, uncovered, about 8 minutes or until beans are tender. Drain and add vinegar, salt, and pepper; cook 5 minutes longer. Add sugar to dissolve. Remove whole cloves; then drain and serve.

Makes 8 servings at 26 calories per serving.

Chef's Cooking Tip:
Don't add soda to green beans to bring out their color. The alkaline solution destroys the soluble vitamins and gives the vegetable a mushy texture.

TARRAGON GREEN BEANS

1 pound fresh green beans
¼ cup chicken broth
½ teaspoon tarragon
½ teaspoon salt
¼ teaspoon pepper

Place beans in a large kettle of boiling salted water. Bring water back to a boil, reduce heat and cook, uncovered, about 10 minutes, or until tender. Drain immediately and run under cold water to stop the cooking process and preserve the color. Just before serving, sauté in a large nonstick skillet with remaining ingredients until heated through.

Makes 4 servings at 25 calories per serving.

Chef's Cooking Tip:
Fresh green beans can be cooked in a large amount of boiling water or broth, uncovered, until tender; then drained, cooled, and reheated at the very last minute. Or they can be cooked in a small amount of water or broth in a covered saucepan until tender and served immediately. The first method retains the bright green color of the beans, while the second method retains more of the bean's natural flavor and nutrients.

Steaming

Steaming is the technique of cooking vegetables wholly or partially by steam. The various methods of steaming vegetables are direct steaming, waterless cooking, pressure steaming, and steam-baking.

Direct steaming is cooking vegetables over—not in—boiling water. The vegetables are placed on a rack or in a perforated steamer basket, and the cooking utensil tightly covered. The steam generated by the boiling water recirculates continuously inside the sealed utensil, thus cooking the vegetables.

The waterless cooking method steams the vegetables in a tightly covered pan or skillet with little or no liquid added—the exact amount needed varying with the size of the pan and the water content of the vegetables. In the little-or-no-water method of cooking, there's very little nutritive loss; the vegetables absorb practically all of the cooking liquid. The success of this method lies in controlling the degree of heat during the cooking process. If the heat is not lowered after the pan is covered, the liquid may boil away, and the vegetables will scorch and dry out.

Steaming in a pressure cooker is an excellent method for cooking vegetables, provided you watch the cooking time carefully as overcooking results very quickly. The real advantage of pressure steaming lies in its ability to cook most vegetables in one-third the time needed for conventional methods of moist heat cooking.

Vegetables that are steamed by the waterless cooking method on top of the stove can be cooked by the same procedure in the oven. The prepared vegetables are placed in an ovenproof casserole dish with a small amount of liquid and seasoning, and the dish is tightly covered to hold in steam. Steam-bake in a preheated moderate to moderately hot oven until the vegetables are crisp-tender, from 30 to 60 minutes, depending on the size of the vegetables and the temperature of the oven. Turn the vegetables in the casserole at least once during cooking.

As a moist heat cooking method, steaming—like stir-frying—has a number of advantages over boiling: steamed vegetables retain more of their natural color, taste, and food value. They also cook drier and taste less watery than vegetables that are boiled.

BASIC STEAMING TECHNIQUES
1. *Peel, trim, and wash the vegetables.* Shred, slice, or dice.
2. *Bring the cooking liquid to a boil* in a heavy pan with a tight-fitting lid.
3. *Add the vegetables and seasoning* to the pan; cover tightly. When the cooking liquid is allowed to evaporate in the air or to be absorbed completely, the vegetables need not be placed on a rack or in a steamer basket over the boiling liquid.
4. *Steam the vegetables* until crisp-tender. Allow from 4 to 8 minutes more cooking time than for the same vegetables processed in boiling liquid.

CARROTS LYONNAISE

4 medium carrots, peeled and sliced
¼ cup chopped onion
1 teaspoon imitation-butter flavoring

¼ teaspoon whole thyme
salt and pepper to taste
2 tablespoons dry white wine, broth or water

In a small saucepan, combine carrots with remaining ingredients. Cover and cook until tender over medium heat about 7 minutes, shaking pan occasionally to prevent sticking.

Makes 4 servings at 30 calories per serving.

Chef's Cooking Tip:
Before storing carrots, be sure to cut off tops so carrot roots remain fresh. If left on, they will continue to live off the root, causing it to dry out.

CARAWAY CABBAGE

1 pound (1 small head) green cabbage
2 tablespoons minced onion
¼ cup chicken broth
½ teaspoon caraway seeds
salt and pepper to taste

Rinse cabbage and discard wilted outside leaves. Shred cabbage and put in a large nonstick skillet; add chicken broth and onion. Sprinkle caraway seed over the top of the cabbage, cover and cook over high heat about 5 minutes to steam. Stir occasionally. Lower heat and simmer until the cabbage is tender. Don't overcook. Drain and season with salt and freshly ground pepper.

Makes 4 servings at 16 calories per serving.

Chef's Cooking Tip:
With the exception of braised cabbage, which is cooked for several hours, overcooking vegetables in the cabbage family (cabbage, Brussels sprouts, broccoli, cauliflower, kale, kohlrabi, and collard) will liberate the sulfur compounds they contain and make them strong-tasting. Cook cabbage only until crisp-tender.

DILLED CARROTS

4 medium carrots
1 minced clove garlic
¼ teaspoon dill weed
2 tablespoons dry white wine, broth, or water

Peel and slice carrots. In a small saucepan, combine carrots with remaining ingredients; cover tightly and cook over moderate heat approximately 7 minutes, or until liquid is absorbed and carrots are barely cooked.

Makes 4 servings at 25 calories per serving.

Chef's Cooking Tip:
Yellow vegetables will keep their color unless they are overcooked. Overcooking or exposure to high temperatures for too long a time will give the vegetables an unpleasant flavor and destroy their nutritional value.

STEAMED VEGETABLE MEDLEY

4 medium carrots, sliced
3 celery ribs, sliced
1 medium onion, sliced
½ cup chicken broth or water
1 teaspoon imitation-butter flavoring
¼ teaspoon dill weed
salt and pepper to taste

Place ingredients in a saucepan. Cover and cook over low heat about 15 minutes, or until vegetables are tender and liquid is absorbed. Stir occasionally.

Makes 4 servings at 40 calories per serving.

Chef's Cooking Tip:
No other method of cooking retains the flavor, texture, and color of vegetables better than steaming. Remember to use only enough liquid to prevent scorching and to use low to moderate heat.

Braising

In *haute cuisine*, uniformly cut or shredded vegetables simmered slowly with a small amount of fat and liquid in a covered pan are said to be braised. During the cooking, the braising liquid is reduced to a rich, flavorful glaze and used as a sauce.

To adapt a classic braising recipe to low-calorie cookery, the most obvious thing to do, of course, is to reduce or eliminate the high-calorie fat. To replace a butter flavor, for instance, I like to use imitation butter flavoring, but seasonings like wine or soy sauce added to the braising liquid or used to deglaze the pan after the vegetables are cooked work equally as well. Incidentally, removing the fat from a recipe often increases the risk of the vegetable's scorching. To discourage this, I prefer to braise vegetables in the oven rather than on top of the stove—a slower but safer braising technique.

At first, braising vegetables in the oven may seem to be the same as steaming, but there is more liquid in braising and the cooking times are much longer. Don't be afraid to experiment with various kinds of vegetables. You'll discover, however, that onions, root vegetables, cabbage, lettuce, celery, fennel and artichokes all take particularly well to this method of preparation.

BASIC BRAISING TECHNIQUES

1. *Slice, dice, or shred the vegetables,* removing any tough cores, stems, or ribs.

2. *Coat a shallow skillet or baking dish* with nonstick cookware spray. Place the pan over moderate heat.

3. *Add the braising liquid* to a depth of 1 inch; bring to a rolling boil.

4. *Add the vegetables and seasonings* and immediately cover the pan to hold in the steam. The boiling liquid will sear the outer surface of the vegetables and help seal in the juices.

5. *Cook the vegetables,* covered, over low heat, on top of the stove or in the oven. Add additional amounts of liquid, if necessary. Stir or shake the pan occasionally to prevent sticking.

6. *Remove the vegetables* to a warm platter. Deglaze the pan and boil down the braising liquid to a few tablespoons and sprinkle over the vegetables.

BRAISED BELGIAN ENDIVE

8 small Belgian endive
1 tablespoon lemon juice
½ cup chicken or beef broth
2 tablespoons diet margarine
1 teaspoon sugar
salt and pepper to taste

Trim the ragged leaves from the endive and trim the butt end. Wash under cold running water; then dry with paper toweling. Arrange the endive, snugly, in a single layer in a small nonstick skillet with a tight-fitting cover. Mix the ingredients and pour over the endive. Bring the liquid to a boil, then cover and cook over low heat, about 30 to 45 minutes, or until the endive is tender when pierced with a fork and the liquid has evaporated. Uncover the last 5 minutes of cooking to allow the vegetables to brown slightly. Turn at least once during cooking.

Makes 4 servings at 40 calories per serving.

Chef's Cooking Tip:
The small amount of sugar is added to aid in the browning.

BRAISED CELERY

4 cups sliced celery ribs
½ cup chicken broth
¼ teaspoon salt
⅛ teaspoon pepper

Combine ingredients in a large saucepan. Cover and simmer 15 to 20 minutes, or until crisp-tender.

Makes 4 servings at 16 calories per serving.

Chef's Cooking Tip:
Vegetables that are braised can be successfully reheated over low heat in a covered saucepan.

BRAISED ONIONS

2 medium-size red Italian onions
salt and pepper to taste

chopped parsley garnish

Peel the onions and cut off a slice from each end; cut in half crosswise. Put the onion halves in a baking dish, season with salt and pepper. Add about ¼ inch of water to the bottom of the baking dish. Cover and braise in a moderate 375° F. oven for 30 minutes. Uncover and test for tenderness with a fork. Continue to bake, uncovered, for another 15 minutes if necessary to make the onions tender. Garnish with parsley and serve.

Makes 4 servings at 40 calories per serving.

Chef's Cooking Tip:
Ironically, onions contain a large amount of sugar and are therefore relatively high in calories. The dieter should use onions sparingly. Substitute shallots for onions whenever possible.

BRAISED CARROTS AND CELERY

1 pound pared and sliced carrots
6 celery ribs, cut in 2-inch lengths

1 cup chicken broth
½ teaspoon chopped parsley

Put chicken broth in saucepan and bring to a boil. Put vegetables in broth, cover and simmer until tender. Uncover and continue to simmer until most of the liquid is evaporated. Sprinkle and garnish with parsley flakes.

Makes 6 servings at 25 calories per serving.

Chef's Cooking Tip:
If possible, peel vegetables only when the skin is too uneven to be thoroughly cleaned. The nutrients in root vegetables lie close beneath the skin, and peeling only destroys the vegetables' nutritional value.

CELERY JULIENNE

6 celery ribs
1 cup chicken broth
1 teaspoon onion powder
¼ teaspoon cumin

salt and pepper to taste
1 teaspoon freshly chopped parsley

Cut celery ribs in half lengthwise, then in half again. Cutting on the bias, cut julienne strips between 1 and 1½ inches long. Arrange julienned celery in a large nonstick skillet and add the rest of the ingredients, reserving the chopped parsley. Heat to boiling, then reduce heat, cover, and simmer 15 minutes or until celery is tender-crisp. Reserve the liquid. Arrange celery in a serving dish. Reduce liquid by half over high heat; pour over celery. Garnish with parsley and serve.

Makes 4 servings at 16 calories per serving.

Chef's Cooking Tip:
To retain the nutritional value in vegetables, prepare them as nearly whole as possible, in as little liquid as possible, and eat them immediately after cooking.

FRENCH-STYLE PEAS

1 tablespoon butter or margarine
2 sliced green onions, white part only
1 cup finely shredded lettuce
1 package (10-ounce) frozen peas, defrosted

2 tablespoons chicken broth or water
½ teaspoon salt
1 can (5-ounce) water chestnuts, drained and sliced

Melt the butter in a small saucepan or nonstick skillet. Add the remaining ingredients except water chestnuts and cook over very low heat for 10 minutes. Add the water chestnuts, cover, and cook 5 minutes longer.

Makes 4 servings at 60 calories per serving.

Chef's Cooking Tip:
To preserve a vegetable's flavor and color, blanch (parboil) in a large amount of boiling water until barely cooked, then drain and cool quickly under cold water. Reheat in a small amount of boiling water until just heated through and serve immediately.

HOT SWEET AND SOUR CABBAGE

6 cups shredded red cabbage
   (about a 3-pound head)
1 cup apple juice
¼ cup red wine vinegar
2 whole cloves
1 small bay leaf
1 tablespoon brown sugar

   Cut the cabbage vertically into quarters; remove the white hard core. Shred cabbage wedges through shredder blade on a food processor or cut lengthwise with a sharp knife into thin strips. Combine ingredients in a large saucepan; mix well.

   Bring the liquid to a boil, then cover lightly and simmer for two to three hours, stirring occasionally. Use as little liquid as possible, adding either apple juice or vinegar if cooking liquid gets too low. Before serving, remove cloves and bay leaf and adjust seasoning to taste.

Makes 8 servings at 28 calories per serving.

MIXED VEGETABLE CASSEROLE

6 medium carrots
1 medium turnip
1 medium rutabaga
1 medium onion
6 celery ribs
2 tablespoons diet margarine
⅓ cup dry white wine
½ teaspoon dill weed
   salt and pepper to taste
2 tablespoons finely chopped
   parsley

   Peel vegetables and cut julienne style, about ¼ inch wide and 2 to 3 inches long. Melt margarine in casserole over low heat and add remaining ingredients except parsley. Cover and simmer for 25 minutes, or until vegetables are tender. Garnish with parsley and serve.

Makes 6 servings at 60 calories per serving.

SALADS AND DRESSINGS

As every dieter knows, when you're struggling to keep slim, salads are the best things you can eat. Besides being crisp, delicious, and filling, they are colorful and beautiful to look at and add variety to your meals without adding calories. What's more, salads are rich in vitamins and minerals and add much-needed roughage to the diet. But best of all, by curbing your appetite, they help diminish your craving for higher-calorie foods.

So don't forget to put plenty of salads on your diet menus—whether tossed, molded, marinated, or frozen, you'll be surprised how many ways there are to serve them. For lunch or for dinner—as an appetizer, as a side dish, as a main dish, as part of a buffet, or even as a dessert—salads are versatile and can be altered to suit your own personal taste. With innumerable varieties of foods to choose from, use your culinary inventiveness and resourcefulness to create your very own low-calorie salad combinations.

Salad-making is beautifully easy, but even the simplest salads must be prepared with care or the results will be less than sumptuous. The salad ingredients, either raw or cooked, must be the freshest and the best available—selected to include a wide range of flavor, color, texture, and nutrients, and be thoroughly chilled before being combined. Dressing must be used sparingly and enhance rather than disguise the main ingredients. Purchase one of the convenient low-calorie salad dressings now on the market or make your own.

Finally, salads—simple or elaborate—must harmonize with the other foods they are served with. And pay particular attention to the arrangement of the salad ingredients and to the garnishments. Garnishes give a salad its finished look and contribute to its attractiveness and palatability, but don't overdo it. As a rule, the simple garnishes such as a sprig of parsley, a strip of pimiento, or a sprinkling of chopped chives are the most effective.

ASPARAGUS SALAD

16 white asparagus spears, canned
4 green pepper rings
4 teaspoons chopped hard-cooked egg white
4 teaspoons diced red peppers
4 large lettuce leaves
4 ounces low-calorie dressing

Place 4 stalks of cold canned asparagus spears through a pepper ring for each serving. Place on lettuce leaf and garnish with chopped hard-cooked egg white and diced red peppers. Serve with 1 ounce of low-calorie dressing.

Makes 4 servings at 25 calories per serving.

Chef's Cooking Tip:
When opening a can of asparagus spears, open the can from the bottom so the spears can be withdrawn without damaging the tips.

CARROT AND RAISIN SALAD

2 cups grated carrot
4 tablespoons raisins
4 tablespoons drained crushed pineapple
2 tablespoons pineapple juice
4 tablespoons plain yogurt
salt and pepper to taste
4 small lettuce cups
4 parsley sprigs

Grate the carrots and mix with raisins and drained crushed pineapple. Blend reserved pineapple juice, yogurt, and seasoning. Mix ingredients together and serve on lettuce cups. Garnish with parsley sprigs.

Makes 4 servings at 60 calories per serving.

Chef's Cooking Tip:
Don't store fresh lettuce too near fresh ripening fruit in your refrigerator. Ripening fruit can give off gases that can cause the lettuce to develop tiny unappetizing brown spots. As an added safeguard, store lettuce in sealed plastic bags.

CHICKEN SALAD

2 cups cooked white meat of chicken or turkey, diced
¾ cup minced celery
¼ cup minced onion
¼ cup minced green pepper
2 tablespoons diced pimiento
6 tablespoons low-calorie creamy salad dressing or plain yogurt
salt and pepper to taste
4 lettuce cups
paprika

Combine ingredients and toss lightly. Fill 4 lettuce cups with the tossed salad and sprinkle with paprika. Chill thoroughly before serving.

Makes 4 servings at 155 calories per serving.

Chef's Cooking Tip:
Cooked poultry should be kept in a covered container in the refrigerator no longer than 2 days. For extended storage, freeze in heavy-duty foil up to 3 to 4 weeks.

CHICKEN SALAD SUPREME

3 cups cooked chicken or turkey meat, diced
1 cup celery, diced
2 tablespoons fresh lemon juice
¼ cup imitation mayonnaise
¼ cup water chestnuts, sliced
¼ cup green onions, sliced
¼ cup green pepper, chopped
dash paprika
salt and pepper to taste
1½ cups alfalfa sprouts
2 cantaloupes, sliced
1 small head endive

Combine first seven ingredients. Chill. Cut melons horizontally into 1-inch-thick slices. Place melon slices on individual plates; line the inside of each with ¼ cup alfalfa sprouts. Mound ½ cup chilled chicken salad over sprouts. Serve on endive leaf and garnish with a sprinkling of paprika.

Makes 6 servings at 255 calories per serving.

CRAB SALAD

2 cans (7½-ounce) crabmeat
2 tablespoons diced onion
½ cup diced celery
1 teaspoon Worcestershire sauce
  salt and pepper to taste
¼ cup diet salad dressing or
  mayonnaise
paprika
4 crisp lettuce leaves

In a medium-size mixing bowl, lightly mix crabmeat, onion, celery, Worcestershire sauce, seasoning, and salad dressing. Chill thoroughly. Serve on crisp lettuce leaves and garnish with paprika, parsley sprigs, and lemon wedges.

Makes 4 servings at 150 calories per serving.

Chef's Cooking Tip:
Cooked fresh, frozen, or vacuum-packed canned crabmeat can all be substituted for canned crabmeat. Be sure to keep all these varieties under constant refrigeration, however.

COLESLAW WITH CREAMY DRESSING

4 cups cabbage, shredded
½ cup plain yogurt
¼ cup buttermilk
1 tablespoon vinegar
½ teaspoon mustard
½ teaspoon paprika
1 teaspoon sugar
salt and pepper to taste

Blend yogurt, buttermilk, vinegar, and seasonings in a mixing bowl. Add the cabbage and toss lightly until well coated with the dressing.

Makes 6 servings at 34 calories per serving.

Chef's Cooking Tip:
Cabbage is easier to shred if it's well chilled. For crunchier coleslaw, cut the cabbage heads in half, then soak them in salted ice water for 1 hour. Drain well. Also, mix with the dressing just before serving.

CREAMY PINEAPPLE COLESLAW

2 cups cabbage, shredded
½ cup pineapple tidbits
¼ cup grated carrot
½ cup plain yogurt
½ cup unsweetened pineapple juice
1 teaspoon prepared horseradish
salt and pepper to taste

Blend yogurt, pineapple juice, horseradish, and seasoning to make dressing. Toss with remaining ingredients. Chill for at least 1 hour before serving.

Makes 4 servings at 60 calories per serving.

Chef's Cooking Tip:
To prevent low-calorie salads from becoming monotonous, it's a good idea to vary the vegetable or fruit ingredients (in this case, apple tidbits along with unsweetened apple juice would be good substitutions) and to change the flavor of the dressing.

CRISP AND TANGY COLESLAW

3 cups (about ½ head) shredded cabbage
½ cup shredded carrot
½ cup sliced radishes
½ cup sliced celery
2 cups unsweetened pineapple juice
½ cup white vinegar
2 teaspoons prepared horseradish
pepper to taste

Combine all ingredients in a large mixing bowl. Marinate the slaw in the refrigerator about 1 hour. Drain before serving. Garnish with paprika for added color, if desired.

Makes 4 servings at 25 calories per serving.

CUCUMBER YOGURT SALAD

2 cucumbers, peeled and sliced
2 green onions, sliced
½ cup low-fat plain yogurt
½ tablespoon lemon juice
¼ teaspoon sugar
dash pepper

Combine all ingredients and chill.

Makes 4 servings at 31 calories per serving.

Chef's Cooking Tip:
Cucumber slices will be crisper if you chill them in salted ice water for at least 1 hour. Rinse and drain them thoroughly before blending them with the dressing.

FARMER-STYLE COTTAGE CHEESE SALAD

½ cup cucumber, peeled and diced
½ cup firm tomato, peeled, seeded, and diced
¼ cup diced celery
¼ cup diced green onions
¼ cup grated carrot
1 carton (16-ounce) large-curd uncreamed cottage cheese
6 paper-thin slices, red or yellow onion
½ head curly endive
dash cayenne pepper
paprika

Combine vegetables, cottage cheese, and cayenne pepper. Scoop on slices of onion. Garnish with sprigs of endive; sprinkle each serving with paprika.

Makes 6 servings at 85 calories per serving.

Chef's Cooking Tip:
When purchasing tomatoes, it's a good idea to buy them in various stages of redness and allow them to ripen at room temperature (tomatoes won't ripen in the refrigerator) as you do bananas or pears. This way you'll be guaranteed a daily supply of ripened tomatoes without fear of waste.

HERBED BEAN SALAD

1 package (10-ounce) frozen cut green beans
1 celery rib, thinly sliced
1 red onion, thinly sliced and separated into rings
½ cup low-calorie Italian-style dressing
2 small heads Boston lettuce

Wash and trim lettuce; tear into bite-size pieces. Place in medium-size salad bowl; chill. Cook beans according to package directions. Chill immediately under cold running water and drain thoroughly. In a bowl, combine beans, celery, onion rings, and Italian dressing. Cover and marinate in refrigerator 2 hours or longer, stirring occasionally. When ready to serve, toss vegetable mixture together with lettuce.

Makes 4 servings at 50 calories per serving.

Chef's Cooking Tip:
Even the most aromatic onions can be sliced without tears if they are placed in the freezer for 10 minutes before being cut.

ITALIAN GREEN SALAD

3 cups romaine lettuce, chopped
4 tomato wedges
¼ cup green pepper, chopped
¼ cup red pepper, chopped
¼ cup red onion, chopped
4 radishes, sliced

1 clove garlic, minced
1 can (4 to 5) anchovies, shredded
2 ounces low-calorie Italian dressing
2 parsley sprigs
salt and pepper to taste

Combine the lettuce, tomatoes, green pepper, red pepper, red onion, radishes, garlic, anchovies, and Italian dressing in a large bowl; mix well. Chill for at least 1 hour. Serve on chilled salad plates and garnish with parsley sprigs. Salt and pepper to taste.

Makes 2 servings at 50 calories per serving.

Chef's Cooking Tip:
Don't fill yourself with unwanted calories just because you don't know what to do with your hands! Crackers are about 15 calories each, but a single pat of butter is 50 calories. These are calories that you take in without even realizing it.

KIWI AND PAPAYA SALAD

2 ripe kiwi fruits
1 ripe papaya

4 lettuce leaves
½ cup low-calorie fruit dressing

Peel, halve, and seed fruits; cut into ¼-inch slices. Arrange in overlapping rows on lettuce leaves. Chill. Add dressing just before serving.

Makes 4 servings at 111 calories per serving.

Chef's Cooking Tip:
When selecting various citrus fruits like oranges, lemons, melons, and grapefruits, heft them in your hand. If they feel heavy for their size, they will be juicy.

MARINATED CUCUMBER SLICES

2 medium-size cucumbers,
  unpeeled and thinly sliced
1 teaspoon salt
½ cup white vinegar
1 tablespoon chopped chives
1 tablespoon diced red pepper
1 teaspoon sugar
salt and pepper to taste
4 lettuce leaves

Layer cucumber slices with 1 teaspoon salt in a shallow baking dish. Let sit for 10 minutes. With a flat-bottomed dish, press cucumbers lightly and pour off excess liquid. Add remaining ingredients, tossing gently to mix well. Cover and marinate for at least 30 minutes to blend flavors. Drain and serve on chilled lettuce leaves.

Makes 4 servings at 30 calories per serving.

Chef's Cooking Tip:
Toasted sesame seeds at 27 calories a teaspoon make a good low-calorie substitute for croutons.

MARINATED RADISH AND CUCUMBER SALAD

4 large radishes, thinly sliced
2 medium-size cucumbers, peeled
  and thinly sliced
1 teaspoon salt
½ cup cider vinegar
1 teaspoon sugar
salt and pepper to taste
4 lettuce leaves

Layer cucumber slices with 1 teaspoon salt in a shallow baking dish. Let sit for 10 minutes. With a flat-bottomed dish, press cucumbers lightly and pour off excess liquid. Add vinegar and seasonings, tossing gently to mix well. Cover and marinate for at least 30 minutes to blend flavors. Drain and serve on chilled lettuce leaves.

Makes 4 servings at 30 calories per serving.

MARINATED THREE BEAN SALAD

1 can (16-ounce) cut green beans
1 can (16-ounce) cut yellow wax
  beans
1 can (16-ounce) red kidney beans
½ cup diced onion
¼ cup diced green pepper
¼ cup diced red pepper
1 cup unsweetened pineapple juice
½ cup cider vinegar
½ teaspoon pepper
1 teaspoon celery salt
1 head red leaf lettuce

Drain liquid from vegetables. Combine all ingredients, cover, and chill for several hours or overnight. Just before serving, line a large salad bowl with the lettuce leaves. Remove salad from refrigerator, toss lightly; drain. Put drained beans in salad bowl and serve immediately.

Makes 10 servings at 50 calories per serving.

MIMOSA SALAD

4 heads bibb or butter lettuce
2 tablespoons shoestring beets
4 teaspoons chopped hard-cooked egg white
1 teaspoon chopped chives
4 ounces low-calorie dressing
freshly ground pepper to taste

Remove outer leaves from lettuce heads. Cut in half and place hearts only in chilled salad bowls. Add beets, chopped egg white, and chives. Serve with 1 ounce dressing and ground pepper to taste.

Makes 4 servings at 30 calories per serving.

Chef's Cooking Tip:
In classical cuisine, a mimosa salad is made with chopped egg yolk rather than egg white. Substituting egg white for egg yolk, however, not only saves calories, it's nutritionally better for you.

MUSHROOMS À LA GRECQUE

1 pound small fresh mushrooms
1 tablespoon fresh lemon juice
3 cups water
1 cup tarragon wine vinegar
1 tablespoon vegetable oil
1 tablespoon sugar
1 bay leaf, crushed
1½ teaspoons garlic salt
¼ teaspoon thyme
¼ teaspoon coarsely ground black pepper

Rinse mushrooms under cold water and place in saucepan with remaining ingredients. Bring to a boil, then cover and simmer for 3 minutes. Let mushrooms cool in liquid. When cold, cover and refrigerate for several hours. Just before serving, drain and garnish with chopped parsley or other green herbs.

Makes 6 servings at 25 calories per serving.

ORANGE AND GRAPEFRUIT SALAD

2 navel oranges, segmented
1 grapefruit, segmented

1 small head Boston lettuce
½ cup low-calorie fruit dressing

Arrange alternating segments of orange and grapefruit in overlapping rows on lettuce leaves. Chill. Spoon 2 tablespoons dressing on each salad just before serving.

Makes 4 servings at 70 calories per serving.

Chef's Cooking Tip:
When squeezing fresh grapefruit and oranges for juice, extricate the seeds, but don't strain out the pulp; it adds extra vitamins, minerals and fiber to the diet.

ORANGE AND ONION SALAD

2 navel oranges, peeled
1 small onion, thinly sliced
4 scallions

1 small head Boston lettuce
½ cup low-calorie French dressing

Make scallion brushes by cutting into 3-inch lengths; trim off root ends. Make vertical cuts from the bulb end deep into the stalk up to the green end. Chill in ice water for 1 hour, then drain. Cut peeled oranges into eight cartwheels. Arrange orange cartwheels and onion slices alternately on lettuce leaves. Garnish plate with scallion brush. Chill. Spoon 2 tablespoons dressing on each salad just before serving.

Makes 4 servings at 65 calories per serving.

Chef's Cooking Tip:
When preparing fresh fruit salads that tend to darken, like pear and apple salads, put the dressing or marinade into the bowl first and slice the fruit directly into the bowl. When they are covered or soaked quickly in this way, there's less chance for the fruits to darken.

PICKLED BEETS

2 cans (16-ounce) thin-sliced beets
2 tablespoons vinegar
2 teaspoons sugar
½ medium-size onion, sliced
salt and pepper to taste

Drain liquid from both cans of beets into a 2-quart saucepan; reserve beets. Add remaining ingredients and heat to boiling. Place drained beets in a deep bowl. Pour hot mixture over beets. Allow to cool to room temperature. Cover and chill several hours or overnight. Stir occasionally to coat beets evenly. Drain before serving, or serve with juice.

Makes 6 servings at 40 calories per serving.

Chef's Cooking Tip:
Cooking red vegetables like beets in acidulated water (with vinegar, lemon juice, or apples) helps to retain their color. Alkaline water makes them fade and turn a bluish-gray.

PINEAPPLE MOLD

1 can (20-ounce) sliced or crushed pineapple packed in juice
2 tablespoons plain gelatin
2 cups water
2 cups unsweetened pineapple juice

Drain pineapple; reserve juice. Coat the surface of a 5- to 6-cup mold with a food release agent. Arrange pineapple in the bottom of the mold. Sprinkle gelatin over 2 cups of cold water to soften. Stir over low heat or boiling water to dissolve. Remove saucepan from stove. Add enough unsweetened pineapple juice to reserved juice to make 2 cups. Stir juice into gelatin mixture. Pour over pineapple slices and chill 3 to 4 hours to firm.

Makes 8 servings at 70 calories per serving.

Chef's Cooking Tip:
Use canned or parboiled fresh pineapple in a gelatin dish. Fresh pineapple has an enzyme that must be destroyed with heat or the gelatin mold will not set.

SPINACH SALAD

1 pound fresh spinach
4 cucumber slices
4 cherry tomatoes
8 paper-thin oinion slices
4 teaspoons chopped hard-cooked egg white
4 ounces low-calorie dressing
freshly ground pepper to taste

Trim off stems from leaves and wash in a sink of tepid water. Rinse under cold running water, then drain thoroughly. Wrap leaves in paper toweling or put them in a plastic bag or covered container. Refrigerate until serving time. Assemble salad at the last moment on chilled plates. Serve with 1 ounce of dressing per serving and ground pepper to taste.

Makes 4 servings at 30 calories per serving.

Chef's Cooking Tip:
For really clean salad leaves, lift them out of the water before draining the sink. This will prevent the sand floating in the water from clinging again to the leaves.

TOMATO ASPIC

2 tablespoons unflavored gelatin
¼ cup water or broth
2 tablespoons lemon juice
3¼ cups tomato juice
1 teaspoon Worcestershire sauce
¼ teaspoon Tabasco sauce
¼ teaspoon white pepper

Combine lemon juice and water in a 1-quart saucepan. Sitr in gelatin to soften. Place saucepan over low heat or over boiling water for 2 to 3 minutes until gelatin is dissolved. Stir constantly. Remove pan from heat and add the remaining ingredients. Stir well. Pour mixture into a 1-quart ring mold; chill until firm, about 4 hours.

Makes 6 servings at 30 calories per serving.

Chef's Cooking Tip:
Loosen the set aspic from the mold by dipping it in warm water about 4 seconds. If necessary, loosen around the edge of the mold with the tip of a knife. Place a plate larger than the mold on top. Sandwich the mold and plate between your hands and quickly turn it upside down. If the aspic doesn't unmold, dip it in the water a few more seconds. Blot up any excess water from the serving platter with paper toweling. Refrigerate before serving.

TOSSED CHERRY TOMATO SALAD

½ head iceberg lettuce
½ head curly endive
½ dozen cherry tomatoes, stemmed
½ medium-size cucumber, sliced
½ cup low-calorie dressing

Wash, drain, and chill salad greens. Tear into bite-size pieces and toss lightly with remaining ingredients. Serve immediately.

Makes 4 servings at 45 calories per serving.

Chef's Cooking Tip:
A simple way to core a head of iceberg lettuce is to grasp the head firmly in your hand and whack the head, stem-end down, on a hard surface. The core should twist and lift out easily.

TOSSED TUNA SALAD

1 large head iceberg lettuce, coarsely chopped
¼ head red cabbage, shredded
½ green pepper, julienned
½ small onion, sliced
2 small ripe tomatoes, cut into wedges
1 small carrot, grated
1 small cucumber, sliced
1 celery rib, sliced
1 can (7-ounce) water-pack tuna, drained and flaked
½ cup low-calorie French or vinaigrette dressing

Toss all ingredients lightly in a large salad bowl. Chill. When ready to serve toss lightly with dressing.

Makes 4 servings at 75 calories per serving.

Chef's Cooking Tip:
Keep plenty of cut-up green peppers, carrots, celery, cucumbers, and zucchini strips on hand to use as snack foods. Place them in ice water to keep them fresh and crisp.

TOSSED SALAD WITH FRESH MUSHROOMS

2 cups bite-size pieces romaine lettuce
2 cups bite-size pieces Boston lettuce
2 cups sliced fresh mushrooms
1 cup peeled and sliced cucumber
1 small onion, thinly sliced
½ cup low-calorie salad dressing

Toss all ingredients lightly just before serving.

Makes 4 servings at 30 calories per serving.

Chef's Cooking Tip:
For a really crisp salad, always add salad dressings just before serving and add only enough dressing to coat the salad leaves lightly. If excess dressing forms a puddle at the bottom of the bowl, you have used too much and your salad is likely to be limp and soggy instead of crisp and refreshing.

VEGETABLE SALAD BOWL

1 package (10-ounce) frozen broccoli spears
1 head iceberg lettuce, shredded
4 tomato wedges
8 cucumber slices
4 tablespoons low-calorie French dressing

Cook the broccoli as directed on the package. Drain, cover, and chill. Mound shredded lettuce on each of 4 salad plates. Arrange broccoli spears, tomato wedges, and cucumber slices on top. Pour 1 tablespoon of dressing over each.

Makes 4 servings at 53 calories per serving.

Chef's Cooking Tip:
Most vegetables used in combination foods, such as carrots, celery, peas, or onions freeze well. Fresh tomatoes, however, change in flavor and color and become limp and watery when frozen. Frozen tomatoes can only be used in cooking, as in sauces, etc.

WALDORF SALAD

2 small red apples, unpeeled, cored and diced
2 tablespoons orange or pineapple juice
2 celery ribs, diced
2 tablespoons raisins
1 small banana, diced
4 tablespoons imitation mayonnaise
4 lettuce leaves
4 parsley sprigs

Sprinkle diced apples with fruit juice. Combine with remaining ingredients. Serve on a lettuce leaf and garnish with parsley sprig.

Makes 4 servings at 115 calories per serving.

Chef's Cooking Tip:
Once cut, apples turn brown very quickly. To keep them fresh-looking, slice them into water to which a pinch of salt or a tablespoon of lemon juice has been added. If not used immediately, then should be covered and chilled as they tend to lose crispness rapidly when they are warm.

BUTTERMILK HERB DRESSING

1 cup buttermilk
1 cup tomato juice
1 cup red wine vinegar
1 tablespoon finely chopped chives
1 teaspoon dill weed
1 teaspoon chervil
½ teaspoon tarragon
½ teaspoon garlic salt

Mix ingredients and refrigerate until cold.

Makes 3 cups at 10 calories per tablespoon.

Chef's Cooking Tip:
If you still want that olive oil flavor in your salad dressing without the unwanted calories that go with it, simply add a few minced olives (1 large olive has about 8 calories compared to 125 calories for each tablespoon of olive oil!) to your favorite style of salad dressing. The taste is there, but the calories are not.

CREAMY BLUE CHEESE DRESSING

1 cup plain yogurt
1 package (4 ounces) crumbled
    blue cheese

2 teaspoons sugar
½ teaspoon celery seed
dash Tabasco sauce

Combine yogurt, sugar, celery seed, Tabasco sauce and 2 ounces of the blue cheese and blend until smooth. Stir in remaining blue cheese and keep refrigerated in a covered jar.

Makes 1¼ cups at 36 calories per tablespoon.

CREAMY BUTTERMILK DRESSING

1½ cups buttermilk
½ cup low-fat cottage cheese
1 tablespoon chopped chives
1 tablespoon freshly chopped
    parsley

1 teaspoon onion salt
½ teaspoon prepared mustard
½ teaspoon alginate powder
    (optional)
dash of Tabasco sauce

Combine all ingredients in a blender and mix until smooth. Cover and refrigerate for at least 2 hours to marry flavors and thicken.

Makes 2 cups at 6 calories per tablespoon.

CREAMY ITALIAN DRESSING

½ cup plain yogurt
1 cup pot-style cottage cheese

1 envelope (7- or 10-ounce) Italian
    salad dressing mix

Place yogurt in the bottom of a blender container. Add cottage cheese and dressing mix and blend until smooth and creamy. Cover and refrigerate at least 2 hours to marry flavors and thicken.

Makes 1½ cups at 20 calories per tablespoon.

CREAMY YOGURT SALAD DRESSING

Here's a wonderful salad dressing you can make when you're left with a few extra egg yolks.

2 cups plain yogurt
2 egg yolks
2 tablespoons vinegar
2 tablespoons honey
1 tablespoon prepared mustard

1 teaspoon alginate powder (optional)
½ teaspoon onion salt
¼ teaspoon paprika
¼ teaspoon cayenne pepper

Combine all ingredients and blend until smooth and creamy. Cover and refrigerate at least 2 hours to allow dressing to thicken.

Makes 2½ cups at 15 calories per tablespoon.

FRENCH DRESSING

1 can (11-ounce) condensed tomato soup
6 tablespoons wine or cider vinegar
1 small clove garlic, minced
1 tablespoon Worcestershire sauce

1 bay leaf, crushed
½ teaspoon dry mustard
½ teaspoon salt
¼ teaspoon oregano
½ teaspoon alginate powder (optional)

Combine all ingredients in a blender and mix until smooth. Cover and refrigerate for at least 2 hours to marry flavors.

Makes 1¾ cups at 9 calories per tablespoon.

FRUIT SALAD DRESSING

1 carton (8-ounce) plain yogurt
2 cartons (8-ounce) low-fat cottage cheese

⅓ cup orange juice
2 teaspoons sugar
1 teaspoon vanilla extract

Combine ingredients in a blender and blend until smooth and creamy. Chill thoroughly before serving.

Makes 3 cups at 16 calories per tablespoon.

ITALIAN DRESSING

⅓ cup unsweetened apple juice
⅓ cup white vinegar
⅓ cup fresh lemon juice
1 clove garlic, crushed
½ teaspoon dry mustard
½ teaspoon onion powder
½ teaspoon whole oregano
½ teaspoon paprika
½ teaspoon thyme
½ teaspoon sugar
⅛ teaspoon rosemary
⅛ teaspoon salt

Combine all ingredients in a blender and mix well. Cover and refrigerate overnight to develop flavors.

Makes 1 cup at 6 calories per ounce.

QUICK LOW-CALORIE DRESSING

1 carton (8-ounce) plain yogurt
2 tablespoons chopped chives
¼ teaspoon onion salt

Combine ingredients in a small bowl and stir until smooth.

Makes 1 cup at 8 calories per tablespoon.

Chef's Cooking Tip:
Variations: ¼ teaspoon of most any seasoning (dill weed, mustard, garlic salt, etc.) can be substituted for the onion salt, if preferred.

THOUSAND ISLAND DRESSING

4 ounces plain yogurt
1 ounce catsup
1 hard-cooked egg
1 small tomato, peeled, seeded and diced
2 tablespoons minced celery
2 tablespoons minced green pepper
1 tablespoon minced green onion (white part only)
2 teaspoons minced yellow jalapeño pepper (omit seeds)
salt and pepper to taste

Blend all ingredients in a mixer at low speed. Blend until well combined. Chill for several hours before serving.

Makes 1 cup at 14 calories per tablespoon.

Chef's Cooking Tip:
Jalapeño pepper seeds are really hot to the uninitiated. Be sure to wash your hands immediately after handling them.

VINAIGRETTE DRESSING

½ cup wine vinegar
¼ cup water
2 tablespoons oil
1 tablespoon fresh lemon juice
1 tablespoon grated onion

1 tablespoon chopped parsley
1 tablespoon chopped chives
½ teaspoon salt
½ teaspoon chervil
¼ teaspoon pepper

Combine all ingredients together and stir or shake vigorously before serving. Store in the refrigerator.

Makes 1 cup at 30 calories per serving.

Chef's Cooking Tip:
Try to serve salads on large chilled plates; it will tempt you to fill it with plenty of low-calorie foods.

SAUCES AND MARINADES

No other food preparation inspires greater creativity and inventiveness on the part of a cook than the art of making sauces. To the cook who loves cooking and derives great pleasure from it, a sauce is the highest expression of the culinary arts; it is the crowning touch that subtly transforms ordinary dishes into the class of memorable culinary experiences. Creative cooks have ever improvised, for sauce-making does not lend itself to precise formulas. It is, instead, a flexible form of cooking that reflects one's own personal taste, and is limited only by the confines of one's technical skills in the kitchen and the resources on hand.

Not surprisingly, sauces play an important role in low-calorie cooking. They enhance both the appearance and the flavor of the foods to which they are added. They add variety and interest to the diet. They expand your cooking repertoire and banish monotony. They add moisture to lean meat, fish, and poultry and make them more attractive to the eye and to the palate. Remember that any sauce should be used to compliment and enhance a dish, not disguise inferiority or mask bad cookery. In all, your cooking won't seem so much like diet cooking if good-tasting, low-calorie sauces are occasionally used. A sauce must contain all the necessary ingredients for superb taste and be used as a complement to good foods. There should be no other criterion.

COCKTAIL SAUCE

1 bottle (11-ounce) dietetic catsup
¼ cup minced celery
¼ cup chopped chives
1 tablespoon creamy horseradish
1 teaspoon Worcestershire sauce
2 teaspoons lemon juice
dash Tabasco sauce

Combine all ingredients together in a small mixing bowl. Chill before serving.

Makes 1½ cups at 6 calories per tablespoon.

CUCUMBER SAUCE

2 cucumbers
½ cup plain yogurt
1 tablespoon creamy-style horseradish
2 teaspoons prepared mustard
2 teaspoons lemon juice
1 teaspoon alginate powder (optional)
⅛ teaspoon onion salt
dash Tabasco sauce

Pare cucumbers; remove seeds. Combine all ingredients in a blender and mix until smooth. Cover and refrigerate for at least 2 hours to allow sauce to thicken.

Makes 2 cups at 10 calories per tablespoon.

DILL SAUCE

1 carton (8-ounce) plain yogurt
1 celery rib, minced
2 teaspoons freshly chopped parsley
½ teaspoon celery salt
½ teaspoon dill weed
¼ teaspoon sugar

Blend ingredients with a wire whip. Cover and chill.

Makes 1 cup at 5 calories per tablespoon.

Chef's Cooking Tip:
Dill weed and dill seed are from the same aromatic plant. Dill weed is the finely chopped leaves and branches, while dill seed is the dried fruit.

SALSA FRIA (COLD SAUCE)

2 large tomatoes, peeled, seeded, and diced
1 can (4-ounce) green chiles, diced
1 celery rib, diced
½ medium-size onion, diced
½ cup tomato juice
1 tablespoon vinegar
1 teaspoon ground coriander
dash pepper

Combine ingredients and chill. Use on hot or cold foods to impart a Mexican flavor.

Makes 2 cups at 5 calories per tablespoon.

SHALLOT SAUCE

1 carton (8-ounce) plain yogurt
2 small shallots, minced
2 tablespoons freshly-chopped parsley
¼ teaspoon dill weed
salt and pepper to taste

Combine the ingredients. Cover and chill. Use for meat, seafood, or vegetables.

Makes 1 cup at 5 calories per tablespoon.

TARTARE SAUCE

1 carton (8-ounce) plain yogurt
1 medium-size sweet gherkin, chopped
½ medium-size dill pickle, chopped
½ small onion, chopped
2 tablespoons chile sauce
2 tablespoons freshly chopped parsley
1 tablespoon lemon juice
½ teaspoon alginate powder (optional)
½ teaspoon dry mustard
¼ teaspoon Worcestershire sauce
salt and pepper to taste

Combine all ingredients in a blender and blend until smooth and creamy. Chill 1 hour before serving.

Makes 1½ cups at 8 calories per serving.

WHITE SAUCE, ROUX METHOD

4 tablespoons diet margarine
4 tablespoons flour
2 cups skim milk
½ teaspoon imitation-butter-flavored salt
¼ teaspoon white pepper
dash paprika

Melt the margarine over a low flame in a small nonstick suacepan. Slowly sprinkle in the flour; stir until margarine and flour are well blended. Cook the roux about 2 minutes; do not brown. Remove pan from heat. Slowly pour in milk, stirring constantly with a wire whisk. Return saucepan to heat and simmer, stirring constantly, until sauce thickens. Add the seasonings and allow the sauce to simmer a few minutes to blend the flavors.

Makes 2 cups at 15 calories per tablespoon.

Chef's Cooking Tip:
By substituting low-calorie ingredients for the high-calorie ingredients in this basic recipe, you have just saved yourself 342 calories!

WHITE SAUCE, BLENDING METHOD

¼ cup water
¼ cup flour
2 cups skim milk
½ teaspoon imitation-butter-flavored salt
¼ teaspoon white pepper
dash paprika

Blend the ¼ cup water and flour to make a paste. Combine with remaining ingredients in a nonstick saucepan and heat over low heat, stirring constantly with a wire whisk until thickened.

Makes 2 cups at 9 calories per tablespoon.

CREAMY FISH SAUCE

½ cup nonfat milk
½ cup bottled clam juice
½ teaspoon onion juice (optional)
dash turmeric

2 tablespoons cold water
1 tablespoon cornstarch
white pepper to taste

In a small, heavy saucepan, combine milk, clam juice, and turmeric; bring just to the boil. Dissolve cornstarch in cold water. Stir slowly into liquid and cook, stirring, until sauce returns to the boil. Season with white pepper to taste.

Makes 1 cup at 9 calories per tablespoon.

BROWN SAUCE, ROUX METHOD

¼ cup diced carrots
¼ cup diced onion
¼ cup diced celery
4 tablespoons diet margarine
4 tablespoons flour
2 cups beef broth
1 cup dry red wine

¼ cup tomato purée
¼ teaspoon marjoram
¼ teaspoon thyme
1 bay leaf
1 teaspoon chopped parsley
salt and pepper to taste

Melt margarine over low heat in a thick-bottomed saucepan. Add diced vegetables; sauté until soft and tender. Sprinkle with flour, blend well, and cook until browned. Remove from heat; slowly add broth, stirring constantly with a wire whisk. Return to heat and continue stirring until sauce thickens. Meanwhile, in a second saucepan, combine the remaining ingredients, except the salt and pepper, and reduce over high heat, uncovered, to ⅓ cup. Add this mixture to the first pan. Cover. Simmer gently for ½ hour. Ladle off accumulated fat; strain through a cheesecloth and season to taste with salt and pepper.

Makes 2 cups at 13 calories per tablespoon.

BROWN SAUCE, BLENDING METHOD

¼ cup diced carrots
¼ cup diced onion
¼ cup diced celery
½ cup dry red wine
2 cups beef broth

1 bay leaf
2 parsley stems
2 tablespoons arrowroot
4 tablespoons Madeira wine

Combine the diced vegetables, wine, broth, bay leaf, and parsley stems in a heavy saucepan. Bring to a boil; reduce the heat and simmer for ½ hour. Thoroughly blend the arrowroot with the Madeira wine. Strain sauce through a dampened cheesecloth. Return to the heat. When sauce is just under the boiling point, slowly pour the arrowroot mixture into the sauce, stirring constantly with a wire whisk. When thickened to desired consistency (arrowroot thickens instantly and does not require further cooking), remove from heat and serve.

Makes 2 cups at 6 calories per tablespoon.

BARBECUE SAUCE

1 can (8-ounce) tomato sauce
2 tablespoons honey
2 tablespoons vinegar
1 tablespoon soy sauce
1 tablespoon Worcestershire sauce

1 clove garlic, minced
½ teaspoon ginger
½ teaspoon Tabasco
¼ teaspoon dry mustard
3 drops liquid smoke

Combine all ingredients in a small saucepan. Bring to a boil, reduce heat, and simmer 15 minutes.

Makes 1 cup at 13 calories per tablespoon.

Chef's Cooking Tip:
Liquid smoke can be obtained readily from most supermarkets. Ask for it, it's worth it! This sauce seems high in calories but remember that it is a basting sauce and only a very small amount actually sticks to the meat that's barbecued.

MARINARA SAUCE

2 cups peeled and diced tomatoes
1 cup beef broth
1 clove garlic, minced
¼ cup diced onion
¼ cup diced green pepper
¼ cup finely chopped mushrooms

salt and pepper to taste
1 bay leaf
1 tablespoon freshly chopped parsley
½ teaspoon whole oregano

Sauté garlic, onion, green pepper, and chopped mushrooms in the bottom of a saucepan with ¼ cup of the beef broth over medium heat for about 5 minutes; do not brown. Add remaining ingredients, cover, and simmer for 1 hour. Remove bay leaf and cool sauce at room temperature. The sauce is even better if you make it one day ahead and chill it in the refrigerator to marry the flavors.

Pour sauce into a blender and blend until smooth. Return to stove, heat, uncovered, and cook until sauce thickens to desired consistency.

Makes 1 cup at 10 calories per tablespoon.

SPANISH SAUCE

¼ cup diced onion
¼ cup diced bell pepper
½ cup diced celery
1 cup tomatoes, peeled, seeded, and diced
1 can (8-ounce) tomato sauce

1 tablespoon freshly chopped parsley
1 teaspoon salt
1 teaspoon whole oregano
½ teaspoon chile powder
⅛ teaspoon garlic powder

Sauté the onion, pepper, and celery in a large nonstick skillet with ¼ cup of boiling water over medium heat, about 5 minutes. Add the remaining ingredients and simmer, uncovered, about 20 minutes.

Makes 3 cups at 10 calories per tablespoon.

Chef's Cooking Tip:
To store unused portions of canned tomato products, spoon the contents into a clean glass jar with a tight-fitting lid; refrigerate up to 6 days or freeze.

SPAGHETTI SAUCE

2 cans (16-ounce) Italian-style plum tomatoes in purée
2 tablespoons instant minced onions
2 tablespoons freshly chopped parsley
¼ cup dry white wine

¼ teaspoon garlic powder
¼ teaspoon sugar
¼ teaspoon whole basil
¼ teaspoon whole oregano
¼ teaspoon salt
¼ teaspoon black pepper
1 small bay leaf

Combine ingredients in a heavy saucepan. Bring to a boil, then reduce heat; simmer, uncovered, for 30 minutes. Stir occasionally. Thin sauce with a small amount of boiling water if necessary. Allow sauce to cool. Reheat when needed.

Makes 3 cups at 6 calories per tablespoon.

Chef's Cooking Tip:
This sauce is about half the calories of the prepared variety. So if you like a lot of sauce on your pasta, try this recipe. Italian sauces are always better when they're made a day ahead, refrigerated, and then reheated. Also, I personally like to blend this sauce in an electric blender for a smoother consistency.

HOLLANDAISE SAUCE

1 carton (8-ounce) plain yogurt
2 egg yolks, beaten
1 tablespoon lemon juice

salt and white pepper to taste
dash Tabasco sauce

Combine ingredients in top of a double boiler or in a heavy saucepan. Cook, stirring constantly, until thickened and smooth. Do not boil.

Makes 1¼ cups at 13 calories per tablespoon.

CURRY SAUCE

1 small chopped onion
1 chopped carrot
1 chopped celery rib
1 small, cored and pared, tart apple
½ banana
1½ cups chicken broth
1½ cups unsweetened pineapple juice

2 teaspoons curry powder
½ teaspoon mace
⅛ teaspoon ground ginger
⅛ teaspoon garlic powder
⅛ teaspoon turmeric
salt and white pepper
dash of cayenne pepper

Combine vegetables, fruits, liquids, and seasonings in a 2-quart saucepan. Bring to a boil; reduce heat to simmer and cook for one hour. Remove from heat and purée in blender, two cups at a time. Return sauce to pan, adjust seasoning with salt, pepper, and cayenne pepper. Reheat and serve.

Makes 3 cups at 20 calories per tablespoon.

Chef's Cooking Tip:
Good low-calorie curry dish accompaniments: unsweetened coconut, chopped chives, minced cooked egg whites, chopped bell pepper, diced banana in orange juice, grated carrot in lime juice.

LEMON SAUCE

1 cup chicken broth
2 teaspoons arrowroot
1 egg

1 tablespoon lemon juice
salt and pepper to taste
dash turmeric

In a small saucepan, combine cold broth and arrowroot powder. Beat in egg. Add lemon juice and seasoning; cook over medium heat until mixture thickens. Do not boil.

Makes 1 cup at 7 calories per tablespoon.

MUSTARD SAUCE

1 cup chicken broth
1 teaspoon dry mustard
1 teaspoon lemon juice
1 teaspoon Worcestershire sauce

1 teaspoon sugar
1 tablespoon cornstarch
2 tablespoons vinegar

Combine the chicken broth, dry mustard, lemon juice, Worcestershire sauce, and sugar in a small saucepan. Bring slowly to a boil over medium heat, stirring occasionally. In a small cup, blend the cornstarch and vinegar to form a paste. With the sauce just under the boil, slowly stir in the cornstarch mixture until the desired degree of thickness is obtained. Simmer for 3 minutes.

Makes 1 cup at 6 calories per tablespoon.

SWEET AND SOUR SAUCE

2 cups unsweetened pineapple juice
½ cup cider vinegar
¼ cup tomato sauce
3 tablespoons sugar
2 tablespoons soy sauce
2 tablespoons cornstarch
¼ cup water

Combine the pineapple juice, vinegar, tomato sauce, sugar, and soy sauce in a small saucepan. Bring slowly to a boil over medium heat, stirring occasionally. In a small cup, blend the cornstarch and water to form a paste. With the sauce just under the boil, slowly stir in the cornstarch mixture until the desired degree of thickness is obtained. Simmer for 3 minutes.

Makes 2 cups at 12 calories per tablespoon.

Chef's Cooking Tip:
The blending or "slurry" method of thickening sauces saves you time and calories. Cornstarch (or arrowroot) has twice the thickening power of flour, so you only need half as much. And since you're substituting water for the high-calorie fat, you'll save 255 calories over the roux method for every cup of liquid thickened.

TERIYAKI SAUCE

½ cup beef broth
½ cup soy sauce
2 tablespoons dry sherry
1 tablespoon sugar
1 tablespoon ginger root, shredded

Combine all ingredients in a small saucepan. Bring to a boil over medium heat, then reduce heat and simmer for 10 minutes. Use hot as a basting sauce for meat, poultry, or seafood, or use cold as a marinade.

Makes 1 cup at 10 calories per tablespoon.

MARINADES

When you talk of a marinade, you're referring to an aromatic liquid, cooked or uncooked, in which meats or vegetables are soaked to absorb flavors. Where fruits are concerned, the word "macerate" is used; we usually say that meats or vegetables are marinated, while fruits are macerated.

Foods have actually been marinated for centuries. Originally, its purpose was to replace salt as the only preservative. In fact the word "marinate" comes from the French *mariner,* meaning to soak or steep in a brine. But today we use a marinade primarily to season and tenderize less-tender cuts of meat. It can also be used to flavor bland-tasting food and, in some instances, to mask off-flavor.

Marinades usually include some kind of food acid (wine, vinegar, lemon, orange, or tomato juice) that can adversely affect metal, thereby changing the character and taste of the marinade. So use only glass, ceramic, or stainless steel receptacles when these acids are present. You'll find that plastic storage bags are also ideal for this purpose.

The length of time a food should marinate depends on what it is and how much added flavor or tenderness it needs. Large or tough cuts of meat, for instance, often require overnight or even several days' soaking. These longer marinating times, of course, give more flavor and tenderness than shorter marinating times.

Marinades can be saved and used again, by the way. Simply bring the marinade to a boil in a saucepan, allow it to cool, then store it, covered, in the refrigerator or freezer to be used when needed.

MARINADE FOR LAMB NO. 1

½ cup dry red or white wine
½ cup vinegar
¼ cup fresh lemon juice
½ cup onion, minced
1 clove garlic, minced

1 bay leaf, crumbled
1 tablespoon fresh parsley, chopped
1 teaspoon salt
3 whole peppercorns, crushed

Combine the ingredients and place in a shallow dish. Add meat and marinate several hours, turning occasionally. Strain marinade and use as a basting liquid.

MARINADE FOR LAMB NO. 2

½ cup tomato juice
½ cup lemon juice
¼ cup onion, minced
1 clove garlic, minced

½ teaspoon turmeric
½ teaspoon ginger
¼ teaspoon ground red pepper
¼ teaspoon ground coriander

Combine the ingredients in a shallow dish. Add meat and marinate several hours, turning occasionally. Strain and use as basting sauce.

WINE MARINADE FOR MEAT

½ cup dry red wine
¼ cup tomato juice
2 tablespoons soy sauce
1 tablespoon Worcestershire sauce

1 tablespoon minced onion
⅛ teaspoon each: garlic salt, black pepper, thyme, marjoram, and rosemary

Combine the ingredients and place in a shallow dish just large enough to hold the meat. Cover and marinate meat in the refrigerator several hours or overnight; turn occasionally.

MARINADE FOR STEAK

¼ cup fresh lemon juice
¼ cup minced onion
1 tablespoon olive oil
1 tablespoon Worcestershire sauce

1 teaspoon prepared mustard
1 teaspoon garlic salt
salt and pepper to taste

Combine all ingredients and pour over steak. Marinate at room temperature for several hours or overnight in the refrigerator.

MARINADE FOR FISH

1 cup water
½ cup dry white wine
1 tablespoon fresh lemon juice
1 small onion, thinly sliced
1 small bay leaf

3 peppercorns
¼ teaspoon celery salt
¼ teaspoon freshly chopped parsley

Combine the ingredients in a small saucepan and simmer five minutes. Cool, then add fish or shellfish.

SWEET AND SOUR MARINADE FOR FISH AND SHELLFISH

1 cup water
¼ cup red wine vinegar
1 small onion, thinly sliced
1 tablespoon whole pickling spice
4 whole peppercorns, crushed
1 teaspoon sugar

Combine all ingredients and pour over seafood. Cover and marinate several hours or overnight in the refrigerator. Cook in marinade until just underdone, then allow to cool without removing from liquid.

MARINADE FOR VEGETABLES

½ cup low-calorie Italian salad dressing
1 tablespoon minced onion
1 tablespoon diced red peppers
½ teaspoon dried parsley flakes
½ teaspoon whole oregano
¼ teaspoon salt
⅛ teaspoon pepper

Combine all ingredients thoroughly. Pour marinade over vegetables. Cover and refrigerate for several hours.

SOY MARINADE FOR CHICKEN NO. 1

4 tablespoons soy sauce
4 tablespoons dry white wine
1 teaspoon curry powder
1 clove garlic, minced
¼ teaspoon dry mustard
¼ teaspoon pepper

SOY MARINADE FOR CHICKEN NO. 2

4 tablespoons soy sauce
1 tablespoon dry sherry
1 clove garlic, minced
1 teaspoon pepper
1 ½-inch-slice ginger root, minced
¼ teaspoon dry mustard

Combine all ingredients and use as a marinade and for basting.

MARINADE FOR FRUITS

1 cup unsweetened pineapple juice
¼ cup orange juice
1 tablespoon honey

½ teaspoon dried mint leaves, crushed
¼ teaspoon vanilla extract

    Combine all ingredients and pour over fruits. Stir gently to mix. Cover and marinate in refrigerator several hours. Stir occasionally.

BREADS AND CEREALS

Carbohydrates (starches and sugars) are an important part of a good diet, but most of us have particular notions about them when we're dieting. Mainly, we consider them evil and synonymous with calories. But the fact is that so-called "starchy" foods, such as pasta, rice, pancakes, and bread, at approximately 80 calories per half-cup serving or 70 calories a slice, in and of themselves, are lower in calories than many foods we think of as "diet" foods.

Ironically, it is the diet that is excessively low in carbohydrates that is usually high in calories. This is because low-carbohydrate diets tend to be disproportionately high in fats—and there is nothing more fattening than fat! It has twice the energy value of carbohydrates or protein. Starches only become villains to the weight-conscious when fats are added to them in the form of calorie-laden sauces, butter, syrups and jams, or when they are consumed in excess amounts. When high-carbohydrate foods are cooked properly and served with low-calorie ingredients, you can eat enough to be satisfied without feeling guilty.

Bear in mind that to be successful, a good reducing diet must not only be low in calories, it must also be nutritionally balanced and be able to satisfy your stomach's need for bulk as well. One-food regimens and fad diets that continually leave you feeling psychologically deprived or physically starving are almost certainly doomed to failure. Starches, on the other hand, give you a feeling of fullness after a meal and help curb the impulse to overeat. Moreover, they are economical and have a marvelous way of making a small amount of high-priced protein go a long way.

Dieting should not be a period of deprivation and suffering, but rather a positive, revised approach to food that makes low-calorie, sensible eating and cooking a habit. And once these habits become established, choosing wholesome, nutritious, low-calorie foods over empty-caloried junk foods stops being a matter of choice and becomes a natural inclination. You'll find that you don't have to starve yourself or eliminate your favorite foods to wage an all-out war on overweight. But you will have to count calories, eat in moderation, and learn to stay within your energy needs. Render high-carbohydrate foods low-calorie by using commercial or homemade low-calorie sauces, spreads, syrups, and jams.

A low-calorie diet will necessitate cutting down on high-carbohydrate foods. But rather than indiscriminately eliminating them from your diet, learn to be selective. Restrict your intake of overly refined and processed foods that add little else but calories, and rely instead on the less-refined ones, such as fresh fruits and vegetables and whole grains that contribute important nutrients to the body, primarily vitamins and minerals.

Remember that it's not necessary to go on a dull, monotonous diet to lose weight. Avoid getting into food ruts by choosing from a variety of food groups each day. The right kind of carbohydrates prepared without high-calorie ingredients will add variety to your meals and help keep "fat" calories under control.

BASIC CREPE RECIPE

3 eggs
⅔ cup flour
1 cup skim milk

1 tablespoon vegetable oil
½ teaspoon salt

Combine ingredients in a blender or mixer and process at high speed for 30 seconds. Cover container; refrigerate for 2 hours. Place a 7-inch nonstick skillet over moderately high heat. Lift skillet off the heat. Using a 1-ounce ladle, pour in the batter and quickly tilt the pan from side to side so as to cover the bottom surface with a thin layer of batter. Return skillet to heat; cook crepe about 1 minute, or until slightly browned on the bottom. Turn the crepe by sliding a spatula under the crepe and flipping it over. Cook second side for about 30 seconds; then remove. Wipe skillet with paper toweling; then reheat pan for next crepe.

Makes 12 servings at 60 calories per serving.

Chef's Cooking Tip:
The second side of a crepe is seldom as evenly browned as the first side, so make the second side the inside of the crepe when you add the filling.

DESSERT CREPES

1 egg
⅓ cup buttermilk pancake mix
⅔ cup skim milk
1 tablespoon sugar

1 teaspoon vegetable oil
½ teaspoon vanilla extract
⅛ teaspoon salt

Combine ingredients in a blender or mixer and process at high speed for 30 seconds. Cover and refrigerate for 2 hours. Place a 7-inch nonstick skillet over moderately high heat. Remove from heat. Pour 1 ounce of batter into skillet; quickly tilt the pan from side to side to cover the entire bottom surface with batter. Return to heat and cook crepe about 1 minute, or until slightly browned. Turn crepe and cook second side 30 seconds longer. Wipe skillet with paper toweling and reheat skillet for next crepe.

Makes 6 crepes at 50 calories per serving.

DIET POULTRY DRESSING

½ cup diced onion
½ cup diced celery
½ cup diced apple, peeled and cored
½ cup chicken broth

4 slices toasted diet bread, diced
1 tablespoon chopped parsley
½ teaspoon poultry seasoning
⅛ teaspoon white pepper

Sauté the diced onion, celery, and apple in a large nonstick skillet with ¼ cup chicken broth for 5 minutes to tenderize vegetables. Remove from stove; stir in diced bread and seasonings. Add remaining broth only if needed to moisten. Bake, uncovered, in a preheated 350° F. oven for 30 minutes.

Makes 4 to 6 servings at 50 calories per 2-ounce serving.

Chef's Cooking Tip:

Remember that daily selections from the four food groups (milk, meats, vegetables and fruits, breads and cereals) combined with a good exercise program are the best way to assure a permanent, low-calorie, nutritious pattern of eating.

NOODLES

1 package (8-ounce) extra-wide
　noodles
1 gallon boiling water

1 tablespoon salt
1 teaspoon cooking oil

Bring water to a boil in a large saucepan. Add salt and cooking oil. Add noodles; cook uncovered, stirring occasionally, until tender, about 10 minutes. Pour noodles into a strainer; rinse under hot running water to remove excess starch. Drain and serve.

Makes 4 servings at 215 calories per serving.

Chef's Cooking Tip:
To cook pasta ahead of time, undercook slightly, then drain and rinse under cold water. Cover with a damp cloth and let it stand in the refrigerator until serving time. To serve, simply return pasta to boiling water or stock to heat through, about 2 minutes. Drain and serve.

BAKED RICE

2 cups boiling water
1 cup uncooked long-grain rice

1 teaspoon fresh lemon juice
½ teaspoon salt

Preheat oven to 350° F. Combine ingredients thoroughly in a 1-quart Dutch oven casserole. Cover tightly and bake 18 to 25 minutes, or until liquid is absorbed. For brown rice, increase the cooking time by 15 to 20 minutes.

Makes 6 servings at 75 calories per serving.

Chef's Cooking Tip:
Variations: Substitute broth or fruit juice for plain water.

BAKED SAFFRON RICE

½ cup minced onion
¼ teaspoon garlic powder
1 small green pepper, thinly sliced
2 tablespoons water
¼ cup pimiento, thinly sliced
1 small tomato, peeled, seeded, and diced
1 cup uncooked long-grain rice saffron threads or turmeric powder
1¾ cups chicken broth
salt and pepper to taste

In a 10-inch nonstick skillet or Dutch oven, combine onion, garlic powder, green pepper, and water. Cover and cook over medium heat for 5 minutes to tenderize vegetables. Uncover; stir in pimiento, tomato, and rice. Add enough saffron threads or turmeric powder to color rice a bright yellow. Stir in chicken broth and seasonings. Cover tightly. Bake in a 400° F. oven 25 minutes, or until liquid is absorbed.

Makes 6 servings at 100 calories per serving.

Chef's Cooking Tip:
Saffron is our most expensive spice. Turmeric will give you the exact color of saffron in a dish, but to approximate the flavor of saffron, try combining ground ginger, cumin, and cayenne pepper (a dash of each will do) with the turmeric before adding it to the dish.

BOILED RICE

3 quarts boiling water
½ teaspoon salt
1 cup uncooked rice

Add salt to boiling water. Pour in rice, ¼ cup at a time, so that the water remains at a rolling boil continuously. Boil rice rapidly, uncovered, 10 to 12 minutes. When tender, drain into a colander; rinse under hot running water to remove excess starch.

Makes 6 servings at 92 calories per serving.

Chef's Cooking Tip:
To reheat cooked rice, place in a fine-meshed sieve and steam in a covered pan with a small amount of water or broth.

FLUFFY STEAMED RICE

1 cup uncooked long-grain rice
3 cups water

1 teaspoon fresh lemon juice
½ teaspoon salt

Combine ingredients in a 2-quart saucepan. Bring to a boil; reduce heat, then cover tightly. Cook very slowly for about 20 minutes or until the liquid is completely absorbed. Test for doneness with a fork only. Using a spoon crushes the grains and makes them sticky.

Makes 6 servings at 75 calories per serving.

Chef's Cooking Tip:
The minerals in hard water will sometimes make rice turn grayish or greenish in color. To avoid this, add 1 teaspoon lemon juice or 1 tablespoon vinegar to the water.

RICE PILAF

1 tablespoon diet margarine
2 tablespoons dry white wine or sherry
2 tablespoons minced onion

½ cup diced celery
1¾ cup chicken broth
1 cup uncooked long-grain rice
salt and pepper to taste

In a 10-inch nonstick skillet, warm margarine and wine over moderate heat. Add onion, celery, and rice. Stir lightly until rice is well coated. Add broth; cover and simmer about 15 to 20 minutes, or until liquid is absorbed. Season with salt and pepper and serve.

Makes 6 servings at 90 calories per serving.

Chef's Cooking Tip:
Leftover cooked rice can be frozen. To reheat, thaw, then drop in boiling water for 2 minutes to heat through. Drain immediately and serve. Do not recook.

SEASONED FRENCH BREAD

4 slices French bread, cut 1 inch thick

2 tablespoons diet margarine
½ teaspoon garlic powder

Spread French bread slices with margarine; sprinkle with garlic powder. Broil under moderate heat until browned.

Makes 4 servings at 87 calories per serving.

GARNISHES

Some people think that the little extras one adds to a dish to make it more attractive are relatively unimportant, but they're wrong. Without these sprightly and colorful garnishes, most foods would be sadly lacking. Garnishes—be they simple sprigs of parsley or watercress or fanciful fluted mushroom caps and intricately cut vegetables—are statements of color and texture that succeed in delighting our senses. They provide that little something that turns an otherwise ordinary dish into a work of art.

There are few restrictions when it comes to garnishing, but in all cases, they should finish off, not overpower or dominate the foods they're served with. They should be simple, appropriate, and easy to prepare. For example, any cut of lamb becomes more pleasing to the eye and palate when it is accompanied with a dab of mint jelly. And lemon wedges or slices are almost always served with seafood.

Garnishes can be as simple or as elaborate as you desire, but you'll soon discover that nothing is more exciting than putting your imagination and creative instincts to work. With a little ingenuity in garnishing, you can turn any dish into something special.

FRUIT GARNISHES

Apple Cup
Cut off top quarter of unpeeled apple. Remove pulp and core with a melon-ball scoop, leaving ½-inch-thick shell. Notch edge or leave plain. Brush cut portions with lemon juice to prevent darkening. Fill with fruit, cheese, or meat fillings.

Frosted Grapes
Wash grapes and separate them into clusters. Beat egg whites in a small bowl until just broken up and runny. Dip grapes in egg white, let excess drip off, then roll in superfine sugar. Place on wire rack until dry.

Fruit Kabobs
Arrange any combination of equal-size fruits with contrasting colors (watermelon balls, grapes, kumquats, strawberries, pineapple chunks, etc.) on skewers. Skewer size can range from 3 to 5 inches.

Grapefruit or Orange Baskets
Mark the outline of a basket on the grapefruit or orange peel, making a handle at least ⅓ of an inch thick. Cut through the peel horizontally and vertically to free the quarter sections of fruit that form the handle. With a paring knife cut the fruit and pulp from inside the handle. Scoop out the basket with a melon-ball scoop.

Lemon Baskets
Make the outline of a basket on the lemon rind. Cut on each side of the handle halfway down the lemon. Make a horizontal cut on both sides and remove the quarter sections so you are left with a handle in the middle. Remove the pulp from inside the handle with a small knife. Scoop out pulp and fill basket with sprigs of parsley or small whole fruits.

Lemon or Lime Roses
With a small paring knife, cut a thin slice across the bottom of fruit, but do not cut all the way through. This forms the base that the rose will stand on. Leave the blade in place and continue to cut the peel in one long strip from the base, cutting through the outer skin only. Recoil the strip from the base, keeping the bottom a little tighter than the top.

Serrated Fruit Halves
Cut a thin slice off each end of fruit. With a sharp-pointed paring knife, cut a zigzag or "N"-type teeth into the center of a melon, orange, or lemon all the way around the middle. Pull halves apart. For melons, scoop out seeds and fill with melon balls, cottage cheese, or various meat fillings.

Single Twist and Tandem Fruit Slices
Cut ⅛-inch-thick slices from limes, lemons, or oranges. Lay slices on cutting board and make one cut from the outer edge to the center; then twist cut edges in opposite directions. Repeat with another slice of the same fruit or a fruit of a contrasting color for tandem.

Pear Halves
Use water-packed canned pears or fresh pear halves that have been brushed with lemon juice. Fill centers with low-calorie jams or small fruits.

VEGETABLE GARNISHES

Carrot Curls
Pare carrot. Using a sharp vegetable peeler or electric slicer, cut carrot lengthwise into paper-thin slices. Roll around finger and fasten with picks. Chill in ice water and remove picks before serving.

Celery Curls
Cut celery ribs into 3-inch lengths. Slit each end into narrow strips almost to center. Place in ice water to allow ends to curl.

Cucumber Baskets
Use 3-inch pieces of cucumber. Cut notches on one cut edge. Scoop out center almost to the bottom and fill with dairy or meat fillings.

Cucumber Cartwheels
Wash but do not pare cucumbers. Score skin in ¼-inch strips, then cut crosswise into ⅛-inch-thick chips.

Fluted Cucumber Slices
Score length of unpeeled cucumber with tines of fork or a lemon stripper. Slice crosswise into desired thickness. Place in ice water to crisp.

Fluted Mushroom Caps
Wipe off caps with damp cloth. Remove stems. Hold a sharp paring knife almost flat on the top of the cap. Pull the knife blade slowly to the bottom while twisting the cap with the other hand to remove a ⅛-inch slice. Repeat around mushroom.

Green Onion Brushes
Cut the onions into pieces 3 inches long. Trim off root ends. Make vertical cuts from the bulb end into the stalk up to the green end. Chill in a bowl of ice water for 1 hour, then drain.

Narcissus

Peel a turnip and cut into thin slices. With a knife, scissors, or cookie-cutter, cut out "V"-shaped pieces all around the slice about ½ inch apart. Trim corners to form petals. Top with carrot cutout dipped in paprika.

Onion Chrysanthemums

Peel a round, well-shaped onion. Cut down from center to within ½ to ¼ inch from the bottom—first in quarters, then in eighths etc., until the onion is cut into ⅛-inch-wide petals. Hold the cut onion under gently running water to spread sections slightly. To color, place onion in cold water to cover that has been tinted with food coloring. Let stand until tinted, then drain. Gently separate flower "petals" from center until the onion resembles a chrysanthemum.

Pickle Fans

Use small sweet or dill pickles. Make several thin lengthwise cuts to ¼ inch from end. Hold end and spread slices gently to form fan.

Potato, Turnip, or Rutabaga Roses

Cut a pointed shape from a peeled vegetable to resemble a child's top. Make parallel slits around the base to form petals. With the point of a knife cut down and in ¼-inch-around petals. Cut around vegetable, removing ¼ inch from sides above petals. Start second row midway between petals and cut down and in as before. Continue making rows until rose is complete. Dip in water tinted with food color, if desired.

Radish Accordions

Trim tops and bottoms of radish. Cut crosswise in thin strips without cutting through. Chill on ice for one hour.

Radish Roses

Trim tops and bottoms from radishes, leaving some of the green on the bottom for extra decoration. Make several parallel cuts around outside of radish from top to bottom without cutting through. Chill in ice water to open "petals."

Tomato Roses

Prepare as for lemon roses, then cut another straight strip of tomato peel as long as the first and roll it into a tight scroll. Place it in the middle of the flower to form the heart. To make stems and leaves, blanch the green part of a leek or scallion in boiling water for 30 seconds. Chill immediately in ice water.

Zucchini Boats
Cut zucchini into halves lengthwise. Scoop out pulp and fill with any mixture desired.

MISCELLANEOUS GARNISHES

Garnishes for Soups
Croutons, noodles, sliced and sieved hard-boiled eggs, cut vegetables, a dollop of yogurt, chopped herbs, grated cheese, diced or flaked meat or seafood.

Garnishes for Gelatin Salads
Sprigs of parsley, watercress or mint, fresh and canned fruits, lettuce, grapes, chopped nuts.

Garnishes for Other Salads
Sprigs of parsley; shredded beets; hard-cooked eggs; wedges, slices, and sieved or julienned meats, cheeses, and vegetables; olives, pickles, green pepper rings, tomatoes, carrot curls, radishes, pimiento, onion, chives, chopped fruit.

DESSERTS

For most of us, the greatest pitfall in dieting is an excessive craving for sweets. It does not, however, arise spontaneously. We are not born with a sweet tooth—it just seems that way. The compulsive desire for sweets is an acquired habit and one that, once established, is difficult, if not impossible, to change. If you have tried to change your eating habits or restrict the foods you crave, you know how difficult it is. Even for the most devout adherents, it takes strong motivation and a great deal of patience. Unfortunately, few of us have the vigilance or self-discipline needed to make the effort permanent. All too often, we find a suitable diet and lose impressive amounts of weight, only to have resentment and feelings of deprivation over not being able to enjoy our favorite foods drive us back to our old dietary habits, and the weight we lost is quickly regained.

If you've dieted in the past, this seesaw existence of weight loss and gain is undoubtedly familiar to you. It happens because most diets, especially fad diets, just don't work. They are unnatural, either too rigid or unimaginative, and you simply can't stick to them.

To lose weight—and keep it off—be realistic and choose a diet plan you can live with. Learn to look at dieting as a means of self-fullfillment rather than as self-denial and make the eating of low-calorie foods a habit. Believing that it's not necessary to alter your life-style and adjust your eating habits to a lower calorie diet is a delusion. For the only way to achieve lasting control over your weight is to have a continuous, sincere, inner wish to do so. In other words, for the rest of your life, you must want to be slim, healthy, and attractive—more than you want to eat. If you can achieve this, you can achieve anything!

You will recall from previous chapters how it is possible to enjoy the kinds of foods you like by learning how to eliminate the unwanted extra calories from your favorite foods and recipes. Not only is this a positive, commonsense approach to dieting you can stick to, but as a creative cook, you are developing sound, low-calorie cooking habits you will use the rest of your life. Remember that all foods contain calories and counting those calories is still the most effective method of reducing. To lose weight, you need to build up a calorie deficit by taking in fewer calories in the form of food than you expend in energy, thus forcing your body to metabolize its own reserves of fat.

Shedding pounds on diets that force you to restrict drastically the kinds of foods you have been used to eating all your life, to my mind, isn't the answer. Although it's quite true that most people become overweight by eating too much of the wrong kinds of foods, you're more likely to stick with a diet regimen that teaches you how to control the intake of your favorite foods rather than one that forces you to eliminate them altogether. In this way, you are able to enjoy what you eat and even indulge in excesses once in a while without feeling guilty.

Controlling the kind and the amount of food you eat and using low-calorie methods of preparation are the best ways I know of to make a diet plan work permanently. But while substituting low-calorie ingredients for high in a recipe works for most kinds of foods, it is not, in my opinion, the best solution for controlling a craving for sweets. First, low-calorie substitutes are difficult to make and rarely taste as good as their high-calorie counterparts. Secondly, most diet recipes for sweet foods rely heavily on artificial sweeteners as a substitute for sugar. And while there is nothing wrong with this per se, it has been my experience (and I have helped thousands of dieters lose weight with its use) that artificial sweeteners—besides being a questionable health risk—only encourage the dieter to retain his craving for highly sweetened foods. I am convinced that most overweight people would be better off cultivating a taste for savory rather than sweet foods and re-educating their palates to prefer them.

It's not easy to control a craving for sweets, but it can be done. By developing a preference for savory foods, you'll find your desire for calorie-laden sweets will gradually disappear. But if you continue to use artificial sweeteners, the task is almost impossible.

While trying to re-educate your sweet tooth, you'll want to avoid—or at least reduce to a minimum—all those popular "goodies" that provide only "empty calories"—that is, calories but no nutrients. They are ruinous to a diet. Remember that only people who have been slim all their lives have the ability to keep their energy intake and expenditure in balance. Overweight people, unfortunately, lack any kind of physiological control over the amount of food they eat. They must continually exercise their willpower and make a conscious effort to achieve this balance.

Overindulging yourself with the wrong kinds of foods might be psychologically comforting, but it will physically trigger a craving for more of the same. Thus your desire for sweets becomes reinforced rather than suppressed. Obviously, the more times you give in to temptation, the harder it will be to diminish your craving for sugary foods and the more you will be adding to your obesity.

Bear in mind that compulsive eating rarely results from physical hunger. For most of us, eating is associated with pleasure, and self-destructive emotions are inevitable when we deny ourselves this pleasure. Combat them by adopting a positive mental attitude toward food. And above all, acquire good eating habits that encourage moderate eating of the right kinds of foods.

Of course you are bound to cheat and go overboard once in awhile. That's all right. Relax and enjoy it. Accept the fact that you won't be able to train your taste away from sweets overnight. There are bound to be setbacks. But if you accept these transgressions in a positive way, the will power you'll need to continue on your diet will return more easily. Once you assert yourself and learn to appease your craving for sweets with savory foods like fresh fruit, guilt feelings and overindulgences will vanish and eating desserts becomes a pleasurable experience. In no time at all you'll find that you'll be able to eat an interesting and satisfying variety of foods without feeling deprived.

Fruits are high in natural sugar, but in such a diluted form as compared to refined sugar that they are comparatively low in calories. They are also excellent sources of vitamins, minerals, and natural fibers. What's more, fruits are versatile, beautiful, delicious, and finally, they are readily available year round.

AMBROSIA

1 cup pineapple chunks
2 oranges, peeled and sectioned
2 bananas, sliced

2 tablespoons shredded coconut
½ cup orange juice

Prepare fruits. Toss ingredients lightly in a medium-size bowl. Chill for at least 1 hour before serving.

Makes 6 servings at 90 calories per serving.

Chef's Cooking Tip:
The easiest way to clean and section an orange is to place it in a hot oven for a few minutes. You'll find that the white stringy inner fibers will come off easily when the skin is peeled.

APPLESAUCE WHIP

¼ cup cold water
2 tablespoons fresh lemon juice
1 tablespoon unflavored gelatin
1 tablespoon sugar
¾ cup boiling water
1 cup cinnamon-flavored applesauce
2 drops red food coloring (optional)
½ cup stiffly beaten egg whites

In a medium bowl, sprinkle gelatin over cold water and lemon juice to soften. Add boiling water to dissolve gelatin, stirring thoroughly. Blend in applesauce and food coloring; then refrigerate in bowl until mixture begins to thicken. Fold the beaten egg whites into the thickened gelatin mixture. Spoon into dessert dishes. Refrigerate about ½ hour before serving.

Makes 4 servings at 86 calories per serving.

Chef's Cooking Tip:
The red coloring will look dark when blended with the applesauce mixture, but when the egg whites are folded in, there will be only a slight suggestion of color.

CINNAMON BAKED APPLES

4 small baking apples
¼ cup apple juice
¼ cup water
1 tablespoon lemon juice
2 whole cloves
2 teaspoons cinnamon

Core the apples and peel ½ inch from the top. Place in a shallow baking pan; sprinkle with the lemon juice and cinnamon. Cover the bottom of the dish with the apple juice and water. Add the cloves; bake, uncovered, at 375° F. for 35 to 45 minutes, basting with the pan juices during baking.

Makes 4 servings at 40 calories per serving.

Chef's Cooking Tip:
Be sure to use firm apples like Gravensteins and Rome Beauties for baking. Some other good choices are: Cortland, Rhode Island Greening, Baldwin, Stayman, and Winesap.

POACHED APPLE SLICES

½ cup apple juice
½ cup dry white wine
1 tablespoon lemon juice
1 tablespoon brown sugar
1 cinnamon stick cut 3 inches long
2 large cooking apples
4 tablespoons low-calorie whipped topping

In a medium saucepan, combine apple juice, wine, lemon juice, sugar, and cinnamon stick; bring to a boil. Wash and core apples. Cut into ¼-inch slices. Add slices to saucepan; cover and simmer 3 to 5 minutes, or until apples are barely tender. Gently stir occasionally so slices are poached uniformly. Remove from heat; serve hot or chill before serving. Garnish with 1 tablespoon whipped topping.

Makes 4 servings at 100 calories per serving.

Chef's Cooking Tip:
Sliced fruits can be prevented from turning brown by soaking them in acidulated water. Drain on paper toweling before using.

BOYSENBERRY PARFAIT

1½ teaspoons unflavored gelatin
½ cup cold water
2 tablespoons sugar
1 cup boysenberry juice
2 teaspoons fresh lime juice
2 cups (2 pounds) frozen boysenberries

Allow berries to thaw; reserve juice. Add enough water to juice to equal 1 cup total; set aside. In a small saucepan, sprinkle gelatin and sugar over ½ cup cold water. Place over low heat to dissolve, stirring constantly, about two minutes; remove from heat. Add the 1 cup boysenberry juice; stir to blend and refrigerate for 30 minutes to set. Add the lime juice and berries. Chill an additional 30 minutes. Fill five (6-ounce) parfait glasses. Refrigerate at least 2 hours to set.

Makes 5 servings at 60 calories per serving.

Chef's Cooking Tip:
Canned fruits like peaches, pears, and pineapple slices can be frozen in the can. For a quick and easy dessert, simply open up both ends of the can, slide the fruit out and slice with a large knife that has been dipped in hot water.

BAKED CHERRY CUPS

1 can (No. 2) water-pack cherries (2¼ cups)
1 tablespoon sugar
½ teaspoon cinnamon
¼ teaspoon almond extract
1 tablespoon slivered almonds

Combine cherries, liquid, sugar, cinnamon, and almond extract in a small mixing bowl to blend flavors. Spoon into five 6-ounce ramekins. Preheat oven to 350° F. Bake in a hot water bath for 30 minutes. Sprinkle slivered almonds over cherries the last 5 minutes of baking.

Makes 5 servings at 60 calories per serving.

Chef's Cooking Tip:
Different varieties of water-packed fruit can be substituted for the cherries in this recipe. Try apricots, fruit cocktail, peaches, pears, or plums.

FRESH FRUIT CUPS

1 cup fresh pineapple, cubed
1 papaya, peeled, seeded, and cubed
1 small orange, peeled and diced
1 small apple, cored and diced
12 small seedless grapes
1 cup sliced strawberries
1 cup water
1 tablespoon honey
6 mint leaves

Mix all fruits except strawberries in a glass or ceramic bowl. Combine water and honey in a small saucepan. Bring to a boil. Pour honey water over fruit; cover at once. When cooled, refrigerate for 6 hours, or overnight. Just before serving, gently fold in sliced strawberries; drain. Serve in stemmed dessert glasses. Garnish with mint leaves.

Makes 6 servings at 60 calories per serving.

Chef's Cooking Tip:
When possible, substitute fresh whole fruit for juices. The whole fruit adds bulk to the diet and satisfies the body longer.

POLYNESIAN FRUIT CUP

1 medium orange
1 small grapefruit
1 papaya
¼ fresh pineapple
1 medium-size banana

1 tablespoon lime juice
1 tablespoon sugar
6 raspberries
6 mint sprigs

Peel and halve orange and grapefruit; remove sections. Peel, seed, and cube papaya. Cut rind from pineapple wedges; cut meat into ¼-inch slices. Peel and slice banana. In a shallow bowl, mix fruits; sprinkle with lime juice and sugar. Cover; chill thoroughly. Serve in sherbet glasses with marinade. Garnish with raspberries and mint sprigs.

Makes 6 servings at 75 calories per serving.

Chef's Cooking Tip:
To section an orange or grapefruit, cut a thin slice from the top and bottom of the fruit. Hold the fruit on a cutting board, and with a sharp knife, cut the peel off in 1-inch slices as close to the flesh as possible. Remove sections by cutting down as close to the membrane as possible between each section. Discard seeds.

BROILED GRAPEFRUIT

2 medium-size grapefruit
1 tablespoon brown sugar

1 teaspoon cinnamon

Cut grapefruits in half horizontally. Core and loosen sections. Place grapefruit in a shallow baking dish, cut-side up; season with sugar and cinnamon. Broil under low heat until grapefruit is warmed through and the outer edge begins to darken.

Makes 4 servings at 70 calories per serving.

Chef's Cooking Tip:
Purchase grapefruits that are firm to the touch and heavy for their size. Heavy fruits are generally juicier and meatier.

MARINATED SLICED PEARS

2 ripe pears
1 cup orange juice
½ cup dry white wine
2 teaspoons honey
2 teaspoons fresh lemon juice
½ teaspoon vanilla extract
1 tablespoon shredded coconut, toasted
4 mint leaves

Peel, core, and slice pears. In a small bowl, combine pears with orange juice, wine, honey, lemon juice, and extract. Cover; marinate in the refrigerator for 2 hours; stir occasionally. Divide pears and marinade among 4 sherbet glasses. Garnish with toasted coconut and mint leaves.

Makes 4 servings at 110 calories per serving.

Chef's Cooking Tip:
Pears are picked green. Allow them to ripen at room temperature before refrigerating.

BAKED PEARS IN WINE

2 medium-size ripe pears, peeled
1 tablespoon lemon juice
½ cup rosé wine
¼ cup water
2 teaspoons sugar
½ teaspoon cinnamon
mint sprigs

Peel, stem, and core fresh pears. Cut in half through the stem; brush each half with lemon juice. Place pear halves in a small casserole dish; add wine, water, sugar, and cinnamon. Cover and bake in a preheated 350° F. oven for 10 minutes. Remove dish from oven. Baste or turn pear halves. Return dish to oven and bake, uncovered, about 10 to 15 minutes longer, or until fork-tender. Place halves in individual dessert dishes; pour hot juices over each. Garnish with mint sprigs and serve.

Makes 4 servings at 65 calories per serving.

Chef's Cooking Tip:
The winter varieties of pears (anjou, bosc, and comice) are the best pears for baking, but they should be firm when purchased.

PRUNE WHIP

2 teaspoons unflavored gelatin
½ cup water
⅛ teaspoon vanilla extract
1 teaspoon lemon juice

1 can (16-ounce) water-packed stewed prunes
2 egg whites
1 teaspoon sugar

Pit prunes, reserving juice. Place water in a small saucepan. Sprinkle gelatin over water and stir over low heat or over boiling water about 1 minute to dissolve gelatin. Combine vanilla, lemon juice, pitted prunes, reserved juice, and dissolved gelatin in a blender; process until smooth. Refrigerate for 30 minutes. Beat the 2 egg whites to form soft peaks. Add sugar a little at a time; continue to whip until stiff but not dry. Fold the egg whites into the prune/gelatin mixture. Spoon into 6 half-cup dessert dishes and chill.

Makes 6 servings at 45 calories per serving.

Chef's Cooking Tip:
Beaten egg whites remain firmer longer if a little sugar is added toward the end of the beating. Don't add the sugar too soon, however, or the egg whites won't stiffen properly.

BAKED COCONUT CUSTARD

3 eggs
¼ cup sugar
⅛ teaspoon coconut extract
⅛ teaspoon salt

2½ cups skim milk
1 tablespoon toasted shredded coconut

Preheat oven to 350° F. Beat eggs slightly. Add sugar, coconut extract, and salt, and continue to beat until just blended. Gradually stir in milk. Pour into seven 5-ounce custard cups or ramekins that have been placed in a shallow baking pan. Fill the bottom of the pan with 1 inch of hot water; place pan in oven. Bake, uncovered, for 40 to 60 minutes, or until a knife inserted in the custard comes out clean. Garnish with toasted shredded coconut. Remove from water bath and cool.

Makes seven ½-cup servings at 104 calories per serving.

Chef's Cooking Tip:
If you're watching your cholesterol count, you may substitute 2 egg whites for each egg yolk in this recipe.

HONEY CUSTARD

3 eggs
2 tablespoons honey
1 teaspoon vanilla extract
¼ teaspoon salt
2½ cups skim milk
dash nutmeg or cinnamon

Preheat oven to 350° F. Beat eggs slightly. Add honey, vanilla extract, and salt, and beat gently just until blended. Gradually stir in the milk. Pour into seven 5-ounce custard cups or ramekins that have been placed in a shallow baking pan. Fill the bottom of the pan with 1 inch of hot water; place pan in the oven. Bake, uncovered, for 40 to 60 minutes, or until a knife inserted in the custard comes out clean. Garnish with a sprinkling of nutmeg or cinnamon before serving.

Makes seven ½-cup servings at 86 calories per serving.

Chef's Cooking Tip:
The cooking time can be cut almost in half by scalding the milk before mixing it with the other ingredients.

PUMPKIN CUSTARD

1½ cups canned pumpkin mix
½ teaspoon ginger
¼ teaspoon salt
⅛ teaspoon nutmeg
2 teaspoons cinnamon
2 eggs
2 tablespoons honey
½ teaspoon vanilla extract
1½ cups skim milk

Preheat oven to 350° F. Combine the pumpkin mix, ginger, salt, nutmeg, and cinnamon in a mixing bowl and blend thoroughly. Beat eggs slightly. Add honey and vanilla extract and continue to beat until just blended. Combine egg mixture with pumpkin mix. Gradually stir in milk. Pour into seven 5-ounce custard cups or ramekins that have been placed in a shallow baking pan. Fill the bottom of the pan with 1 inch of hot water. Place pan in oven; bake, uncovered, for 40 to 60 minutes, or until a knife inserted in the custard comes out clean. Remove from water bath and cool.

Makes seven ½-cup servings at 82 calories per serving.

Chef's Cooking Tip:
Don't overbeat the eggs or you'll have a light, porous custard rather than a firm, smooth one.

BANANA SHERBET

4 very ripe bananas
1 cup orange juice
½ cup water
½ cup skim milk

1 tablespoon lemon juice
2 tablespoons sugar
1 teaspoon alginate powder
 (optional)

Combine all ingredients in a blender; blend until smooth. Pour mixture into a metal bowl or pan and freeze until almost firm. Remove from freezer, break up into chunks, and beat until mixture is ice cream consistency. Pour back into pan and freeze until firm. Repeat at least once. Allow sherbet to soften slightly in the refrigerator before serving.

Makes 6 servings at 90 calories per serving.

BUTTERMILK SHERBET

3 cups buttermilk
1 cup skim milk
¼ cup honey
2 teaspoons vanilla extract
1 teaspoon lemon juice

1 teaspoon alginate powder
 (optional)
2 teaspoons unflavored gelatin
¼ cup water

Combine buttermilk, skim milk, honey, vanilla, lemon juice, and alginate powder in a blender; process for 5 seconds. Pour mixture into a metal bowl or baking pan. Cover and freeze until almost firm. Sprinkle gelatin over ¼ cup of water to soften; dissolve over very low heat or over boiling water. Remove sherbet from freezer. Break into chunks and return to blender. Add dissolved gelatin; rewhip until smooth. Recover pan and freeze. Allow sherbet to soften in the refrigerator 10 minutes before serving.

Makes 8 servings at 80 calories per serving.

Chef's Cooking Tip:
Always keep still-frozen desserts tightly covered to prevent dehydration and the formation of large ice crystals.

CANTALOUPE SHERBET

½ large cantaloupe, peeled, cleaned, and cubed
1 cup orange juice
1 teaspoon fresh lime juice
2 tablespoons honey
1 teaspoon alginate powder (optional)
2 egg whites
dash salt

Combine the cantaloupe cubes, orange juice, lime juice, honey, and alginate powder in a blender and process until smooth. Pour mixture into a metal bowl or pan; freeze until almost frozen. Meanwhile, beat the 2 egg whites until foamy. Add the dash of salt and continue to beat until egg whites are stiff. Return frozen mixture to blender and process until smooth and creamy. Pour sherbet back into freezer tray. Fold in stiffly beaten egg whites and chill until firm.

Makes 6 servings at 60 calories per serving.

ORANGE SHERBET

1 can (6-ounce) frozen orange juice concentrate
2 cups buttermilk
1 teaspoon lemon juice
1 teaspoon grated orange rind
2 drops orange food coloring (optional)
2 tablespoons honey
¼ teaspoon vanilla extract
2 egg whites
dash salt

Combine the orange juice concentrate (undiluted), buttermilk, lemon juice, orange rind, food coloring, honey, and vanilla extract in a blender and process for 5 seconds. Pour into a metal mixing bowl or pan; freeze until almost firm. Meanwhile, beat the 2 egg whites until foamy. Add the dash of salt and continue to beat until egg whites are stiff. Return frozen mixture to blender and process until smooth and creamy. Pour back into freezer tray. Fold in stiffly beaten egg whites and chill until firm.

Makes 8 servings at 85 calories per serving.

PEACH SHERBET

2 cups sliced fresh peaches
1 cup plain yogurt
2 tablespoons honey
½ cup orange juice

1 teaspoon vanilla extract
1 teaspoon alginate powder
  (optional)

Combine all ingredients in a blender and process until smooth and creamy. Pour mixture into a mixing bowl or pan and freeze until almost solid. Remove from freezer, break into chunks; return mixture to blender and process to ice cream consistency. Pour back into pan and freeze until firm. Allow to soften slightly in the refrigerator before serving.

Makes 6 servings at 80 calories per serving.

FROZEN BANANA YOGURT

3 large ripe bananas
1 carton (16-ounce) plain yogurt
2 tablespoons sugar
1 teaspoon vanilla extract
½ teaspoon alginate powder
  (optional)

⅛ teaspoon cinnamon
1 teaspoon unflavored gelatin
¼ cup skim milk

Combine bananas, yogurt, sugar, vanilla, alginate powder, and cinnamon in a blender and process for 10 seconds. Pour mixture into a metal bowl or baking pan. Cover and freeze until almost firm. Sprinkle gelatin over ¼ cup of milk to soften. Dissolve gelatin over a very low heat, stirring constantly, or over boiling water. Remove sherbet from freezer. Break into chunks and return to blender. Add dissolved gelatin; rewhip until smooth. Recover pan and freeze. Allow sherbet to soften in the refrigerator 10 minutes before serving.

Makes 6 servings at 105 calories per serving.

Chef's Cooking Tip:
Bananas are best picked green and ripened at room temperature. When ripe and flecked with brown, they should be eaten or refrigerated in tightly sealed glass jars to inhibit further ripening.

FROZEN STRAWBERRY YOGURT

2 cups fresh strawberries, sliced
1 cup plain yogurt
2 tablespoons honey
2 teaspoons lemon juice

½ teaspoon alginate powder
   (optional)
1 teaspoon unflavored gelatin
¼ cup skim milk

Combine strawberries, yogurt, honey, lemon juice, and alginate powder in a blender and process for 10 seconds. Pour mixture into a metal bowl or baking pan. Cover and freeze until almost firm. Sprinkle gelatin over ¼ cup milk to soften. Dissolve gelatin over a very low heat, stirring constantly, or over boiling water. Remove sherbet from freezer. Break into chunks and return to blender. Add dissolved gelatin; rewhip until smooth. Recover pan and freeze. Allow sherbet to soften in the refrigerator 10 minutes before serving.

Makes 5 servings at 83 calories per serving.

Chef's Cooking Tip:
Strawberries should be washed before you hull them. This prevents the berries from absorbing some of the water and diluting their flavor.

FROZEN VANILLA YOGURT

1 cup skim milk
2 cups plain yogurt
3 tablespoons lemon juice
2 tablespoons sugar

2 teaspoons vanilla extract
1 teaspoon alginate powder
   (optional)
1 teaspoon grated lemon rind

Combine all ingredients in a blender and process until smooth. Pour mixture into a metal mixing bowl or baking pan; freeze until almost solid. Remove from freezer. Break into chunks and rewhip to ice cream consistency. Cover and refreeze until almost solid; then repeat above procedure. Refreeze. Allow to soften for 10 minutes in the refrigerator before serving.

Makes 6 servings at 72 calories per serving.

Chef's Cooking Tip:
Although nutritious, at 250 calories per cup, commercial fruit-flavored yogurts are anything but low in calories! Use plain yogurts and various flavoring extracts and you'll be cutting the calories in half.

PINEAPPLE FRAPPÉ

1 can (20-ounce) crushed pineapple in unsweetened juice

1 can (6-ounce) unsweetened pineapple juice

Combine ingredients in a blender and process for 5 seconds. Pour mixture into a metal bowl or baking pan and freeze until almost firm. Remove from freezer. Break into chunks and rewhip until just smooth. Quickly recover and refreeze. Allow to soften slightly in the refrigerator before serving.

Makes 6 servings at 60 calories per serving.

Chef's Cooking Tip:
It's hard to tell when a fresh pineapple is truly ripe, but here are some points to look for: a small, compact crown (top); a solid, rather hollow sound when tapped at the base; a fresh, bright appearance rather than a dull brown look; an odor that is fragrant.

ANGEL FOOD CAKE

1¼ cups egg whites (10 to 12 whites)
¼ teaspoon salt
1 teaspoon cream of tartar

1¾ cups granulated sugar, divided
½ teaspoon vanilla extract
¼ teaspoon almond extract
1 cup sifted cake flour

Bring egg whites to room temperature. In a large mixing bowl, beat egg whites, salt, and cream of tartar on medium speed until foamy. Add 1 cup sugar, ¼ cup at a time, on high speed until stiff peaks form. Don't add the sugar too soon or the whites won't stiffen properly. Fold in flavor extracts. Sift flour before measuring; then resift 2 more times with remaining ¾ cup sugar. Sprinkle sifted flour, ¼ cup at a time, over beaten egg whites, folding gently after each addition. Turn batter into an ungreased 9-inch tube pan. Gently cut through batter with a knife to remove air bubbles. Place on the lowest rack in a preheated 375° F. oven; bake for 30 to 40 minutes, or until top is delicately browned and cake is springy to the touch. Invert pan on a funnel or bottle to allow air to circulate underneath; allow to cool for 2 hours. Loosen around edges with a knife and turn out. If cake is made ahead, you can leave it in the pan until ready to be served.

Makes 16 servings at 125 calories per serving.

BEVERAGES

Between-meal snacks are practically the American way of life, so how can we cope with them without going overboard on calories? One way to handle this situation is to always have delicious hot and cold low-calorie beverages on hand. They're guaranteed to fill in those hungry hours during the day for precious few calories, indeed. If you were to approach your next meal feeling too hungry, however, you might be tempted to overeat and go off your diet.

Remember, there is no law that says you have to suffer to be slim. What dieter could feel deprived being able to enjoy thirst-quenching Cantaloupe Coolers or tall, frosty Tropical Fruit Shakes? Some of these drinks are not without calories by any means, but when compared to sugary soft drinks and even fresh fruit juices that keep sending you back for more, they're actually a bargain in calories.

So for between-meal and late-night snackers alike, here are some nutritious, low-calorie beverages you can enjoy without worrying about extra pounds.

APRICOT NECTAR COOLER

2 cans (6-ounce) apricot nectar
1 carton (8-ounce) plain yogurt

2 ice cubes, cracked
dash of cinnamon

Combine apricot nectar and yogurt in an electric blender and process until smooth and creamy. Add ice cubes; cover and blend until ice is completely crushed.

Makes 2 servings at 172 calories per serving.

CANTALOUPE COOLER

½ medium cantaloupe
1 cup plain yogurt

1 tablespoon sugar
2 ice cubes, cracked

Remove seeds and rind from cantaloupe. Combine with remaining ingredients in a blender. Process until smooth. Serve immediately.

Makes 2 servings at 113 calories per serving.

COFFEE MILKSHAKE

3 tablespoons nonfat dry skim milk powder
1 cup cold black coffee

½ teaspoon vanilla extract
1 teaspoon sugar
4 ice cubes

Place all ingredients in blender and blend until ice is crushed and liquid is foamy.

Makes one serving at 75 calories per serving.

ORANGE PINEAPPLE PUNCH

1 cup orange juice
½ cup unsweetened pineapple juice
1 tablespoon fresh lime juice

4 ice cubes
1 bottle (10-ounce) plain soda

Chill all ingredients at least 1 hour before using. Combine all ingredients except soda in a blender and blend until ice is crushed. Add soda and pour over ice. Serve immediately.

Makes 4 servings at 60 calories per serving.

SPARKLING FRUIT PUNCH

1 cup orange juice
½ cup apricot juice
½ cup unsweetened pineapple juice
4 ice cubes
1 bottle (10-ounce) plain soda

Chill all ingredients at least 1 hour before using. Combine all ingredients except soda in a blender and blend until ice is crushed. Add soda and pour over ice. Serve immediately.

Makes 4 servings at 60 calories per serving.

STRAWBERRY MILKSHAKE

1 cup fresh strawberries
1½ cups nonfat milk
1 tablespoon powdered sugar
dash ground cinnamon

Clean and wash berries; place in plastic bag or airtight container and freeze for 30 minutes. Remove from freezer and combine with remaining ingredients in blender. Blend until smooth and serve immediately.

Makes 2 servings at 109 calories per serving.

THICK TROPICAL FRUIT SHAKE

1 ripe banana
1 carton (8-ounce) plain yogurt
¼ cup orange juice
¼ cup unsweetened pineapple juice
4 ice cubes
¼ teaspoon coconut extract

Chill all ingredients at least 1 hour before using. Combine all ingredients in a blender and blend until smooth. Garnish with fruit slices and mint sprigs and serve immediately.

Makes 2 servings at 144 calories per serving.

TROPICAL PUNCH

1 ripe banana
1 cup fresh pineapple chunks
1 can dietetic apricot nectar
¼ teaspoon coconut extract
1 can (12-ounce) diet cream soda

Combine all ingredients except cream soda in a blender and blend for 1 minute. Add cream soda and process about 30 seconds longer. Pour over ice, garnish with fruit slices and mint sprigs, and serve immediately.

Makes 4 servings at 54 calories per serving.

UNCLOUDY LEMON ICED TEA

4 cups cold *water*
8 tea bags
lemon wedges

Combine water and tea bags in a pitcher; cover and refrigerate overnight. When ready to serve, remove tea bags and stir. Serve over ice with a lemon wedge garnish.

Makes 8 servings. Calorie count insignificant.

MENUS

By this time, I hope that you've come to agree with me that discipline and moderation rather than deprivation and monotony are the keys to successful dieting. I hope that you've discovered that with the proper cooking method and a little common sense about food, you can look forward to a slimmer, more attractive figure and enjoy eating at the same time. Most of all, I'd like to think that this book has given you a new approach to the whole business of cooking and eating and has encouraged you to experiment and devise low-calorie recipes of your own.

From the beginning, I've suggested that counting calories is what dieting is all about—less calories means less weight. However, while calories do count, so does the nutritive value of the food you eat. And heavily. The menus in this book have been carefully planned as balanced meals. I have tested each recipe, not just once, but many times, so I'm sure they work. Every menu has been designed to include a variety of flavors, colors, and textures. They are not only low in calories, but delicious, and appealing to the eye, as well.

Sticking with your diet program long enough to make low-calorie cooking and eating a habit requires motivation and perseverance, but the rewards in improved looks, health, and vigor certainly make it worthwhile.

LOW-CALORIE DINNER MENUS

FILLET MIGNON DINNER

Vegetable Juice Cocktail Supreme	43
Spinach Salad Mimosa w/French Dressing	30
Fillet Mignon Bordelaise	280
Braised Belgian Endive	40
Ambrosia	90
1 slice rye bread	70
1 teaspoon diet margarine	17
Coffee or Tea	0

Total Calories: 570

ROAST CHICKEN DINNER

Shrimp Cocktail	50
Carrot and Raisin Salad	60
Roasted Chicken	270
Ratatouille en Casserole	50
Baked Potatoes	80
1 tablespoon diet margarine	50
Baked Pears in Wine	55
Coffee or Tea	0

Total Calories: 615

BROILED STEAK DINNER

French-style Onion Soup	80
Lettuce Wedges with French Dressing	25
Broiled Beef Fillets	260
Herbed Broiled Tomatoes	56
Broiled Mushrooms	35
Seasoned French Bread	87
Broiled Grapefruit	55
Coffee or Tea	0

Total Calories: 598

LOBSTER DINNER

Manhattan Clam Chowder	100
Cucumber-Onion Salad	50
Steamed Rock Lobster Tails	224
Rice Pilaf	145
Asparagus Spears with Pimiento	16
Spicy Peach Compote	60
Coffee or Tea	0

Total Calories: 595

VEAL DINNER

Cauliflower Soup	50
Italian Green Salad	50
Veal Cacciatore	220
Fresh Broccoli with Lemon	25
½ cup Mashed Potatoes	92
1 slice Italian bread	70
1 teaspoon diet margarine	17
Prune Whip	40
1 tablespoon Cool Whip	16
Coffee or Tea	0

Total Calories: 580

BAKED TROUT DINNER

Tomato Bouillon Soup	30
Cucumber Salad	30
Baked Trout with Wine Sauce	175
Zucchini Provencale	16
Parslied Potatoes with Margarine	116
1 slice rye bread	70
1 teaspoon diet margarine	17
Strawberry Yogurt Whip	40
Coffee or Tea	0

Total Calories: 494

BARBECUED CHICKEN DINNER

Gazpacho	50
Crisp and Tangy Coleslaw	25
Barbecued Chicken	270
Noodles Parmesan	150
Tarragon Green Beans	25
Frozen Banana Yogurt	80
Coffee or Tea	0

Total Calories: 600

WEIGHTS, MEASURES, AND EQUIVALENTS

ABBREVIATIONS

Teaspoon	tsp.	Gram	g.
Tablespoon	tbsp.	Kilogram	kg.
Cup	c.	Milliliter	ml.
Pint	pt.	Centiliter	cl.
Quart	qt.	Deciliter	dl.
Gallon	gal.	Liter	l.
Ounce	oz.	Degree Fahrenheit	°F.
Pound	lb.	Degree Celsius	°C.
Bushel	bu.	Sodium	Na.

COMMON CAN SIZES AND CONTENTS

CAN SIZE	APPROXIMATE CUPS	APPROXIMATE WEIGHT
6 ounce	¾ cup	6 ounces
Buffet (8 ounce)	1 cup	8 ounces
Picnic	1¼ cups	10½ ounces
2 vacuum (12 ounces)	1½ cups	12 ounces
No. 300	1¾ cups	14 to 16 ounces
No. 303	2 cups	16 to 17 ounces
No. 2	2¼ to 2½ cups	1 pound, 4 ounces
No. 2½	3¼ to 3½ cups	1 pound, 12 ounces
No. 3	4 to 4½ cups	2 pounds, 1 ounce
No. 3 cylinder	5¾ cups	3 pounds
46 ounce	5¾ to 6 cups	3 pounds, 3 ounces
No. 5	6½ to 7 cups	3 pounds, 8 ounces
No. 10	12 to 13 cups	7 pounds

EQUIVALENT WEIGHTS AND MEASURES

FRUITS:

Apples	1 pound	4 small or 3 cups, sliced
Bananas	1 pound	4 small or 2 cups, mashed
Berries	1 pint	2 cups
Cantaloupe	2 pounds	3 cups, diced
Cherries	1 pint	1 cup, pitted
Grapefruit	1 small	1 cup, sections
Grapes	¼ pound	1 cup
Lemon	1 medium	2 tablespoons juice
Orange	1 small	¾ cup, sections
Peaches	1 pound (3)	2 cups, chopped
Pears	1 pound (3)	2 cups, chopped
Pineapple	3 pounds	2½ cups, chopped
Plums	1 pound (4)	2 cups, chopped
Prunes	1 pound (5)	2 cups, chopped

VEGETABLES:

Asparagus	1 pound	18 spears
Avocado	1 medium	2 cups, chopped
Beans, green	1 pound	3 cups, cooked
Beets	1 pound	2 cups, cooked and sliced
Bell Pepper	½ pound (1)	1 cup, chopped
Broccoli	1 pound	6 cups, cooked
Cabbage	1 pound	4 cups, shredded; 2½ cups, cooked
Carrots	1 pound	4 cups, chopped
Cauliflower	1½ pounds	6 cups, chopped and cooked
Celery	2 ribs	1 cup, finely chopped
Cucumber	1 medium	1½ cups, sliced
Eggplant	1 pound	6 cups, cubed
Lettuce	1 head	6 cups, chopped
Mushrooms	¼ pound	1 cup, sliced
Onion	1 medium	1 cup, finely chopped
Potatoes	1 pound (4)	2½ cups, cooked and diced
Pumpkin	3 pounds	4 cups, cooked and mashed
Rutabagas	1½ pounds	2 cups, cooked and mashed
Spinach	1 pound	2 cups, cooked
Tomatoes	1 pound (3)	1¼ cups, cooked and chopped
Zucchini	1 pound	4 cups, sliced

PROTEIN:

Cheese, cottage	½ pound	1 cup
Cheese, grated	¼ pound	1 cup
Eggs	6 eggs	1 cup
Egg whites	8 to 10	1 cup
Crab, cooked	½ pound	1 cup
Lobster, cooked	½ pound	1 cup
Oysters, raw	½ pound	1 cup
Scallops, cooked	½ pound	1 cup
Shrimp, cooked	1 pound	3 cups
Tuna, canned	7 ounces	¾ cup

METRIC CONVERSIONS FOR LIQUID MEASURES

The basic unit of liquid volume in the metric system is the liter, with decimal multiples being the deciliter (divided into tenths) and the centiliter (divided into hundreths). A milliliter (one one-thousandth of a liter) is the other commonly used unit.

$$1 \text{ liter} = 10 \text{ deciliters}$$
$$1 \text{ liter} = 100 \text{ centiliters}$$
$$1 \text{ liter} = 1000 \text{ milliliters}$$

To convert cups to liters, multiply cups by 0.24.
To convert liters to cups, multiply liters by 4.17.
To convert quarts to liters, multiply quarts by 0.95.
To convert liters to quarts, multiply liters by 1.057.
To convert gallons to liters, multiply gallons by 3.8.
To convert liters to gallons, multiply liters by 0.26.
To convert ounces into centiliters, multiply ounces by 2.96.
To convert centiliters to ounces, multiply centiliters by 0.34.

LIQUID MEASURE	APPROXIMATE METRIC EQUIVALENT
¼ cup	½ dl. or 6 cl.
⅓ cup	¾ dl. or 8 cl.
½ cup	1 dl. or 12 cl.
⅔ cup	1½ dl. or 15 cl.
¾ cup	1¾ dl. or 18 cl.
1 cup	¼ liter or 24 cl.
1 quart	1 liter or 95 cl.
1 gallon	3¾ liter or 375 cl.

METRIC CONVERSIONS FOR WEIGHT

The basic unit of measurement in the metric system for weight is the gram (g.), with decimal multiples being the milligram and the kilogram

$$1 \text{ gram} = 1{,}000 \text{ milligrams}$$
$$1 \text{ kilogram} = 1{,}000 \text{ grams}$$
$$2{,}205 \text{ pounds} = 1{,}000 \text{ kilograms}$$

To convert ounces to grams, multiply ounces by 28.35.
To convert grams to ounces, multiply grams by 0.035.
To convert kilograms to pounds, multiply kilograms by 2.2.
To convert pounds to kilograms, multiply pounds by 0.45.

OUNCES/POUNDS	APPROXIMATE GRAM/ KILOGRAM EQUIVALENT
1 oz.	30 g.
2 oz.	60 g.
3 oz.	85 g.
4 oz.	115 g.
5 oz.	140 g.
6 oz.	180 g.
8 oz.	225 g.
10 oz.	285 g.
12 oz.	340 g.
14 oz.	400 g.
16 oz.	454 g.
20 oz.	567 g.
24 oz.	680 g.
30 oz.	850 g.
¼ lb.	115 g.
½ lb.	226 g.
¾ lb.	340 g.
1 lb.	454 g.
1¼ lb.	567 g.
1½ lb.	680 g.
1¾ lb.	794 g.
2 lb.	908 g.
2.2 lb.	1 kilogram

TOMATO PRODUCT SUBSTITUTIONS

Tomato sauce—Equal amount tomato purée with added seasonings.

Tomato sauce (8 ounces)—1 can tomato paste plus 1½ cans water and seasonings.

Whole tomatoes (1 cup)—1⅓ cups cut-up fresh tomatoes simmered for 10 minutes.

Stewed tomatoes—Equal amount whole peeled fresh tomatoes, chopped, plus diced onion, celery, and green pepper.

Tomato purée—1 can tomato paste plus equal amount of water.

Tomato juice (3 cups)—1 can tomato paste plus 3 cans water, dash of salt and sugar.

Chile sauce, catsup, and cocktail sauce—Interchangeable with only slight variations in flavor. Cocktail sauce includes horseradish, garlic, and spice oils.

OVEN TEMPERATURES

To convert Fahrenheit to Celsius (also called Centigrade) temperature, subtract 32, multiply by 5, and divide by 9. To convert Celsius to Fahrenheit temperature, multiply by 9, divide by 5, and add 32.

FAHRENHEIT (°F.)	CELSIUS (°C.)	TERM
160	71	Warm
170	77	
200	93	
205	96	Simmer
212	100	Boil
225	107	
250	121	Very slow
275	135	
300	149	Slow
325	163	
350	177	Moderate
375	190	
400	204	Hot
425	218	
450	232	
475	246	Very hot
500	260	
525	274	
550	288	Extremely hot

SEASONINGS

Garlic, minced	1 clove	⅛ teaspoon
Garlic powder	⅛ teaspoon	1 whole garlic clove
Herbs, fresh	1 tablespoon	1 teaspoon dried
Herbs, dried	1 teaspoon	1 tablespoon fresh
Horseradish, prepared	2 tablespoons	1 tablespoon fresh
Onion, dried minced	1 tablespoon	¼ cup minced raw onion
Onion, dried chopped	2 tablespoons	1 medium raw onion
Onion powder	1 teaspoon	1 medium raw onion
Parsley, dry	1 tablespoon	3 tablespoons, fresh
Prepared mustard	1 tablespoon	1 teaspoon dry mustard

WEIGHTS AND MEASURES

1 teaspoon	60 drops or ⅓ tablespoon
1½ teaspoon	½ tablespoon
3 teaspoons	1 tablespoon
2 tablespoons	⅛ cup or 1 ounce
4 tablespoons	¼ cup
5 tablespoons + 1 tsp.	⅓ cup
8 tablespoons	½ cup
10 tablespoons + 2 tsp.	⅔ cup
12 tablespoons	¾ cup
14 tablespoons	⅞ cup
16 tablespoons	1 cup or 8 ounces
1 cup	½ pint or 8 ounces or 227 grams
2 cups	1 pint or 16 ounces
4 cups	1 quart or 2 pints
½ pint	1 cup
1 pint	2 cups or ½ quart
2 pints	4 cups or 1 quart
1 quart	4 cups or 2 pints or 32 ounces
4 quarts	1 gallon
8 quarts	1 peck
1 gallon	4 quarts or 16 cups
2 gallons	1 peck
1 peck	8 quarts
4 pecks	1 bushel
1 pound	16 ounces (dry) or 454 grams
1 ounce	2 tablespoons or 28.35 **grams**
2 ounces	¼ cup
4 ounces	½ cup
8 ounces	1 cup or ½ pint
16 ounces	2 cups or 1 pint or ½ quart
32 ounces	4 cups or 2 pints or 1 quart
1 dram	1/16 ounce
pinch or dash	⅛ teaspoon
dash (liquid)	6 to 8 drops

GLOSSARY OF COOKING TERMS AND FOREIGN PHRASES

abricot: (F.) Apricot.
agneau: (F.) Lamb.
à la: (F.) "In the manner of" or "the house specialty."
à l'ancienne: (F.) In the old style.
à la bourgeoise: (F.) Family style.
à la broche: (F.) Cooked on a spit over an open fire.
à la carte: (F.) Menu item to order, priced separately.
à la king: (F.) Foods served in white cream sauce.
à la mode: (F.) "In the fashion," as pie with ice cream. Also applied to various ways of serving.
à la Russe: (F.) The Russian way.
al dente: (I.) "To the tooth"—used to describe the degree of doneness of spaghetti or other pasta as felt between the teeth.
allemande: (F.) White sauce of stock, egg yolks, and cream.
agar agar: Seaweed gelatin used for thickening.
aiguillettes: (F.) Strips of breast of duck and other poultry.

aile: (F.) Wing tip of poultry or game.
allumette: (F.) Cut like large matchsticks.
amandine: (F.) Made with almonds or garnished with same.
ananas: (F.) Pineapple.
anchois: (F.) Anchovy.
andalouse: (F.) Prepared the Andalusian (Spanish) way.
angelica: Candied leafstalk of an herb. Usually used for dessert decoration.
anglaise: (F.) In the English style.
antioxidant: Substance capable of preventing oxidation in foods.
antipasto: (I.) "Before the meal." Food served before the main course.
appareil: (F.) Mixture of different ingredients as preparation for a dish.
appetizer: Food served before the main course.
argenteuil: (F.) With asparagus.
aromates: (F.) Herbs and vegetables like *mirepoix* used for flavoring and aroma.

[285]

arrowroot: Starch obtained from the root of a tropical plant used for thickening.

arroz con pollo: (Sp.) Main course dish of chicken, rice, tomatoes, garlic, red and green peppers.

artichaut: (F.) Globe artichoke.

asado: (Sp.) Roasted meat.

ascorbic acid: Vitamin C available in powder or tablet form.

asperge: (F.) Asparagus.

aspic: A clear gelatin made from vegetable or meat broth.

assaisonner: (F.) To season.

attereaux: (F.) Partially cooked skewered foods; metal skewers.

aubergine: (F.) Eggplant.

au beurre: (F.) With or cooked in butter.

au beurre noir: (F.) With nut-brown or black butter.

au blanc: (F.) "To keep white" by cooking with a *blanc,* a mixture of acidulated water, flour, and seasoning.

au gras: (F.) Meat cooked with rich sauce.

au gratin: (F.) Baked with a topping of crumbs and/or cheese and baked or browned in oven or broiler.

au jus: (F.) With natural juices of the meat.

au lait: (F.) With milk.

au maigre: (F.) Cooked with fish or vegetable stocks.

au naturel: (F.) Plainly cooked; foods cooked in a simple style.

au rouge: (F.) Foods prepared with or served in a red sauce.

au ruban: (F.) The stage of cooking when a mixture reaches a ribbonlike texture when dropped from a spoon.

au vert: (F.) Foods prepared with a green sauce.

aux croutons: (F.) With bread cut in small dice and fried.

avgolemono: (Greek) Egg and lemon soup.

baba: (F.) A yeast raised cake flavored with rum or fruit sauce.

bain marie: (F.) Steam table or water bath; double boiler.

bake: Cook in the oven by dry heat, usually uncovered.

barbecue: To cook or roast food over hot coals or grill, basting with sauce.

bard: To wrap meat, fish or poultry with thin slices of fat.

bar le duc: (F.) Jam made of red currants.

baron d'agneau: (F.) The saddle and legs of lamb in one piece.

baron of beef: Double sirloin of beef in one piece.

baste: To moisten or ladle food with drippings.

batter: Flour and liquid mixture thin enough to pour or stir.

Bayonne ham: French raw ham, like prosciutto or Westphalian ham.

béarnaise: (F.) Sauce derived from Hollandaise containing egg yolks, vinegar, butter, onion, and spices.

beat: To stir vigorously with a rapid motion to incorporate air into a mixture.

béchamel: (F.) A cream sauce or white sauce.

bellevue: (F.) Well decorated; beautiful to look at.

beurre manie: (F.) Mixture of flour and butter used to thicken.

beurre noir: (F.) Butter cooked to dark brown.

beurre noisette: (F.) Butter cooked to light brown.

bien cuit: (F.) Medium well done.

bifteck haché: (F.) Chopped steak.

bigarad: (F.) Bitter oranges.

bind: To add ingredients (egg yolks, thick sauce) to hold a mixture together.

bisque: (F.) A thick, rich soup from fish, shellfish or game.

blanc: (F.) White color.
blanch: To scald quickly in boiling water, then chill.
blancmange: (F.) A milk dessert shaped in a mold.
bland: Food that is smooth textured but not stimulating to the taste.
blanquette: (F.) Light cream sauce of egg and cream.
blanquette d'agneau: (F.) Stewed lamb in white sauce.
blanquette de veau: (F.) Veal stew in a light cream sauce.
blau: (G.) Literally, "blue;" undercooked fish; rare meat.
blend: To thoroughly mix two or more ingredients until smooth.
blini: (Russian) A thin pancake leavened with yeast and egg whites.
boeuf: (F.) Beef.
boil: To cook in boiling liquid. 212° F. at sea level.
boiled dressing: Cooked dressing for salads.
bombe: (F.) A dessert frozen in a melon-shaped mold.
bombe glacée: (F.) A frozen dessert filled with various ice creams.
bone: To remove all bones from meat, fish or poultry.
bonne femme: (F.) Home-style soups and stews, usually with leeks, carrots, onions, and potatoes. Also, cooking with mushrooms and white wine.
bordelaise: (F.) Brown sauce with onion and red wine.
bordure: (F.) With a border of duchesse potatoes as garnish.
borscht: (Russian) A mixed vegetable soup with beets.
bouchée: (F.) Small puff pastry shell filled with meats or fruits.
bouillabaisse: (F.) A fish-based soup, stew combination.
bouillon: (F.) A clear meat stock obtained from broth.
boulangère: (F.) A style of cooking potatoes by placing them under the roasted meat.
bouquet: Volatile oils that give flavor.
bouquet garni: (F.) Aromatic herbs tied together. Usually parsley, thyme, bay leaf, rosemary, or various aromatic vegetables tied in a cheesecloth and removed before the dish is served.
bouquetière: (F.) Vegetables arranged around a plate or platter.
bourgeoise: (F.) Plain, home-style cooking.
bourguignonne: (F.) Sauces flavored with Burgundy wine.
braise: To cook, covered, in a small amount of liquid.
brazier: Heavy-duty cooking utensil with tight-fitting cover.
breading: To coat with bread crumbs before cooking.
breton: (F.) Items that are garnished with beans.
brew: Cook in liquid to extract flavor.
brider: (F.) To truss poultry.
brine: Salt, vinegar and water solution for pickling.
brioche: (F.) A rich, light yeast roll.
brochette: (F.) A skewer or food broiled on a skewer.
brodo: (I.) Bouillon, broth, or chowder.
broil: To cook by the radiation of an open flame.
brule: (F.) A pudding made with egg yolks, then molded.
brunoise: (F.) Vegetables cut in small cubes for soups or sauces.
buffet: A display of foods, usually for self-service.
butt: (G.) Flounder, turbot.
butterpaste: Butter and flour kneaded together for thickening(*beurre manie*).

café: (F.) Coffee.
café au lait: (F.) Coffee served with hot milk.
calvados: (F.) Apple brandy.

camembert: (F.) A soft cheese made from cow's milk.

Canadian bacon: Smoked loin of pork. Extremely lean.

canapé: (F.) An appetizer arranged on a bread base.

cannelloni: (I.) Squares of pasta stuffed with meat or cheese and served with tomato or meat sauce.

capers: Pickled buds from wild caper bush.

capon: A male chicken castrated while young.

carafe: Bottle used for water or wine.

caramelize: To dissolve granulated sugar with water and cook over medium heat to a deep honey color.

carbonize: To burn.

cardinal sauce: Béchamel sauce with coral and lemon juice.

cassolette: (F.) Ovenproof china container or pot used for serving one portion of fine ragouts, eggs, etc.

cassoulet: (F.) French stew made with beans and lamb, goose, or pork.

caviar: Salted egg or roe of fish; black or red.

cayenne: Red powdered seasoning. Hot pepper seasoning.

cèpes: (F.) A species of mushroom.

cerise: (F.) Cherry.

cervelles: (F.) Brains.

chablis: (F.) White burgundy wine.

chafing dish: Deep metal pan used with or without water heated from beneath.

champignons: (F.) Button mushrooms.

chanterelles: (F.) Species of mushrooms.

chantilly: (F.) Foods containing whipped cream.

chapon a l'ail: (F.) Garlic-flavored bread added to a mixed salad.

charlotte russe: (F.) A refrigerator dessert in a mold garnished with lady fingers.

chasseur: (F.) Literally "hunt style." Food basically prepared with tomatoes, mushrooms, and wine.

chateaubriand: (F.) Tenderloin of beef broiled or sautéed and then sliced.

chaud: (F.) Hot.

chaud froid: (F.) Literally "hot-cold." In cooking, cold jellied sauces used to cover cold food buffet platter.

chemiser: (F.) To coat with chaud-froid or aspic.

chiffonade: (F.) Prepared with finely shredded vegetables in soups, salads and dressings.

chill: To refrigerate until cold.

chimaja: Mildly flavored spice used in Mexican cookery.

china cap: A cone-shaped strainer.

chine: (F.) Bone adhering to the fillet of the loin of meats.

chinois: (F.) Literally "Chinese." Fine-mesh conical strainer.

chop: To cut into small pieces.

chorizos: (Mexican) Highly spiced sausages.

chou: (F.) Cabbage.

choucroute: (F.) Sauerkraut.

chou-fleur: (F.) Cauliflower.

chou frise: (F.) Kale.

chou paste: Cream puff dough.

choux de Bruxelles: (F.) Brussels sprouts.

chow-chow: Mixed pickles in mustard.

chutney: Relish made from fruits and vegetables.

cimier: (F.) A saddle of venison, mainly of stag.

ciseler: (F.) To cut or score meat or fish so that it will cook faster and will not crack during cooking.

clafouti: (F.) Baked fruit and batter dessert.

clarify: To make clear by skimming or by adding egg whites to remove unwanted particles.

cloche: (F.) Literally "a bell." A round silver, metal or glass cover to keep food hot.

cloche, sous: (F.) Under bell, usually glass; thus "under glass."

coat: To cover an entire surface with flour, crumbs, sauce, or batter.
cocotte: (F.) An earthenware ovenproof individual casserole.
coddle: Cooking at a simmer, as coddled eggs.
collared: Pickled or salted meat rolled tightly and cooked with herbs and spices; served cold.
compote: Fruit stewed in syrup; a stew of fruits.
concasser: (F.) To chop coarsely, or pound.
consommé: (F.) Clarified broth.
coq au vin: (F.) Chicken cooked with wine, onion, and bacon.
coquilles St. Jacques: (F.) A recipe in which scallops are served.
coulis: (F.) Thick soup made with crustaceans.
coupe: (F.) A low stemmed, shallow cup of glass or silver used for appetizers or desserts.
couronne: (F.) To arrange and serve food in the shape of a crown.
court bouillon: (F.) Literally, a "short broth"; a prepared broth made for poaching fish.
cracklings: Crisp fried or deep-fried pork bits.
crecy: (F.) Food prepared with or garnished with carrots.
crême: (F.) Cream.
creole: Foods containing tomato, green pepper, and onion, and usually a dash of Tabasco.
crêpe: (F.) A very thin pancake.
crêpes suzette: (F.) A thin, sweet pancake that is usually rolled and served with butter or fruit sauces.
cresson: (F.) Watercress.
croquette: A mixture of bound foods, usually breaded and deep-fried. Often cylindrical or cone shaped.
crostacei: (I.) Shellfish.
croustade: (F.) A toast case or shell served with creamed meats, fish, or poultry. Sometimes used with vegetables.
croûtons: (F.) Small cubes of bread that are toasted or fried and used as a garnish for soup or salad.
crudités: (F.) Raw salad vegetables.
crumble: To break into small irregular pieces.
cube: Food cut into one-half-inch squares.
cuisine: (F.) The art of cookery. Also kitchen.
culotte: (F.) Top part of a bottom round.
curing: Pickling in brine.
curry: An eastern Indian dish or stew seasoned with curry powder.
custard: A thickened mixture of egg, milk, and other ingredients.
cut in: To blend shortening into a flour mixture.
cutlet: A small, thin piece of meat for sautéing.

dab: Species of flounder.
dag kebab: Skewered chunks of veal, onion and tomato.
daikon: (Japanese) Radish, eaten raw or cooked.
damson: Small plum with blue skin and greenish flesh.
dariole: Small beaker mold in which pastries or vegetables are cooked.
darne: (F.) Middle of a fish, usually referred to salmon.
dartois: (F.) Tiny snacks served as an hors d'oeuvre.
dash: Less than one-eighth teaspoon in measurement.
dasheen: Plant used as a base for puddings and confections.
daube: (F.) Stew; meat braised in stock or red wine.
daubière: (F.) A casserole dish used for braising.
decant: To pour a liquid from one container into another.

deglaze: To dissolve food particles from a roasting pan or hot skillet using a liquid, usually wine, vinegar, water or stock.
déjeuner: (F.) Lunch or midday meal.
demi-glace: (F.) A reduced sauce.
demi-sec: (F.) A type of champagne that is distinctly sweet.
demitasse: (F.) A small cup of coffee served after dinner.
désosser: (F.) To bone or remove bones from meat, poultry or fish.
devil: To prepare with hot sauce or seasoning.
dice: To cut into uniform quarter-inch cubes.
dindon: (F.) Turkey.
dindonneau: (F.) Young turkey.
ditali: (I.) Elbow-shaped macaroni or other pasta.
dolce: (I.) Sweet.
dolma: (Turkish) A stuffed vegetable dish; eggplant, tomatoes, green peppers, grape, or cabbage leaves.
dot: To scatter bits of butter or other seasoning over food surface.
drain: To pour off liquid from the solids.
draw: To remove the entrails of poultry or game; to eviscerate.
drawn butter: Clarified butter; butter melted slowly until milk solids sink to the bottom of the pan.
dredge: To coat food with dry ingredients, usually flour, prior to frying.
dress: To eviscerate. Also, to add dressing to a salad.
drippings: Fat and sediment that accumulates during frying or roasting.
drizzle: To pour melted butter, marinade, or other liquid over the surface of food slowly in thin streams.
dry: In wine it means a small amount of sugar; less sweet.
du barry: (F.) Garnish of cauliflower.
duchess potatoes: Mashed potatoes mixed with beaten eggs and squeezed through a pastry tube.
dugléré: (F.) Prepared with onions, shallots and tomatoes; method of cooking white fish.
dust: To cover lightly with flour, sugar, or other dry ingredients.
duxelles: (F.) Chopped onions or shallots mixed with chopped mushrooms and cooked until dry. Used to flavor soups, sauces and stuffings.

eau: (F.) Water.
éclair: (F.) A pastry or cake shell filled with whipped cream or custard.
écossaise: (F.) Scottish style.
écrevisse: (F.) Crayfish.
émincé: (F.) To cut fine.
émincé of beef: (F.) Thin slices or cuts of meat.
emulsion: A mixture of mutually insoluble liquids in which one is dispersed in droplets throughout the other so as to be held in suspension.
en chemise: (F.) Cooked with the skins on, like potatoes.
enchilada: (Mexican) Tortillas dipped in hot fat and covered with a hot sauce and grated cheese.
en coquille: (F.) Cooked in the shell as with scallops or oysters on the half shell.
endive: Salad greens with lively flavor. Curly endive is lacy. Belgian endive grows in small finger-shaped heads and is somewhat bitter.
entrecôte: (F.) Rib or rib-eye steak.
entrée: (F.) A dish served before or between courses. In America it is usually considered the main course of the meal.
épinard: (F.) Spinach.
escalope de veau: (F.) Veal scallop.
escargot: (F.) Snail.
eviscerate: To remove internal organs.

farce: (F.) Stuffing. Forcemeat.
farcir: (F.) To stuff or fill.

[290]

farina: A fine meal of wheat used in puddings and breakfast cereal.
farinaceous: Prepared with meal or flour.
fermière: (F.) Literally "Farmer's style." Prepared with coarsely chopped vegetables: carrots, turnips, onions, potatoes, celery, and cabbage.
filet: (F.) A flat slice or steak of lean meat or fish without bone.
fillet: English spelling of filet.
fines herbs: (F.) Minced herbs: chervil, tarragon, and chives, although parsley is often included.
finnan haddie: Smoked haddock.
flake: To break into small pieces with a fork.
flambé: (F.) To set afire, as in chafing dish cookery.
flan: Shallow pastry shell molded in a metal ring set on a baking sheet; a baked custard.
flannel cake: A thin, tender griddle cake.
flapjack: A large pancake.
fleuron: (F.) Puff paste baked in a crescent shape and used as a garnish. Brushed with egg and baked in a hot oven.
florentine: Made with spinach. Literally, "as prepared in Florence."
flute: To crimp the edge of a pie crust in a fluted design.
foie: (F.) Liver.
foie de volaille: (F.) Chicken liver.
foie-gras: (F.) Fatted goose liver.
fold: To mix a light mixture with a heavier one so very little lightness is lots. Lifted from beneath rather than stirred in a circle.
fond: (F.) Basic stock; natural juices.
fondantes potatoes: Parboiled oval-shaped potatoes.
fondue: (F.) Melted Swiss or Gruyère cheese dish.
forcemeat: Meats pounded in a mortar or ground for use as stuffing.
forestière: (F.) Prepared and garnished with mushrooms.

fraises: (F.) Strawberries.
franconia potatoes: Potatoes pared and browned with a roast.
frappé: (F.) A frozen fruit dessert made of ice.
frapper: (F.) To chill.
french: To remove the meat and fat from the end of the bone, as French lamb chops.
fricassee: Cubed pieces of meat or poultry prepared in a white sauce.
frijoles: (Mexican) Beans cooked with fat and seasoning.
fritter: A batter dropped by the spoonful into deep hot fat.
friture: (F.) Frying fat. Also food fried in fat.
frizzle: To pan-fry over intense heat with little fat until crisp.
froid: (F.) Cold.
fromage: (F.) Cheese.
frost: To cover with frosting; also to chill until frosty, as to frost a glass. Icing.
fumet: (F.) A concentrated essence of fish, game or vegetables.
fu yung: (Chinese) An omelet made with shrimp, crab, pork, lobster, chicken, etc.

gado-gado: (Indonesian) Raw and cooked vegetables served with a coconut sauce.
galatine: (F.) Boned poultry stuffed with pâté and coated with aspic.
game: Any edible wild bird or beast.
gammelöst: (Norwegian) Literally "old cheese." Made from sour milk.
gammon: (English) A side of salted, smoked or dried bacon; cured ham.
gänsebraten: (G.) Roast goose.
ganso: (Sp.) Goose.
garbure: (F.) A thick cabbage soup.
garnish: To decorate with food or the actual foods used to garnish.
gastric: Cooking term when items are prepared with white wine, vinegar, shallots, peppercorns and spices.

gâteau: (F.) Cake.
gaufre: (F.) A light, crisp waffle.
gaufrette potatoes: (F.) French-fried potatoes in the waffle iron.
gazpacho: (Sp.) A cold soup made with fresh tomatoes and other vegetables.
gefilte fish: (Jewish) Literally "stuffed fish." Poached fish cakes.
gelato: (I.) Literally "frozen." Ice cream; iced dessert.
gelée: (F.) Jelly; gelatin extracted from meat. To frost or freeze.
gerstensuppe: (Swiss) A thick barley soup with vegetables and ham.
gervais: (F.) French cream cheese.
getmesost: (Swedish) Soft cheese made from goat's milk.
gherkin: A young cucumber used for pickling.
giblets: The heart, liver and gizzard of poultry.
gigot d'agneau: (F.) Leg of lamb.
giouvetsi: (Greek) Leg of lamb with rice shaped pasta.
glacé: (F.) Candied, frozen or glazed.
glaze: To baste or brush with glossy coating such as meat glaze, jelly, or icing; to make glossy with egg, water, sugar or milk; bone stock reduced to thickness of jelly.
gnocchi: (I.) A light dumpling.
gohan: (Japanese) Rice.
goulash: (Hungarian) A thick stew made with beef or veal.
gourmet: (F.) A connoisseur in eating and drinking.
granité: (F.) A water-based frozen dessert.
grate: To scrape into small pieces by rubbing a hard food on a grater.
gratin: (F.) Sprinkled with cheese or bread crumbs. Sometimes used for browning cooked food under the broiler.
gravlax: (Scandinavian) Raw salmon cured with pepper, dill, salt, sugar. Usually served cold.

grecque, à la: (F.) Any dish of Greek origin; tomato-based dishes.
gribiche: (F.) A cold sauce served with cold fish.
grillades: (F.) Meat or fish grilled over high heat.
grissini: (I.) Bread sticks.
grits: Coarsley ground corn served as a side dish.
guacamole: (Mexican) Cold sauce made with avocado.
guava: Fruit cooked to make jellies and jams.
gumbo: (Creole) A thick soup with chicken, onion, green peppers, and okra.

haché: (F.) To hash or to mince.
haricots: (F.) Beans.
haricots blancs: (F.) White kidney beans.
haricots verts: (F.) Small green string beans.
hasenpfeffer: (G.) Rabbit stew.
heifer: A young cow that has not had a calf.
herbs: Aromatic greens for seasoning, dry and fresh.
herb bouquet: Mixed herbs tied together and used for seasoning soups or stocks.
hollandaise: (F.) Sauce of eggs, butter, lemon juice and seasonings, served over hot food.
homard: (F.) Lobster.
homard à l'Américaine: (F.) Lobster seasoned with tomatoes, garlic, and herbs.
homogenize: Emulsified liquid. A technique in milk processing that breaks up fat globules so they will remain evenly distributed rather than floating to the top.
hongos: (Sp.) Mushrooms.
hongroise, à la: (F.) Literally, prepared in the Hungarian way, using onions, sour cream and paprika.

hors d'oeuvre: (F.) Bite-sized portions of food used as a relish or appetizer or as the first course of a meal.
huitres: (F.) Oysters.
hure: (F.) Head of boar or pig.
hydrogenated fat: Fat combined with hydrogen to maintain stability.

ice: Frozen mixture of sweetened fruit juice; to cover with icing.
icing: A sugar mixture used for frosting.
ichiban dashi: (Japanese) Basic Japanese soup stock.
Indian pudding: Baked pudding with corn meal, milk, brown sugar, eggs, raisins, and seasonings.
infuse: To steep or soak without boiling in order to obtain a liquid extract from food, flowers and plants.
Irish stew: Lamb stew mixture.

jalapeño: (Mexican) Bright green, two-inch, hot chile.
jambon: (F.) Ham.
jambonneau: (F.) Small or "picnic" ham.
jamón: (Sp.) Ham.
jardinière: (F.) Mixed vegetables served in their own sauce.
jerusalem artichoke: Tuberous root vegetable with a sweet, tender taste.
jicama: (Mexican) A root vegetable, served hot or cold.
johnnycakes: Bread made from yellow corn meal, eggs and milk.
jook soon: (Chinese) Bamboo shoots.
julienne: (F.) To cut food into one and one-half inch matchlike strips; strips of garnish.
junket: A milk dessert thickened with rennet.
jus: (F.) Literally "juice." Usually the juice of meat.
jus d'herbes: (F.) Herb juices.

kaas: (Dutch) Cheese.
kaftes: (Middle Eastern) Beef patties served with tomato sauce.
kai lang: (Chinese) Broccoli.
kakavia: (Greek) Sardine soup.
kalakeitto: (Finnish) Fish chowder made with onions, potatoes, and milk.
kakamaria: (Greek) Squid.
kalbsleber: (G.) Calf's liver.
kasha: Buckwheat groats.
kielbasa: (Polish) Hard, garlic-flavored pork sausage.
kippered herring: Dried or smoked herring.
kishke: (Jewish) Casing stuffed with beef and matzo meal
kiwi fruit: Fruit with brown, hairy skin and green, soft-seeded flesh.
knead: To work a dough until smooth and elastic, usually with the hands.
kohl: (G.) Cabbage.
korma mahi: (East Indian) Fish curry.
kota: (Greek) Chicken.
kreas: (Greek) Lamb; also meat.
kreplach: (Jewish) Small dough triangles filled with cheese, chicken, chicken livers, or potatoes and cooked in broth or water.
kumquats: Known as the golden orange. A small oval citrus fruit having an acid pulp and an edible rind.
kwas: (Russian) Drink made by fermenting rye flour, yeast, malt and water.

lagosta: (Portuguese) Spiny lobster.
lait: (F.) Milk.
laitue: (F.) Lettuce.
langouste: (F.) Spiny lobster; sea crawfish.
larding: To insert strips of salt pork into lean meat to prevent drying.
leaven: To add a leavening ingredient such as baking powder, baking soda, or yeast to batters and doughs to make them rise.

leeks: A pungent onionlike bulb used for seasoning in soups and stews.

legumes: (F.) Vegetable, usually a seedpod vegetable; dried foods as beans, peas and lentils.

lentil: Round, flattened beans from a leguminous plant; basically used in soups.

liaison: A binding method used for sauces.

limande: (F.) Flounder, lemon sole and sand dab.

limpa: (Swedish) Bread.

line: To cover the bottom or sides of a pan with paper or sometimes thin slices of food.

lychee: (Chinese) Fruit with hard scaly outer covering and white translucent watery flesh.

lyonnaise potatoes: (F.) Literally "in the style of Lyon, France." With parsley and onions.

macaroon: Cakes or cookies made from egg whites, sugar, and almonds.

mace: The outer shell of nutmeg; an aromatic spice.

macédoine: (F.) A mixture of hot or cold fruits and vegetables.

macerate: To soak or steep in wine or spirits; to pickle briefly.

madrilène soup: (F.) Seasoned consommé with tomato.

maitre d'hotel, à la: (F.) A yellow sauce of butter, lemon juice, parsley, egg yolks, and seasoning.

maraschino: Royal Anne cherries, bleached, cooked in syrup with bright color and maraschino flavor added.

marengo, à la: (F.) With mushrooms, tomatoes, olives, and olive oil.

marinade: A liquid of wine, vinegar, oil, bouillon, and aromatic vegetables and seasonings in which meat, fish, or poultry are steeped or marinated.

marinate: To let food steep in a marinade.

marinière, à la: (F.) Mussels and other shellfish prepared in a white sauce.

marmite, petite: (F.) Clear, strong, and savory broth.

marron: (F.) A large sweet chestnut.

marsala: An Italian wine; pale golden, semi-dry.

marzipan: (G.) Almond paste. A confection formed in fruit and vegetable shapes and colored.

masa: (Mexican) Tortilla dough of ground dried corn and oil.

mash: To reduce to a pulp.

mask: To cover with a thick sauce; to hide the flavor.

masquer: (F.) To mask or cover; to coat hot or cold food with sauce, jelly or aspic.

massena, à la: (F.) Garnishing style consisting of artichoke hearts, Béarnaise sauce and beef marrow.

matelote: (F.) Literally, "sailors." Fish stew.

matzo: (Jewish) Unleavened bread with a crisp, crackerlike consistency.

matzo balls: (Jewish) Egg and matzo-meal dumplings; usually poached in soups.

medaillon: (F.) Cut in rounds; small, round or oval cuts of meat or fish.

mejillones: (Sp.) Mussels.

melanzana: (I.) Eggplant.

melba: A dessert of vanilla ice cream, a sauce, whipped cream, and a peach or pear.

melba toast: Very thinly sliced crisp toast baked in an oven.

menthe: (F.) Mint.

menthe, crème de: (F.) A peppermint cordial.

meringue: (F.) Stiffly beaten mixture of sugar and egg white.

meunière, à la: (F.) Fish floured and sautéed in butter. Served with brown butter sauce, lemon, and parsley.

mie-de-pain: (F.) Fresh breadcrumbs used as a food coating.
mignon: (F.) Tenderloin of beef, veal, lamb or veal.
milanaise: (F.) Literally, "as prepared in Milan, Italy." A garnish consisting of a julienne of ham, tongue, mushrooms, and truffles.
mimosa: A garnish of finely chopped hard-boiled eggs.
minceur: (F.) Literally, "slimness;" low-calorie French cuisine.
minestra: (I.) Soup; also first course.
minestrone: (I.) Thick vegetable soup with pasta.
mirepoix: (F.) Vegetable mixture of onions, carrots, and celery used to flavor soups, sauces, or stocks. Also used as a vegetable base in baking and roasting. Generally sweated for a few minutes to bring out its flavor.
miso: (Japanese) Soy bean paste used to flavor soups.
mocha: Coffee-chocolate flavoring.
mole: (Mexican) Sauce or purèe made with chiles.
molletes: (Mexican) Sweet rolls.
mongol soup: Soup with tomatoes, split peas, and julienne vegetables.
monosodium glutamate: A flavor enhancer made from vegetable protein.
monter: (F.) To whip, as with eggs or egg whites; or butter in a sauce.
mornay: (F.) A sauce of cream, eggs, cheese, and seasoning.
moules: (F.) Mussels.
moussaka: (Middle Eastern) Eggplant and ground meat dish.
mousse: (F.) A creamy frozen dessert; also a hot or cold dish bound with egg whites or gelatin.
moutarde: (F.) Mustard.
mouton: (F.) Mutton.
mozzarella: (I.) Soft, unripened cheese with a bland, slightly sweet flavor. Stringy and creamy when melted.

mull: A hot liquid; to heat and spice a beverage such as wine, cider, or ale.
mulligatawny soup: (English) Curry-flavored soup made with lamb or chicken and vegetables.
muscheln: (G.) Shellfish, usually refers to mussels.
muskat: (G.) Nutmeg.
musslor: (Swedish) Mussels.

nabos: (Sp.) Turnips.
nage, à la: (F.) Preparing freshwater crawfish in an herb-flavored stock.
nameko: (Japanese) Tiny wild mushrooms.
natilla: (Mexican) Custard.
naturschnitzel: (G.) Literally "plain veal." Veal cutlets lightly dusted with flour and sautéed with a light seasoning.
navarin: (F.) A stew of mutton with vegetables.
navets glacés: (F.) Glazed turnips.
nedlagt: (Norwegian) Pickled; preserved.
neufchatel: (F.) A cream cheese.
ngah choy: (Chinese) Bean sprouts.
nicoise: (F.) Literally, "prepared in the manner of Nice." With the highly seasoned foods of Provence: tomato sauce with garlic, green pepper, tarragon, chives, and mayonnaise.
noir: (F.) Black.
noisette: (F.) Literally, "hazelnut." Choice small cuts of meat or vegetables cut into round shapes.
noix: (F.) Nut.
nouilles: (F.) Noodles used in soups and garnishes.

obst: (G.) Fruit.
ochsenbraten: (G.) Beefsteak.
oeuf: (F.) Egg.
oie: (F.) Goose.

oignons: (F.) Onions.
oiseaux sans ailes: (F.) Veal slices rolled around stuffing. "Veal birds."
opp: (Chinese) Duck.
orret: (Norwegian) Trout.
osso bucco: (I.) Braised veal shanks or knuckles.
oukha: (Russian) A fish soup made with white wine.
ouzo: (Greek) An anise-flavored aperitif.
oysters bercy: Oysters on the half-shell with a creamy egg sauce; includes shallots, lemon juice, parsley, and white wine.
oysters casino: Oysters on the half-shell broiled with a topping of chile sauce, bacon, and horseradish.
oysters delmonico: Oysters on the half-shell broiled with a topping of green and red peppers with bacon, lemon juice, and buttered breadcrumbs.
oysters rockefeller: Oysters on the half-shell topped with seasoned chopped spinach, shallots, garlic, Pernod, and anchovies; usually baked on a bed of rock salt.

pain: (F.) Bread.
panache: (F.) Mixed colors, as two or more vegetables.
panbroil: To cook in a skillet with very little fat or no fat at all at high heat.
pane: (I.) Bread.
pané: (F.) With breadcrumbs.
papillote, en: (F.) Cooked in parchment paper or foil.
paprika: (Hungarian) Sweet, pungent seasoning made from red peppers.
parisienne, à la: (F.) Literally, "in the Parisian style." Includes potatoes cut into round balls.
parmentier: (F.) Made with potatoes, as potato soup.
parmesan: A hard, dry Italian cheese made from skim milk. Usually grated and served as a garnish.

parmigiano, formaggio: (I.) Parmesan cheese.
parsley: A cultivated herb used mostly as a garnish and for seasoning.
paskha: (Russian) An Easter cake of cottage cheese arranged in the shape of a pyramid.
pasta: (I.) Generic word for all forms of macaroni. Paste or dough made of flour and water, used dried or fresh, like ravioli.
paste: A smooth creamy mixture of two ingredients.
pastrami: (Rumanian) Highly seasoned corned beef brisket.
pastry: A baked paste of flour, water, and shortening.
pasty: (British) A turnover with a filling of seasoned meat or fish.
patatas: (Sp.) Potatoes.
pâté de foie gras: (F.) Paste made of fatted goose livers.
paupiette: (F.) Thin slice of meat, rolled and stuffed.
paysanne: (F.) Literally "peasant style." Vegetables cut into regular square shapes.
pêche: (F.) Peach.
pechuga de ave: (Sp.) The breasts of poultry.
petit: (F.) Small.
petit dejeuner: (F.) Breakfast.
petite marmite: (F.) A meat broth with meat and vegetables.
petits pois: (F.) Small green peas.
pièce de résistance: (F.) The main course or special dish.
pilaf: (Turkish) A steamed rice dish with meat, shellfish, or vegetables in a seasoned broth.
pimiento: Red sweet Spanish pepper.
pipe: To force frosting, whipped cream, mashed potatoes, or other soft mixture foods through a pastry tube.
piquante: (F.) Pleasantly pungent in taste and flavor.
pit: To remove pits; the stone or pit in various fruits.

pizza: (I.) A baked dish consisting of a shallow pielike crust usually covered with a spiced mixture of tomatoes and cheese.

plank: A hard wood board on which food is prepared and served.

pluches: (F.) The leaves of herbs used unchopped.

plump: To soak fruits in liquid until they swell up.

poach: To cook food totally or partially in simmering liquid.

poire: (F.) Pear.

poireau: (F.) Leek.

poisson: (F.) Fish.

polenta: (I.) A thick corn-meal mush, often served with sauce or gravy. Sometimes cooked firm like a cake and cut into wedges.

polonaise: (F.) Literally, "Polish manner or style." Prepared or dressed with browned butter and bread crumbs.

pommes de terre: (F.) Literally, "apples of the earth." Potatoes.

popovers: Individual puffed-up rolls.

potage: (F.) Thickened soup, usually of puréed vegetables.

pot-au-feu: (F.) Meat and vegetables cooked slowly in a meat broth to make soup. Literally, "pot on the fire."

potiron: (F.) Pumpkin.

potpourri: (F.) Mixture. A combination of elements.

pot roast: To brown, then to roast, covered, with some liquid.

poulet: (F.) Chicken.

poultry: Usually referred to as domestic fowls, but includes chickens, turkeys, ducks, geese, Cornish hens, pigeons, and squab.

pound: To flatten by pounding.

prawn: Large shrimp.

prefabricated: Refers to cuts of meat cut by purveyors to a purchaser's specifications, as pre-cut steaks.

preheat: To bring the oven or broiler temperature to the recommended temperature in advance of cooking.

prick: To make holes over the surface of pastry to allow steam to escape.

printanière: (F.) Small diced vegetables used as a garnish.

prosciutto: (I.) Very flavorful ham, usually sliced thin.

provençale, à la: (F.) Southern French style cooking, usually with tomatoes, onions, and garlic.

provolone: (I.) White, medium-hard cheese with a slight smoky flavor.

purée: Mashed; sieved to a smooth consistency; blended. A thick soup.

quahaug: An edible clam of the Atlantic coast of North America.

quenelles: (F.) A dumpling. A forcemeat of meat, poultry, fish, or shellfish formed into balls and poached.

quiche: (F.) A custard dish baked in an unsweetened pastry shell and filled with beaten eggs plus cheese, ham, onions, or seafood.

quiche alsacienne: (F.) Quiche made with onions.

quiche de jambon: (F.) Quiche made with ham.

quiche lorraine: (F.) Quiche made with cheese and bacon.

quin scallops: Deep-sea scallops.

quisquillas: (Sp.) Shrimp.

radis: (F.) Radish.

ragout: (F.) A meat and vegetable stew.

ragu: (I.) Meat stew or sauce.

rakor: (Swedish) Prawns or shrimp.

ramekin: A small individual dish used for both baking and serving; a small tart.

rarebit: (Welsh) Sometimes called Welsh rabbit; a dish of melted cheese over toast.

rasher of bacon: (English) A thin slice of bacon to be fried or broiled.

ratatouille: (F.) Mixed vegetable dish of eggplant, zucchini, tomatoes, onion, and garlic served hot or cold.

ravigote sauce: (F.) Piquant white sauce with vinaigrette and capers, onions and herbs.

ravioli: (I.) Small casings of pasta with various fillings, as chopped meat or cheese, often served with a sauce.

réchauffé: (F.) Reheated or warmed over.

reconstitute: To restore dried or concentrated foods to their natural state.

red snapper: A fish with red or reddish body. Found in tropical and semitropical waters.

reduce: To boil uncovered until quantity of liquid is reduced.

réduire: (F.) To reduce. To concentrate flavors of sauces, soups or other liquids by cooking rapidly, uncovered.

refritos: (Mexican) Refried beans.

rejer: (Danish) Shrimp or prawns.

reker: (Norwegian) Shrimp or prawns.

relish: A spicy or savory condiment served with other food.

remoulade: (F.) A mayonnaise-base sauce; a variation of tartar sauce.

renaissance, à la: (F.) A garnish comprised of small mounds and groups of vegetables; usually arranged around a roast.

render: To reduce, convert, or melt down fat by heating.

rennet: A dried extract of a pig or calf's stomach used to curdle milk.

renverser: (F.) To unmold, to turn food out on a dish.

res: (Mexican) Beef. Also *carne de res.*

rice: A cereal grass cultivated extensively in warm climates.

Richelieu: (F.) Garnished with stuffed tomatoes, mushrooms, artichoke bottoms, braised lettuce, and potatoes.

ricing: To sieve food to the consistency of rice; to put through a perforated ricer or sieve.

ricotta: (I.) An unripened cheese similar to cottage cheese, but smoother.

rinderrouladen: (G.) Rolled filets of beef.

rindfleisch: (G.) Boiled beef.

ris de veau: (F.) Veal sweetbreads.

rissole: (F.) A small, pastry-enclosed croquette with a minced meat or fish filling, usually fried in deep fat; a meat pie or a fried pie.

rissole potatoes: Potatoes cut in the shape of an egg and browned.

riz: (F.) Rice.

roast: To cook in the oven by dry heat.

rôti: (F.) Roast. Rôti de veau; roast veal.

roti: (East Indian) Bread.

rotoli di manzo: (I.) Rolled filets of beef.

rouge: (F.) Red.

rouladen: (G.) Rolled filets of beef braised in sauce.

roux: (F.) Fat and flour liaison mixture used to thicken soups and sauces.

royale: (F.) A savory custard used to garnish consommés.

rumaki: (Hawaiian) Chicken livers, water chestnuts, and bacon; wrapped, skewered, and broiled.

rusks: (English) A light, soft-textured sweetened biscuit.

sabayon: (F.) A creamy dessert or sauce made of egg yolks, sugar, and wine.

sachet: (F.) Mixed herbs and spices tied in a bag.

saffron: Expensive seasoning. The dried stigmas of saffron plant used to color foods such as rice or saffron cakes.

Saint-Germain: (F.) A thick green pea soup; also a garniture of puréed green peas.

salamander: A broiler-type oven with heat from the top and an open front. Used for au gratin dishes or glazing.

salmis: (F.) A highly spiced dish made from roasted game birds, minced and stewed in wine; a sauce.

salpicon: (F.) A cooked food that has been cut into dice and bound together with a thick sauce.

san si yu chi: (Chinese) Shark fins.

sarma: (Armenian) Lamb and rice dish with mint wrapped in grape leaves.

sarmi: (Bulgarian) Stuffed cabbages simmered in water or tomato juice.

sashimi: (Japanese) Thinly sliced raw fish.

satsuma jiru: (Japanese) Chicken soup.

saucissons: (F.) Sausages.

sauerbraten: (G.) A pot roast of beef marinated in vinegar, water, wine, and spices before being cooked.

sauté: (F.) To cook quickly in a skillet over high heat; literally "to jump."

scald: To heat a liquid almost to the boiling point.

scallion: A young bulbless onion; green onions.

scallop: The edible abductor muscle of a scallop. Also, to bake in a casserole with milk or a sauce and often with breadcrumbs.

scaloppine: (I.) Thin slices of meat sautéed quickly over high heat.

scampi: (I.) Large shrimp or prawns.

schnitzel: (G.) Cutlet.

schwartelbraten: (G.) Roast leg of pork.

schweinefleisch: (G.) Pork.

scones: (Scottish/English) Thin cakes of oatmeal baked on a griddle. Known as Scottish quick bread.

score: To mark with a series of shallow, even gashes.

Scotch eggs: (Scottish) Hard-cooked eggs encased with sausage, then rolled in cracker crumbs and deep-fried.

sear: To char, scorch, or burn the surface of meat with intense heat to seal in the juices.

season: To add salt, pepper, herbs, or spices for flavoring.

sec: (F.) Dry, as in dry wine; very low sugar content.

seeg: (Russian) Smoked fish.

sefrina: (Moroccan) Beef stew with saffron and ginger.

serviette: (F.) A table napkin.

set: Allowed to stand until congealed, as with gelatin.

shad: Any of several food fishes related to herring.

shallot: Bulb of the onion family favored by chefs for its pungent flavor. Used mainly for sauces.

sherbet: A sweet-flavored water-ice to which milk, egg whites, or gelatin has been added.

shirred eggs: Eggs cooked by baking in individual china dishes.

shortening: A fat suitable for baking or frying.

sift: To put through a sieve or other straining device.

simmer: To cook in liquid just below the boiling point.

singe: To burn the ends of; to burn off the feathers of poultry by subjecting briefly to flame.

sizzling steak: Steak served on a hot aluminum or steel platter to make the hissing sound characteristic of hot fat.

skewer: A long metal or wooden pin on which food is fastened for grilling, broiling, or roasting.

skim: To remove floating matter from the top of a liquid using a skimmer or ladle.

sliver: To cut into long, slender pieces.

smorgasbord: (Swedish) Tidbits and appetizers arranged on a table and served buffet style.

smother: To cover thickly with another foodstuff; to cook vegetables in a covered kettle until tender.

soak: To let stand in liquid or make saturated by placing in liquid.

soirée: (F.) Evening party.

sommelier: (F.) A wine steward or waiter.

soubise: (F.) A thick onion sauce.

soufflé: (F.) A baked fluffy egg dish combined with various other ingredients and served as a main dish or sweetened as a dessert.

soufflé potatoes: Potato slices puffed up like pillows.

sous cloche: (F.) Under glass.

souse: To cover in wine vinegar and spices; food is usually cooked slowly and allowed to cool in its own liquid.

spaetzle: (Austrian) Fine homemade noodles riced through a colander into boiling water.

Spanish rice: A dish consisting of rice, tomatoes, spices, chopped onions, and green pepper.

spatchcock: Any small bird split down the back, flattened and broiled.

spice: Any of various aromatic and pungent vegetable substances, such as cinnamon or nutmeg, used to flavor foods or beverages.

spiny lobster: Any of various edible crustaceans having a spiny carapace and lacking the large pincers characteristic of true lobsters. Also called langouste, rock lobster, and sometimes crayfish. Only the tail section is edible.

spit: A slender, pointed rod on which meat is impaled for broiling.

spumoni: (I.) A frozen dessert of ice cream, fruit, nuts, or candies.

squab: A young, unfledged pigeon.

steam: To cook, covered, over a small amount of boiling water so that the steam circulates freely around the food. The food must not touch water.

steep: To let soak in liquid until liquid absorbs the flavor and extracts flavor or color, as hot tea.

steer: A young ox, especially one castrated before sexual maturity and raised for beef.

sterilize: To destroy bacteria and microorganisms with boiling water, dry heat, or steam.

stew: To cook food by simmering or boiling slowly. Also, a dish cooked by stewing, especially a mixture of meat, vegetables, and stock. Suited to coarse-fibered meats.

stewed fruit: Fruit simmered in a sweetened liquid or juice.

stir: To mix with a spoon through a liquid to blend or cool the contents.

stock: The strained liquid from the broth of boiled meat, fish, poultry or vegetables used in the preparation of soup, gravy and sauces.

strain: To put through a strainer or sieve.

streusel: (G.) A crumblike topping for coffee cakes and rich breads. Literally, "something strewn together."

stroganoff: (Russian) Sliced beef cooked with onions, mushrooms, and seasonings in a sour cream sauce.

strudel: (G.) A sheet of paper-thin dough rolled up with filling and baked. Usually filled with fruit.

stud: To stick cloves, slivers of garlic, or other seasoning into the surface of food to be cooked.

stuff: To fill the body cavity, usually fish or poultry.

stuffing: Food put in the cavity of meat, fish, poultry or vegetables. Stuffing or dressing in French cooking is called forcemeat; *farces*.

subgum: (Chinese) With mixed vegetables like bamboo shoots, water chestnuts, and fresh mushrooms.

succotash: Kernels of corn and lima beans cooked together.

suet: The hard fatty tissues around the kidneys of cattle and sheep used in cooking and making tallow.

Suisse: (F.) Switzerland; à la Suisse, "Swiss style."

sumo: (Portuguese) Juice.

suprême de volaille: (F.) Boned chicken breast.

svamp: (Swedish) Mushrooms.

sweat: To draw out the flavor from vegetables by steaming or sautéing gently in a covered pan.

sweetbreads: The thymus gland of calf or lamb.

Tabasco: (Mexican) A trademark for a pungent sauce made from the fruit of a pepper; hot red pepper sauce.

table d'hôte: (F.) A full-course meal served at a fixed price at a restaurant or hotel.

taco: (Mexican) A tortilla folded around a filling as of ground meat, cheese, lettuce, onion, and hot sauce.

tallow: A mixture of the whitish, tasteless solid or hard fat obtained from parts of the bodies of cattle, sheep or horses.

tamale: (Mexican) A dish made of fried chopped meat and crushed peppers rolled in cornmeal mush, wrapped in corn husks, then steamed.

tapioca: A beady starch used for puddings and as a thickening agent in cooking.

tartar steak: Raw ground beef mixed with onion, seasoning, and egg. Usually eaten as an appetizer.

tarte: (F.) A small open-faced pie or pastry filled with fruit. Also called flan.

tartelette: (F.) A little tart. Small, round pastry cases around a filling. Used for dessert, garnish, or hors d'oeuvres.

tasse: (F.) Cup.

terrines: (F.) A pâté (a meat pie) without a crust, baked in an oval or rectangular earthenware dish called a terrine. Terrines are always served cold.

tête: (F.) Head.

timble: (F.) A bland, custardlike dish of cheese, chicken, fish or vegetables baked in a drum-shaped pastry mold.

torte: (G.) A kind of rich layer cake made with many eggs and a little bit of flour; usually contains chopped nuts.

tortilla: (Mexican) A thin unleavened pancake made of cornmeal; served hot with various fillings.

tortino: (I.) A savory tart filled with meat, fish, or vegetables.

toss: To mix a salad lightly so as to cover with dressing using either the hands or a large fork and spoon.

tournedos: (F.) Small filets of beef cut from the tenderloin; often wrapped in bacon for flavor.

tourte: (F.) A double crust pie made with flaky short paste.

tramezzino: (I.) A small sandwich.

trifle: (English) A dessert, consisting of sponge cake spread with jam, soaked in wine, sprinkled with crusted macaroons, and topped with custard and whipped cream.

tripe: The light-colored inner lining of the stomach of cattle.

truffles: A species of fungi, similar to mushrooms, dark in color and used as a garnish and seasoning.

truss: To bind or skewer the wings or legs of a fowl into a compact shape before cooking.

tunny: (English) Tuna.

Turkish coffee: Pulverized coffee in a thin sugar syrup.

turnover: Food encased in pastry and baked.

tutti frutti: (I.) Literally, "all fruit." A confection, especially ice cream, containing a variety of chopped candied fruits.

uccelletti: (I.) A small bird, usually spit-roasted.

uova: (I.) Eggs.

uova mollette: (I.) A soft-boiled egg.

uvas: (Sp.) Grapes.

vaca: (Sp.) Beef.

vaca estofada: (Sp.) Beef stew.

valenciana, a la: (Sp.) Valencian style; with rice, tomatoes, and garlic.
vapeur, à la: (F.) Steamed.
veal birds: Thin slices of veal rolled and stuffed with a filling.
veau: (F.) Veal.
velouté: (F.) White sauce made with veal or chicken stock.
veneziana: (I.) Venetian style with onions, white wine, and mint.
verdure: (F.) Green vegetables.
verjus: The juice of unripe fruit, especially sour grapes.
verlorene Eier: (G.) Poached eggs.
vermicelli: A food consisting of wheat flour paste made into long threads; thinner than spaghetti.
véronique: (F.) Garnished with grapes.
viande: (F.) Meat or flesh.
Vichy: (F.) Garnished with carrots.
vichyssoise: (F.) Literally "prepared in Vichy." A thick, creamy potato soup flavored with leeks or onions; usually served cold.
vinaigrette: (F.) French salad dressing of oil, vinegar, herbs, and spices.
Virginia ham: A lean, salty, hickory-smoked ham with dark meat.

waffle: (Dutch) A light, crisp batter baked in a waffle iron until golden brown.
Waldorf salad: A salad of diced raw apples, celery, nuts, whipped cream, and mayonnaise on a bed of lettuce.
Welsh rabbit: (Welsh/British) A dish made of melted cheese, milk or cream, beer or ale, served hot over toast or crackers. Also called "Welsh rarebit."
whip: To beat into a froth; to incorporate air in a mixture as in egg whites.
wiener schnitzel: (G.) Sautéed breaded veal.
wild rice: The grain of a grass of northern North America. It is not a true rice.
won ton: (Chinese) A stuffed noodle paste dumpling served in soup. Also a soup containing such a dumpling.

yaourt: (F.) Yogurt.
Yogurt: A food prepared from curdled milk to a custardlike consistency.
York ham: (English) Excellent, mild ham, thinly sliced.
Yorkshire pudding: (English) A popover baked in beef drippings; the traditional accompaniment to roast beef.

zabaglione: (I.) A rich, custard dessert made with egg yolks, sugar and wine; served either hot or cold.
zalm: (Dutch) Salmon.
zarzuela: (Sp.) Savory stew of assorted fish and shellfish.
zucchero: (I.) Sugar.
zwieback: (G.) A hard crispy bread, sliced thin and baked.
zwiebel suppe: (G.) Onion soup made with red wine and seasoning.

INDEX TO RECIPES

Appetizers, Lunch and Dinner
  Fruit Cocktail, 23
  Jellied Chicken Broth, 24
  Jellied Tomato Consommé, 24
  Shrimp Cocktail, 24
  Vegetable Juice Cocktail Supreme, 25

Beverages
  Apricot Nectar Cooler, 270
  Cantaloupe Cooler, 271
  Coffee Milkshake, 271
  Orange Pineapple Punch, 271
  Sparkling Fruit Punch, 272
  Strawberry Milk Shake, 272
  Thick Tropical Fruit Shake, 272
  Tropical Punch, 273
  Uncloudy Lemon Iced Tea, 273

Breads and Cereals
  Crepes
    Basic Crepe Recipe, 245
    Dessert Crepes, 246
  Diet Poultry Dressing, 246
  Noodles, 247
  Rice
    Baked Rice, 247
    Baked Saffron Rice, 248
    Boiled Rice, 248
    Fluffy Steamed Rice, 249
    Rice Pilaf, 249
  Seasoned French Bread, 249

Combination Main Dishes
  Cheese Enchiladas, 51
  Lasagne Florentine, 52
  Stuffed Crepes Florentine, 53
  The Dieter's Taco, 54

Desserts
  Custards
    Baked Coconut Custard, 263
    Honey Custard, 264
    Pumpkin Custard, 264
  Cakes
    Angel Food Cake, 269
  Fruit Desserts
    Ambrosia, 257
    Applesauce Whip, 258
    Baked Cherry Cups, 260
    Baked Pears in Wine, 262
    Boysenberry Parfait, 259
    Broiled Grapefruit, 261

Fruit Desserts (continued)
  Cinnamon Baked Apples, 258
  Fresh Fruit Cups, 260
  Marinated Sliced Pears, 262
  Poached Apple Slices, 259
  Polynesian Fruit Cups, 261
  Prune Whip, 263
Frozen Desserts
  Banana Sherbet, 265
  Buttermilk Sherbet, 265
  Cantaloupe Sherbet, 266
  Frozen Banana Yogurt, 267
  Frozen Strawberry Yogurt, 268
  Frozen Vanilla Yogurt, 268
  Orange Sherbet, 266
  Peach Sherbet, 267
  Pineapple Frappé, 269

Egg Dishes
  Egg
    Boiled Eggs, 46
    Fried Eggs, 46,
    Poached Eggs, 47
    Scrambled Eggs, 47
    Shirred Eggs, 48
  French Toast, 50
  Omelets
    Cheese Omelet au Gratin, 48
    French Omelet, 49
    Spanish Omelet, 49

Garnishes
  Fruit Garnishes
    Apple Cup, 251
    Frost Grapes, 251
    Fruit Kabobs, 251
    Grapefruit or Orange Baskets, 251
    Lemon Baskets, 251
    Lemon or Lime Roses, 251
    Serrated Fruit Halves, 251
    Single Twist and Tandem Fruit Slices, 252
    Pear Halves, 252
  Vegetable Garnishes
    Carrot Curls, 252
    Celery Curls, 252
    Cucumber Baskets, 252
    Cucumber Cartwheels, 252
    Fluted Cucumber Slices, 252
    Fluted Mushroom Caps, 252
    Green Onion Brushes, 252
    Narcissus, 253
    Onion Chrysanthemums, 253
    Pickle Fans, 253
    Potato, Turnip, or Rutabaga Roses, 253
    Radish Accordians, 253
    Radish Roses, 253
    Tomato Roses, 253
    Zucchini Boats, 254
  Miscellaneous Garnishes
    Garnishes for Gelatin Salads, 254
    Garnishes for Soups, 254
    Garnishes for Other Salads, 254

Marinades
  Marinade for Fish, 241
  Marinade for Fruits, 243
  Marinade for Lamb No. 1, 240
  Marinade for Lamb No. 2, 241
  Marinade for Steak, 241
  Marinade for Vegetables, 242
  Soy Marinade for Chicken No. 1, 242
  Soy Marinade for Chicken No. 2, 242
  Sweet and Sour Marinade for Fish and Shellfish, 242
  Wine Marinade for Meat, 241

Meats
  Braised
    Braised Beef with Mushrooms, 94
    Braised Lamb Chops, 94
    Steak au Suisse, 95
    Sweet and Sour Stuffed Cabbage, 95
    Zesty Pot Roast with Onion Soup Mix, 96
  Broiled
    Barbecued Spareribs, 78
    Broiled Lamb Shish Kabobs, 77
    Broiled Liver, 78
    Broiled Liver and Onions, 75
    Broiled Salisbury Steak, 76
    Broiled Sirloin Tips, 77
    Broiled Steaks, 76
    Hamburgers, 75
    London Broil, 78

Panbroiled
  Beef Curry, 80
  Beef Stroganoff, 81
  Curry of Beef Noisette, 84
  Fillet of Beef Italian, 81
  Marinated London Broil, 82
  Mushroom Burgers, 82
  Panbroiled Steak au Poivre, 83
  Panbroiled Steak Diane, 83
Roasted
  Boneless Roast Loin of Pork, 72
  Beef Loin Strip Roast, 70
  Roast Leg of Veal, 72
  Roast Rack of Lamb à la Française, 71
  Roast Sirloin of Beef, 70
  Roast Tenderloin of Beef, 69
  Rolled Roast Leg of Lamb, 71
  Standing Rib Roast of Beef (Non-Searing Method), 68
  Standing Rib Roast (Searing Method), 68
Sautéed
  Armenian Lamb, 85
  Sautéed Creole Liver, 88
  Sautéed Liver and Onions, 88
  Stir-Fried Beef and Broccoli, 86
  Stir-Fried Beef Curry with Rice, 86
  Stir-Fried Beef and Peppers, 87
  Stir-Fried Pork and Pineapple, 89
  Veal Cacciatore, 89
  Veal Scallopini, 90
Simmered
  Boiled Beef Dinner, 92
Stewed
  Beef Goulash, 98
  Beef Stew, 99
  Chile Con Carne, 100
  Lamb Stew, 99

Party Foods
  Dips
    Clam Dip, 16
    Cranberry Dip, 17
    Curried Avocado Dip, 17
    Curried Horseradish Dip, 17
    Dieter's Plain Sour Cream Dip, 18
    Flavored Sour Cream Dip, 18
    Fruit Dip, 18
    Onion Dip, 19
    Seafood Cocktail Dip, 19
    Tangy Lemon Dip, 19
  Hor d'Oeuvres
    Cold
      Deviled Eggs, 19
      Ham-Wrapped Pickles, 22
      Stuffed Celery, 20
    Hot
      Bacon-Wrapped Water Chestnuts, 20
      Baked Stuffed Mushrooms, 20
      Raw Mushrooms and Roquefort, 21
      Rumaki, 21
  Spreads
    Liver Pâté, 23
    Low-Calorie Cream Cheese Spread, 22
    Sardine Spread, 23

Poultry
  Baked
    Baked Chicken Parmesan, 114
    Barbecued Chicken, 113
    Chicken Cacciatore, 113
    Chicken Kabobs Teriyaki, 114
    Chicken Sauté Sec, 115
    Honey-Baked Drumsticks, 115
    Mexican-Style Baked Chicken, 116
    Oven-Fried Chicken, 116
    Oven-Fried Chicken Breasts, 117
  Broiled
    Broiled Chicken, 118
    Chinese-Style Broiled Drumsticks, 119
    Marinated Chicken Kabobs, 120
    Mustard Broiled Chicken, 119
  Poached
    Poached Chicken, 126
  Roasted
    Roast Chicken, 109
    Roast Chicken à l'Orange, 108
    Roast Duck, 109
    Roast Unstuffed Turkey, 110
    Rock Cornish Hens, 111
  Sautéed
    Basque Chicken, 121

Poultry, Sautéed (*Continued*)
    Glazed Chicken, *122*
    Hawaiian Chicken, *122*
    Kauai Chicken, *123*
    Sautéed Chicken Cacciatore, *124*
    Sautéed Chicken Livers, *124*
Steamed
    Steamed Chicken, *129*
    Steamed Cornish Game Hens, *130*
Stewed
    Coq au Vin, *128*
    Chicken Marengo, *128*
    Chicken with Artichoke Hearts, *127*

Salads
    Asparagus Salad, *212*
    Carrot and Raisin Salad, *212*
    Chicken Salad, *213*
    Chicken Salad Supreme, *213*
    Cole Slaw with Creamy Dressing, *214*
    Crab Salad, *214*
    Creamy Pineapple Coleslaw, *214*
    Crisp and Tangy Coleslaw, *215*
    Cucumber Yogurt Salad, *215*
    Farmer-Style Cottage Cheese Salad, *216*
    Herbed Bean Salad, *216*
    Italian Green Salad, *217*
    Kiwi and Papaya Salad, *217*
    Marinated Cucumber Slices, *218*
    Marinated Radish and Cucumber Salad, *218*
    Marinated Three Bean Salad, *218*
    Mimosa Salad, *219*
    Mushrooms à la Grecque, *219*
    Orange and Grapefruit Salad, *220*
    Orange and Onion Salad, *220*
    Pickled Beets, *221*
    Pineapple Mold, *221*
    Spinach Salad, *222*
    Tomato Aspic, *222*
    Tossed Cherry Tomato Salad, *223*
    Tossed Salad with Fresh Mushrooms, *224*
    Tossed Tuna Salad, *223*
    Vegetable Salad Bowl, *224*
    Waldorf Salad, *225*

Salad Dressings
    Buttermilk Herb Dressing, *225*
    Creamy Blue Cheese Dressing, *226*
    Creamy Buttermilk Dressing, *226*
    Creamy Italian Dressing, *226*
    Creamy Yogurt Salad Dressing, *227*
    French Dressing, *227*
    Fruit Salad Dressing, *227*
    Italian Dressing, *228*
    Quick Low-Calorie Dressing, *228*
    Thousand Island Dressing, *228*
    Vinaigrette Dressing, *229*

Sauces
    Cold
        Cocktail Sauce, *231*
        Cucumber Sauce, *231*
        Dill Sauce, *231*
        Salsa Fria (Cold Sauce), *232*
        Shallot Sauce, *232*
        Tartare Sauce, *232*
    Hot
        Barbecue Sauce, *235*
        Brown Sauce, Blending Method, *235*
        Brown Sauce, Roux Method, *234*
        Creamy Fish Sauce, *234*
        Curry Sauce, *238*
        Hollandaise Sauce, *237*
        Lemon Sauce, *238*
        Marinara Sauce, *236*
        Mustard Sauce, *238*
        Spaghetti Sauce, *237*
        Spanish Sauce, *236*
        Sweet and Sour Sauce, *239*
        Teriyaki Sauce, *239*
        White Sauce, Blending Method, *233*
        White Sauce, Roux Method, *233*

Seafood
    Baked
        Baked Fillet of Sole, *147*
        Baked Fish Creole, *144*
        Baked Fish Fillets Italiano, *144*
        Baked Fish Fillets or Steaks, *143*
        Baked Fish Fillets in Tomato Sauce, *145*
        Baked Fresh Salmon Steaks, *143*

Baked Halibut Steaks, *146*
Baked Trout au Gratin, *149*
Baked Trout in Wine Sauce, *150*
Baked Whole Red Snapper, *147*
Fillet of Sole Bonne Femme, *148*
Fillet of Sole Duglere, *148*
Low-Calorie Baked Flounder, *145*
Boiled
    Boiled Lobster Tails, *155*
    Boiled Salmon, *156*
    Boiled Shrimp, *156*
Broiled
    Broiled Fish Fillets or Steaks, *140*
    Broiled Lobster Tails, *141*
    Seafood Shish Kabobs, *141*
Poached
    Basic Poached Fish, *158*
    Delicious Pickled Salmon, *159*
    Lobster en Casserole, *158*
    Poached Bay Scallops, *160*
    Poached Fillet of Sole, *161*
    Poached Fillet of Sole in Milk, *161*
    Poached Halibut Steaks, *159*
    Scotch Salmon, *160*
Sautéed
    Sautéed Fillet of Sole, *152*
    Sautéed Fillet of Sole à l'Anglaise, *152*
    Sautéed Fillet of Sole à la Meuniere, *151*
    Stir-Fried Shrimp with Snow Peas, *153*
    Stir-Fried Sweet and Sour Shrimp, *153*
Steamed
    Steamed Fish Fillets, *162*
    Steamed Fish Fillets or Steaks (Thick Cuts), *162*
    Steamed Halibut Steaks in Foil, *163*
    Steamed Lobster Tails, *164*
    Steamed Rainbow Trout in Foil, *164*
    Steamed Rock Cod, *163*

Soups
    Clear Soups
        Beef Cabbage Soup, *28*
        Beef Consommé, *27*
        Borscht, *28*
        Chicken Broth Parmesan, *29*
        Consommé Madrilène, *29*
        Fresh Mushroom Soup, *29*
        Homemade Turkey Soup, *30*
        Jellied Tomato Consommé, *30*
        Low-Calorie Vegetable Soup, *30*
        Old-Fashioned Beef Vegetable Soup, *31*
        Onion Soup, *31*
        Vegetable Soup, *32*
        Wine Bouillon Soup, *32*
    Family Soups
        Bouillabaisse, *37*
        Chicken in the Pot, *37*
        Cioppino, *38*
        Cock-a-Leekie Soup, *38*
        Sopa de Albondigas (Mexican-Style Meatball Soup), *40*
    Thick Soups
        Carrot Soup, *33*
        Cream of Cauliflower Soup, *33*
        Fresh Broccoli Soup, *34*
        Fresh Tomato Soup, *34*
        Gazpacho, *35*
        Manhattan Clam Chowder, *35*
        Puréed Asparagus Soup, *36*
        Split Pea Soup, *36*
    Stocks
        Basic Beef Stock, *40*
        Basic Chicken Stock, *41*
        Court Bouillon, *41*
        Fish Stock, *42*
        Lamb Stock, *42*
        Lobster Stock, *42*

Vegetables
    Baked
        American Indian Peppers, *187*
        Baked Acorn Squash, *186*
        Baked Asparagus Parmesan, *187*
        Baked Corn on the Cob, *189*
        Baked Potatoes, *188*
        Baked Stuffed Potatoes, *190*
        Baked Summer Squash, *187*
        Baked Tomatoes Italiano, *188*

Vegetables, Baked (*Continued*)
    Baked Tomato Parmesan, *190*
    Baked Zucchini Italian, *190*
    Ratatouille, *189*
Boiled
    Boiled Cauliflower with Parsley, *197*
    Boiled Potatoes, *198*
    Cauliflower à l'Italienne, *197*
    Fresh Boiled Artichokes, *198*
    Fresh Broccoli with Lemon, *199*
    Green Beans and Stewed Tomatoes, *200*
    Hot Boiled Asparagus Spears, *199*
    Hot Sweet and Sour Beets, *200*
    Hungarian Brussels Sprouts, *201*
    Julienne of Beans with Tomato, *201*
    Mashed Potatoes, *202*
    Sweet and Sour Cut Green Beans, *202*
    Sweet Peas Mandarin, *200*
    Tarragon Green Beans, *203*
Braised
    Braised Belgian Endive, *207*
    Braised Carrots and Celery, *208*
    Braised Celery, *207*
    Braised Onions, *208*
    Celery Julienne, *209*
    French-Style Peas, *209*
    Hot Sweet and Sour Cabbage, *210*
    Mixed Vegetable Casserole, *210*
Broiled
    Broiled Eggplant Parmigiana, *185*
    Broiled Mushrooms, *184*
    Broiled Onion, *184*
    Broiled Zucchini, *184*
    Herbed Broiled Tomatoes, *185*
Sautéed
    Bean Sprouts and Mushrooms Sauté, *192*
    Sautéed Cabbage, *194*
    Sautéed Garden Vegetables, *193*
    Sautéed Mushrooms with Tomatoes, *193*
    Sautéed Zucchini and Cheese, *195*
    Sautéed Zucchini and Onions, *196*
    Spinach in Red Wine, *194*
    Zucchini Provençale, *195*
Steamed
    Carrots Lyonnaise, *204*
    Caraway Cabbage, *205*
    Dilled Carrots, *205*
    Steamed Vegetable Medley, *206*

INDEX

Appetizers, *16-25*
Artichokes, *170*
  boiled, *198*
Asparagus, *170*

Baking, *2*
  poultry, *111-117*
  seafood, *143-150*
  vegetables, *185-190*
Beans, fresh, *170*
  boiled, *200-203*
Beef
  beef tenderloin, *69*
  boiled beef, *92*
  consommé, *27*
  ribs of, *68*
  steaks, *76*
  stock, *40*
  strip loin, *79*
  top sirloin, *79*
Beets, *170*
  boiled, *200*
Belgian endive, *207*
Beverages, *270*
Boiling, *3*
  seafood, *154-157*
  vegetables, *196-203*

Braising, *4*
  meat, *92-96*
  vegetables, *206-210*
Breads and cereals, *244-249*
Broccoli, *171*
  boiled, *199*
Broiling, *2*
  meat, *73-79*
  poultry, *117-120*
  seafood, *139-141*
  vegetables, *183-185*
Brussels sprouts, *171*
  boiled, *201*

Cabbage, *171*
  braised, *210*
  sautéed, *194*
  steamed, *205*
Carrots, *171*
  steaming, *204, 205*
Casseroles, *51*
Cauliflower, *172*
  boiled, *197*
Celeriac, *172*
Celery, *172*
  braised, *207-209*

Cheese, *45*
Chicken
  baked, *114*
  broiled, *118*
  roast of, *108, 109*
  steamed, *129*
  stock, *41*
Chicken livers, *124*
Clams, *136*
Cod, *163*
Cooking methods, *1-5*
  dry heat, *2*
  moist heat, *3*
Corn, *172*
  baked, *189*
Cornish game hens, *111*
  steamed, *130*
Court bouillon, *41, 154, 157*
Crabs, *137*
Crepes
  basic recipe, *245*
  dessert, *246*
  Florentine, *53*
Cucumbers, *173*

Desserts, *255*
Dips, *16-19*
Duck, *109*

Eggs, *44-50*
  boiled, *46*
  fried, *46*
  omelets, *48-50*
  poached, *47*
  scrambled, *47*
  shirred, *48*
Eggplant, *173*
  broiled, *185*
Enchiladas, *51*

Fat
  in cooking, *191*
Fish, (see Seafood)
Fish stock, *42*
Flounder, *145*
French toast, *49*

Garlic, *10*
Garlic bread, *249*
Garnishes, *250-254*

Halibut, *146, 159, 163*
Herbs, *8*
Hors d'Oeuvres, *19-21*

Imitation butter flavoring, *206*

Juices
  as seasoning, *7*
Julienne, how to, *179*

Kabobs
  chicken, *120*
  lamb, *77*
  seafood, *141*

Lamb, *57*
  leg of, *71*
  rack of, *71*
  shish kabobs, *77*
  stock, *42*
Lasagne, *52*
Leeks, *11*
Legumes, *177, 180*
Lettuce, *173*
Liver, *75, 78*
Lobster, *138, 141, 155, 158, 164*
Lobster stock, *42*

Marinades, *240-243*
Meat, *55-100*
  buying, *58-61*
  cuts, *59, 60*
  grading, *57*
  preparation methods, *65*
    braising, *92-96*
    broiling, *73-79*
    panbroiling, *79-84*
    roasting, *66-73*
    sautéing, *84-90*
    simmering, *90-92*
    stewing, *96-100*
    storing, *62-65*
Meat thermometer, *67*

[310]

Mirepoix, 67
Mushrooms, 8, 173
　broiled, 184
　sautéed, 192, 193

Noodles, 247

Okra, 174
Onions, 9-11
　dry, 174, 177
　green, 174
　　braised, 208
　　broiled, 184
　　soup, 31
Oysters, 136

Peas, 174
　braised, 209
Peppers, sweet, 174
　baked, 187
Poaching, 4
　poultry, 125-126
　seafood, 157-161
Pork, 57, 72
Potatoes, 175, 177
　baked, 188, 190
　boiled, 198
　mashed, 202
Poultry, 101-130
　buying, 102
　classifications, 101
　cleaning and trussing, 103
　cutting and boning, 104-106
　preparation methods
　　baking, 111-117
　　broiling, 117-120
　　poaching, 125-126
　　roasting, 106-111
　　sautéing, 120
　　steaming, 129-130
　　stewing, 126-128
　storing and handling, 102-103
Poultry dressing, 246

Quick low-calorie dressing, 228

Ratatouille, 189
Rice, 75
　baked, 247
　boiled, 248
　pilaf, 249
　steamed, 249
Roasting, 2
　meat, 66-73
　poultry, 106-111
Rutabagas, 176

Saffron, 248
Salad dressing, 225-229
Salads, 211-225
Salmon, 143, 156, 159, 160
Salt, 11-12
Sauces, 230-239
Sautéing, 3
　meat, 84-90
　poultry, 120
　seafood, 150-154
　vegetables, 191-196
Seafood, 131-165
　buying, 132-133
　cooking methods
　　baking, 143-150
　　boiling, 154-157
　　broiling, 139-141
　　poaching, 157-161
　　sautéing, 150-154
　　steaming, 161-165
　preparation for cooking, 135
　storing and handling, 133
Seasonings, 6-15
　citrus juices and rinds, 7
　herbs, 8
　mushrooms, 8
　onions, 9-11
　salt, 11-12
　soy sauce, 12
　spices, 12
　vanilla, 13
　vinegar, 13-14
　wine, 14-15
Scallops, 160
Shallots, 10
　sauce, 232

[311]

Shellfish, *136*
Shrimp, *137, 153, 156*
Simmering, *4*
   meat, *90-92*
Snapper, *147*
Sole, *147, 148, 151, 152, 161*
Soups, *26-40*
Soy sauce, *12*
Spices, *12-13*
Spinach, *175*
Spreads, *22-23*
Squash, *175*
   baked, *186, 187, 190*
   broiled, *184*
   sautéed, *195, 196*
Steaming, *1*
   poultry, *129-130*
   seafood, *161-165*
   vegetables, *203-206*
Stewing, *4*
   meat, *96-100*
   poultry, *126-128*
Stir-frying, *3*
   meat, *86, 87, 89*
   vegetables, *191, 192*
Stocks, *40-43*
Storing foods
   meat, *62-65*
   poultry, *102-103*
   seafood, *133*
   vegetables, *177*

Tacos, *54*
Tartare sauce, *232*
Tomatoes, *176*
   baked, *188-190*
   broiled, *185*

Turnips, *176*
Trout, *149, 150, 164*
Turkey
   roasting of, *110*
   soup, *30*

United States Department of Agriculture (USDA), *57*

Vanilla, *13*
Veal, *57*
   roasting of, *72*
Vegetables
   buying, *169-177*
   classifications, *166-168*
   cooking methods, *180-210*
     baking, *185-190*
     boiling, *196-203*
     braising, *206-210*
     broiling, *183-185*
     sautéing, *191-196*
     steaming, *203*
     stir-frying, *191, 192*
   preparation for cooking, *178-180*
   storing, *177*
Vinegar, *13-14*

Wine, *14-15*

Yogurt
   in dips, *17*
   in desserts, *267-268*
   in sauces, *231-237*
   in Stroganoff, *81*
   garnish in soup, *28*

Zucchini, (see Squash)